2ND EDITION

KEY ISSUES IN SPECIAL EDUCATIONAL NEEDS & INCLUSION

ALAN HODKINSON

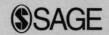

Los Angeles | London | New Delhi
Singapore | Washington DC

Los Angeles | London | New Delhi
Singapore | Washington DC

SAGE Publications Ltd
1 Oliver's Yard
55 City Road
London EC1Y 1SP

SAGE Publications Inc.
2455 Teller Road
Thousand Oaks, California 91320

SAGE Publications India Pvt Ltd
B 1/I 1 Mohan Cooperative Industrial Area
Mathura Road
New Delhi 110 044

SAGE Publications Asia-Pacific Pte Ltd
3 Church Street
#10-04 Samsung Hub
Singapore 049483

Editor: Amy Jarrold
Assistant editor: George Knowles
Production editor: Tom Bedford
Copyeditor: Salia Nessa
Proofreader: Camille Bramall
Indexer: Silvia Benvenuto
Marketing manager: Lorna Patkai
Cover design: Wendy Scott
Typeset by: C&M Digitals (P) Ltd, Chennai, India
Printed and bound by CPI Group (UK) Ltd,
Croydon, CR0 4YY

© Alan Hodkinson 2016

First edition © Alan Hodkinson and Philip Vickerman, published 2009, reprinted 2013

Library of Congress Control Number: 2015935198

British Library Cataloguing in Publication data

A catalogue record for this book is available from the British Library

ISBN 978-1-4739-1224-3
ISBN 978-1-4739-1225-0 (pbk)

At SAGE we take sustainability seriously. Most of our products are printed in the UK using FSC papers and boards. When we print overseas we ensure sustainable papers are used as measured by the Egmont grading system. We undertake an annual audit to monitor our sustainability.

This book is due for return on or before the last date shown below.

SAGE was founded in 1965 by Sara Miller McCune to support
the dissemination of usable knowledge by publishing innovative
and high-quality research and teaching content. Today, we
publish more than 850 journals, including those of more than
300 learned societies, more than 800 new books per year, and
a growing range of library products including archives, data,
case studies, reports, and video. SAGE remains majority-owned
by our founder, and after Sara's lifetime will become owned by
a charitable trust that secures our continued independence.

Los Angeles | London | New Delhi | Singapore | Washington DC

To all the children and professionals whom I have encountered in my journeys into the world of special educational needs and disabilities. I have learnt so much from you and for this I shall always be grateful.

I wish also to acknowledge my indebtedness to Helen, Zac and Fin who, despite the selfishness that a text of this length involves, have offered me throughout the past year their continued support and encouragement.

To Steve and Diana, thank you for the opportunities and support you have offered me. You have been a guiding light to my educational journey.

And finally, to Phil, a researcher and scholar who is a breath of fresh air in a sometimes stagnant world.

Alan Hodkinson

Education Studies: Key Issues Series

In the last two decades Education Studies has developed rapidly as a distinctive subject in its own right. Beginning initially at undergraduate level, this has grown at Masters level and is characterised by an increasingly analytical approach to the study of education. As education studies programmes have developed there has emerged a number of discrete study areas that require in-depth texts to support student learning.

The central book in the series is *Introduction to Education Studies, Fourth Edition* (forthcoming Spring 2016) which gives students an important grounding in the study of education. The 'Key Issues in Education Studies' texts have evolved from this and use the same critical approach. Each volume outlines a significant area of study and all of the books have been written by experts in their area to provide the detail and depth required by students as they progress further in the subject.

Taken as a whole, this series provides a comprehensive set of texts for the student of education. While of particular value to students of Education Studies, the series will also be instructive for those studying related areas such as Childhood Studies and Special Needs, as well as being of interest to students on initial teacher training courses and practitioners working in education.

We hope that this series provides you, the reader, with plentiful opportunities to explore further this exciting and significant area of study and we wish you well in your endeavours.

Steve Bartlett and Diana Burton

Series Editors

Books in the series

Steve Bartlett & Diana Burton: *Introduction to Education Studies, Fourth Edition* (forthcoming Spring 2016)

Diana Burton & Steve Bartlett: *Key Issues for Education Researchers* (2009)

Alan Hodkinson: *Key Issues in Special Educational Needs and Inclusion, Second Edition* (2016)

Emma Smith: *Key Issues in Education and Social Justice* (2012)

Stephen Ward & Christine Eden: *Key Issues in Education Policy* (2009)

CONTENTS

ABOUT THE AUTHOR

Alan Hodkinson was for many years a Special Educational Needs Coordinator (SENCo) and senior manager in the primary school sector. Currently, he is an Associate Professor in the Centre for Culture and Disability Studies at Liverpool Hope University.

PREFACE TO THE SECOND EDITION

The first edition of *Key Issues in Special Educational Needs and Inclusion* provided a starting point for students to engage in an informed debate about the complexity of special educational needs (SEN) and inclusion that existed within the first decade of the twenty-first century. Reviews of the text noted that:

> This is probably one of the most accessible books I have read lately in relation to SEN and inclusion. . . . It would be very accessible to students who are relatively new to the theoretical aspects behind the idea or concept of inclusion.

This second edition updates the text by examining and exemplifying the 'radical overhaul' of SEN, disability and inclusion that has taken place since 2010. This text takes a more critical stance to inclusion and how its conceptual underpinning is defined through policy and the manner in which it has been operationalised in schools. Responding to the constructive criticisms provided by anonymous reviewers, this edition has revised how international elements of inclusive practice are examined. It is hoped that these revisions will enable students to find continued value in this text as an introduction to SEN and inclusion.

Context of the book

SEN, disability and inclusion are areas that are both complex and multifaceted. This is a world where professionals, families and administrators coexist with each other and despite their sometimes competing agendas have to ensure that, through their best endeavours, children's needs are met. This world though has another side – that of government departments, educational and health policies, civil servants and the public at large. This 'underworld' provides the political will that confirms, conforms and constrains the systems and processes of SEN and inclusive provision that children experience in their educational journeys through our schooling system. This world has in recent times been subject to change, as in 2010 the government radically overhauled policies relating to SEN. In creating its policy, government articulated that it was responding to the frustrations of children and families to the landmark educational policy of the last Labour government, namely that of inclusion (see DfE, 2011).

The study of such policy and practice transformation within the context of SEN and inclusion necessitates students' recognition of the complex interplay between these two worlds (Norwich, 2000). SEN exist upon a continuum of abilities and impairments and sometimes there is no clear-cut distinction between those who have SEN and those who have not (Terzi, 2005). Conceptualising differences such as disability, impairment and the SEN of children upon this continuum is complicated and often fraught with difficulties, not least in that we are dealing with an individual's life, hopes and aspirations. There are many competing views about the definitions of SEN, disability and impairment and how these affect children in schools. Perhaps, most contentious of all, certainly in light of the recent government's so called 'radical overhaul' of SEN policies, is how and indeed where educational provision for these children should be organised (Lloyd, 2012).

Uses of the book

This book explores and critically examines the world of SEN, disability and inclusion. It will raise students' awareness of the key issues and concepts that dominate this world by providing a perspective of the ideological and political debates that have shaped its historical and current development. While it is clear that the catalogues of publishing houses (Nind, 2005) and journals are bursting with titles that relate to SEN, disability and inclusion, a closer examination of such material reveals that many texts assume a level of knowledge, understanding and sometimes practical experience, which many students may not possess. The aim of this book, therefore, is to provide a starting point to enable students to develop a basic knowledge and understanding so that they might be better able to engage in meaningful, informed and critical discussion of the issues that dominate SEN, disability and inclusion. Whilst this text is not intended for teacher trainees, many such students did find the first edition of this text a useful supplement to their studies.

A text such as this then, directed as it is towards the novice student, can only provide an overview of the complexity of the issues. As such, some concepts are necessarily subject to simplification and it is accepted that this may, perhaps, cause a distortion of the facts. However, throughout the book the student is directed towards further materials that will help them to develop a more complete grasp of this area. I therefore want to emphasise from the outset that this text is only the beginning of a student's journey into this complex world, as it offers only a basic introduction that provides a point of departure for a deeper exploration and critical examination of SEN, disability and inclusion.

Format of the book

This book is organised into three distinct sections. Section 1 defines the concepts of special needs and SEN and examines how provision for such is maintained in

England, Northern Ireland, Wales and Scotland. In addition, it analyses how the development of the concept of disability has been defined through ideological models that have developed over time. Furthermore, it considers how the attitudes of teachers, parents and non-disabled children have affected the inclusion of disabled children within schools. Section 2 considers the historical development of the world of SEN, disability and the emergence of inclusive education within England and during the latter part of the twentieth century. Section 3 examines the legislation governing SEN, disability and inclusive education in England. It also offers an outline of how the SEN Code of Practice operates. This section also outlines and examines the roles and responsibilities of the education, health and social care professionals involved in the delivery of SEN and inclusive educational provision. Chapter 8 offers a comparative analysis of the legislation and practices that govern the delivery of SEN, disability and inclusion within the English education system, and that of a number of other European and non-European countries.

Throughout the book the terms 'special educational needs' (SEN) will be employed as opposed to the term 'special educational needs and disability' (SEND). This is because 'SEN' has a legal determination, whereas 'SEND' does not. This difference is explained more fully in Chapter 1.

LIST OF FIGURES AND TABLES

Figures

Tables

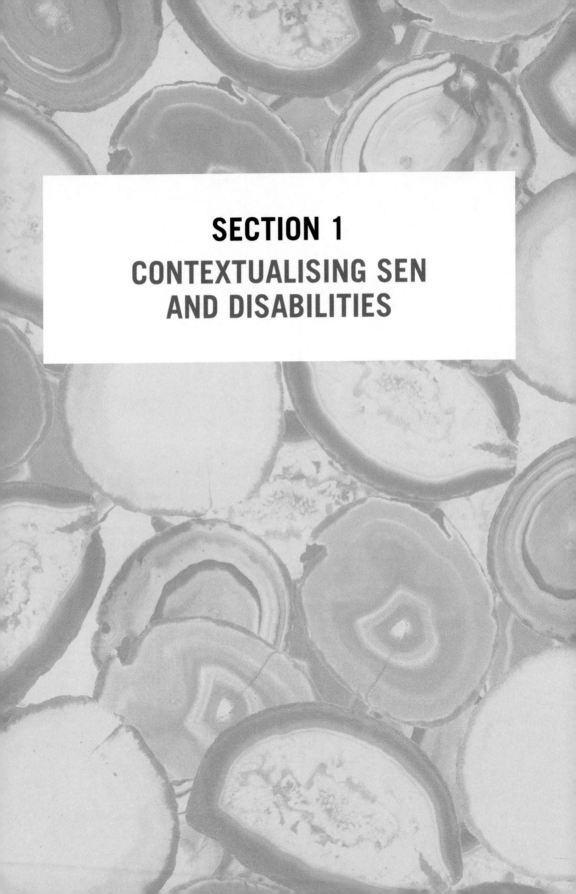

SECTION 1
CONTEXTUALISING SEN AND DISABILITIES

1
INTRODUCING SEN

∶ **CHAPTER OBJECTIVES**

- To introduce the concept of SEN and the scale of the issue in England.
- To define the differences between SEN and special needs.
- To provide an overview of how SEN legislation is employed throughout the UK.

Introduction

This chapter will introduce you to the concept of special educational needs (SEN). It will include definitions of SEN and special needs and will outline the scale of the issue in England. It will also provide a brief overview of how processes of SEN are operationalised in Wales, Scotland and Northern Ireland. In addition, it will provide you with a number of case studies that will help you to develop a better understanding of these key concepts. The final section of the chapter suggests additional reading and offers practical activities that will further develop your knowledge and understanding of SEN and inclusion.

DEFINING SEN IN ENGLAND

Clause 20 of the Children and Families Act 2014 denotes that a child or young person has a SEN when he or she has a learning difficulty or disability that calls for special educational provision to be made for him or her.

According to the Act, a child or young person has a learning difficulty if he or she has:

a) significantly greater difficulty in learning than the majority of others of the same age; or

b) disability that prevents or hinders him or her from making use of facilities of a kind generally provided for others of the same age in mainstream schools.

(Continued)

(Continued)

Following a formal assessment under Section 37 of the Children and Families Act 2014, a local authority may issue an Education, Health and Care Plan (EHCP). This is a legal document specifying the child's needs, the special educational provision required and the outcomes that will be sought for that child.

The phrase 'SEN' was coined by the Warnock Report of the late 1970s (DES, 1978). Previously, children had been labelled by the employment of ten categories of 'handicap' set out in the regulations of the 1944 Education Act (see Chapter 3).

The ten categories of 'handicap' defined by the 1944 Education Act were:

- blind
- partially sighted
- deaf
- delicate
- diabetic
- educationally subnormal
- epileptic
- maladjusted
- physically handicapped
- speech defect.

The Warnock Report in 1978, followed by the 1981 Education Act (DES, 1981), altered the conceptualisation of special education by emphasising that a child's educational need should be prioritised first and not their individual learning disability or impairment. Today, in the context of educational provision, the term SEN has a legal definition that refers to children who have learning difficulties and/or disabilities, which make it more difficult for them to learn or access education than most children of the same age.

The Children and Families Act (DfE, 2014a) (see Chapter 7 for further details) offers guidance that helps teachers and other professionals make decisions upon whether a child has a SEN. For example, it states that:

> A child or young person does not have a learning difficulty or disability solely because the language (or form of language) in which he or she is or will be taught is different from a language (or form of language) which is or has been spoken at home. (Section 20[4])

Furthermore, clause 77 of the Act creates a Code of Practice (henceforth referred to as the 'Code'), which relates to children from 0–25 years of age and provides advice to local authorities, maintained schools and early years educational settings on how to identify, assess and make provision for children's SEN so as to ensure that 'all children achieve their best, become confident individuals living fulfilling lives; and that they make a successful transition into adulthood' (DfE, 2014b: 58). Teachers and professionals must have regard for the Code in all the work they do with children and young adults with SEN. The Code indicates that a child or young person's needs may fall into at least one of four broad categories:

1. communication and interaction
2. cognition and learning
3. social, mental and emotional health
4. sensory and/or physical needs.

The Code also details that behavioural difficulties do not necessarily mean that a child has a SEN (DfE, 2014b). The Code does make it clear though that when behaviour is consistently disruptive or a child has become withdrawn, this can be a sign of an unmet SEN.

The four categories are sub-divided into:

1 Communication and interaction

- **Speech, language and communication (SLCN)** – these children find it more difficult to communicate with others and may have difficulties in taking part in conversations.

- **Autistic spectrum disorder (ASD)**, including Asperger's syndrome and autism. These children have difficulty in communication, social interaction and imagination. In addition, they may be easily distracted or upset by certain stimuli, have problems with change to familiar routines or have difficulties with coordination and fine-motor skills.

2 Cognition and learning

- Children with learning difficulties will learn at a slower pace and may have greater difficulty in acquiring basic literacy or numeracy skills or in understanding concepts. They may also have speech and language delay, low self-esteem, low levels of concentration and underdeveloped social skills.

- Children and young children with a learning difficulty are at increased risk of developing a mental health problem and may need additional support with social development, self-esteem and emotional well-being.

- **Severe learning difficulties (SLD)** – children may have significant intellectual and cognitive impairments. They may have difficulties in mobility and coordination, communication and perception, and the acquisition of self-help skills.

(Continued)

(Continued)

- **Profound and multiple learning difficulties (PMLD)** – these children have severe and complex difficulties as well as significant other difficulties such as a physical or a sensory impairment.

- **Specific learning difficulty (SPLD)** – a child may have a difficulty with one or more aspects of learning, including a range of conditions such as dyslexia (reading and spelling), dyscalculia (maths), dyspraxia (coordination) and dysgraphia (writing).

3   **Social, mental and emotional health**

- Children who have difficulties with their emotional and social development may have immature social skills and find it difficult to make and sustain healthy relationships. These may be displayed through them becoming withdrawn or isolated, as well as through challenging, disruptive or disturbing behaviour.

- Some children may have a recognised disorder, for example, attention deficit disorder (ADD), attention deficit hyperactivity disorder (ADHD), attachment disorder, autism or pervasive developmental disorder.

4   **Sensory and/or physical needs**

- There is a wide variety of sensory and physical difficulties that affect children and some of them may require special educational provision. It is this group that should be identified as having a SEN.

- Visual impairment (VI) or hearing impairment (HI) may require specialist support and equipment to access learning.

- Multi-sensory impairment (MSI) is a combination of visual and hearing difficulties, which makes it much more difficult to access the curriculum.

- Physical disability (PD) requires ongoing support and equipment to access all the opportunities available to their peers.

(DfE, 2014b: 97–8)

The four categories of SEN as defined in the Code are explained more fully in the case studies below.

CASE STUDY 1.1

Specific learning difficulties

Tendrya is ten and is a pupil in a class in an urban primary school. He is normally a well-mannered child and is a well-liked member of the class. Tendrya has satisfactory language skills and has very good conversational skills. Tendrya, however, does have difficulties in transposing and reversing numbers and struggles in most mathematical activities. Tendrya's teacher and parents have worked hard to remediate these difficulties. To date, Tendrya is failing to make progress in his numeracy work in school. Recently, Tendrya has become agitated in numeracy lessons and his inability to keep up with the rest of the class is causing him intense frustration that often leads to incidents of poor behaviour. In view of Tendrya's difficulties he was referred to an educational psychologist for an assessment of his needs. The psychologist detailed that Tendrya was 36 months behind in his computational, directional abilities and in his ability to sequence instructions compared to that expected for a child of his age. It is interesting to note that Tendrya's father, when questioned about his maths work, stated that he had similar difficulties when he was at school.

In terms of the legislation it may be observed that Tendrya will require SEN provision because he has a 'discrepancy between achievement and his general intellectual ability'. If we examine the categories above, we observe that Tendrya would be considered under Section 2 (those of cognition and learning) and that his SEN would be described as a specific learning difficulty, namely that of dyscalculia.

CASE STUDY 1.2

Social, mental and emotional health

Ben is eight years old and a member of a class in a rural primary school. Ben has difficulty making and keeping friends, both at school and in his home environment. In addition, over the past six months Ben has become isolated and withdrawn. His class teacher reports that Ben is failing to achieve and often disrupts the class with outbursts of very challenging behaviour. She has also noticed that Ben has intense difficulties in sitting still and has an inability to concentrate on even simple tasks. Ben's mother has said that he has had difficulties at home with simple tasks such as dressing and feeding himself. Ben's mother is very concerned about her son's progress at school as well as his impulsive and challenging behaviour at home.

Ben is presenting with significant difficulties that are providing a barrier to his learning. In terms of the legislation Ben's behaviour is so severe that he would be classified as having a SEN that falls into the category of social, mental and emotional health. After several assessments by the educational psychologist and paediatric team, Ben was assessed as having the recognised impairment of ADHD.

CASE STUDY 1.3

Sensory and/or physical needs

Bethany is a very happy, polite and well-motivated pupil who is due to sit her GCSEs in two years' time. She is often to be found at the centre of any playground games and has a wide circle of friends. She likes nothing better than reading her

(Continued)

(Continued)

favourite stories to her friends. Bethany's teachers had expected her to do very well in her forthcoming exams. However, recently Bethany's handwriting has become very untidy and she is becoming increasingly slow at copying work from the board during lessons. Her teachers have also noticed that she has been finding it more and more difficult to navigate around the school, and has fallen over several times both in the playground and at home. At a recent hospital assessment, Bethany was found to have a deteriorating eye condition. With this knowledge, the school has begun to make adaptations both to Bethany's classroom and her curriculum. The teachers have made sure that she always sits at the front of the class in lessons that involve reading from the board. They have also provided Bethany with large print books and with these she has rediscovered her love of reading.

For the purposes of the Code, Bethany would be classified as having a SEN that is sensory in nature. This is because her deteriorating eyesight is adversely affecting her ability to learn and her educational progress is therefore being restricted because of this.

SEN in Scotland, Wales and Northern Ireland

Within the UK the educational provision for children with learning difficulties broadly operates under similar legislative systems, although England and Wales are perhaps closest in terms of the operation of their legal and organisational systems. It is important to remember, however, that aspects of the Northern Ireland and especially the Scottish system can differ substantially from those observed within English schools.

For more detailed information that relates to the organisation of SEN support in Scotland, Northern Ireland and Wales, you will need to access the following links.

Scottish Executive: www.gov.scot/Publications/Recent

Northern Ireland Department of Education: www.deni.gov.uk/index/support-and-development-2/special_educational_needs_pg.htm

Welsh Assembly: http://gov.wales/statistics-and-research/?subtopic=Special+educational+needs&lang=en

Scotland

Until 2004, special education in Scotland was organised in a broadly similar manner to that in England. However, the legal framework in Scotland substantially changed in 2005 with the implementation of the Education (Additional Support for Learning) (Scotland) Act 2004. This Act, which was substantially amended in 2009, abolished the term SEN and replaced it with a much broader definition – that of 'additional support need'. Additional support need, as defined by the Act, refers to a child or young person who would benefit from extra help in order to overcome barriers to their learning.

The Act stipulates that some children and young people may require additional support for a variety of reasons, such as those who:

- have motor or sensory impairments
- are being bullied
- are particularly able or talented
- have experienced a bereavement
- are looked after in social care surroundings
- have a learning difficulty
- are living with parents who are abusing substances
- are living with parents who have mental health problems
- have English as an additional language
- are not attending school regularly
- have emotional or social difficulties
- are on the child protection register
- are young carers.

For the most up-to-date edition of the Scottish Code of Practice, see: www.gov.scot/Publications/2011/04/04090720/0.

Wales

In 2014 the system of educational provision in Wales was subject to a major review. This review produced a White Paper that outlined proposals to introduce a new legislative framework for supporting children and young people with additional learning needs. The proposed legislation attempted to provide uniformed provision for learners aged 0 to 25 and replace the terminology of SEN with additional learning needs. The proposed legislation also intended to replace Statements of SEN with a new Individual Development Plan. For the most up-to-date information, see: http://wales.gov.uk/consultations/education/proposals-for-additional-learning-needs-white-paper/?lang=en.

Northern Ireland

Special education in Northern Ireland was governed by the legal framework established within the Education (Northern Ireland) Order 1996 as amended by the SEN and Disability (Northern Ireland) Order 2005 (DoE, 2005). These orders place a duty for the provision for children with SEN upon the education and library boards and the boards of governors within mainstream schools. This Order increased the rights of children with SEN to attend mainstream schools and, for the first time, introduced disability discrimination laws for the whole of the education system in Northern Ireland. Similar to Scotland, Wales and England, the Department for Employment and Learning in Northern Ireland offers advice and guidance on how to operate a system for identifying and assessing children with learning difficulties. This guidance is contained within a Code of Practice, which came into effect in Northern Ireland on 1st September 2005. However, as in Wales in 2014, the Code and legislation that govern SEN became subject to review.

SEN: the scale of the issue

In 1978, the Warnock Report (DES, 1978) initially estimated that as many as 20 per cent of children, during their time at school, might experience a SEN that would necessitate additional educational provision to be made. The report also estimated that around 2 per cent of all children and young people of school age may have an educational need that is so severe that they would require a Statement of SEN. Over 35 years later, data from the Department for Education (DfE, 2013a) revealed that in January 2013 some 229,390 pupils in England had Statements of SEN. The data also revealed that the figure of 2 per cent provided by the Warnock Report in relation to children who would require a Statement underestimated the numbers of children and young people who would need the highest level of special educational provision. The percentage of pupils with Statements in 2013 was 2.8 per cent, which has remained relatively unchanged for some five years (see Figure 1.1). However, it is of interest to note that the number of children with SEN who do not require a Statement has decreased from 18.2 per cent of children in January 2010 (see Figure 1.2) to 16.0 per cent (some 1.55 million children) in January 2013.

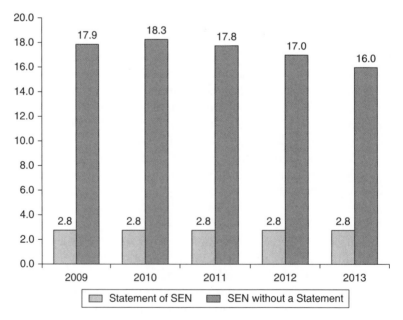

Figure 1.1   Percentage of pupils with SEN in schools in England

(source: DfE, 2013b: 1)

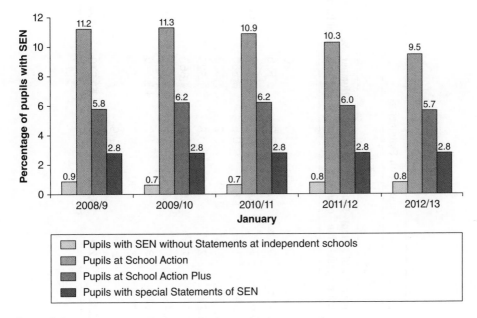

Figure 1.2 Percentage of pupils with SEN 2008/9 to 2012/13

(source: DfE, 2013c: 2)

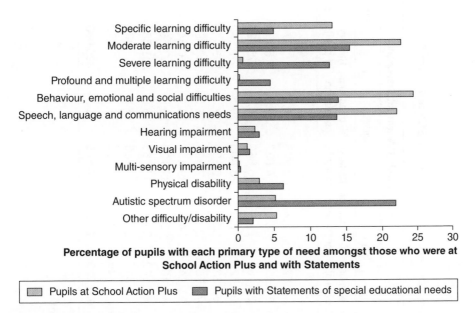

Figure 1.3 Percentage of pupils with each primary type of SEN in 2012/13

(source: DfE, 2013b)

Table 1.1 The age and gender of pupils with SEN in January 2013

| | Pupils with SEN without Statements | | | | | | Pupils with Statements | | | | | |
| | Boys | | Girls | | Total | | Boys | | Girls | | Total | |
Pupils aged:	Number of pupils	% of school population	Number of pupils	% of school population	Number of pupils	% of school population	Number of pupils	% of school population	Number of pupils	% of school population	Number of pupils	% of school population
2 and under	525	2.6	245	1.3	770	1.9	15	0.1	5	0.0	20	0.1
3	10,555	8.0	4,620	3.6	15,175	5.8	405	0.3	220	0.2	625	0.2
4	38,165	11.9	16,860	5.5	55,025	8.8	3,650	1.1	1,460	0.5	5,110	0.8
5	58,725	18.9	28,405	9.5	87,130	14.3	4,690	1.5	1,870	0.6	6,560	1.1
6	68,320	22.7	35,120	12.2	103,440	17.5	5,430	1.8	2,090	0.7	7,520	1.3
7	70,555	24.0	37,305	13.2	107,860	18.7	6,220	2.1	2,305	0.8	8,525	1.5
8	71,240	24.8	39,405	14.3	110,645	19.6	7,095	2.5	2,570	0.9	9,665	1.7
9	68,460	25.2	39,100	15.0	107,560	20.2	7,430	2.7	2,700	1.0	10,135	1.9
10	64,120	24.7	37,465	15.0	101,585	20.0	8,270	3.2	2,905	1.2	11,175	2.2
11	515	27.2	285	18.8	800	23.5	245	13.0	100	6.7	345	10.2
12 and above	45	10.5	30	7.3	75	8.9	20	4.4	10	1.9	25	3.2
Total all ages	**451,220**	**20.5**	**238,840**	**11.3**	**690,060**	**16.0**	**43,465**	**2.0**	**16,245**	**0.8**	**59,710**	**1.4**

(source: DfE, 2013b)

In 2013, government data (DfE, 2013a: 2) denoted that two and a half times more boys than girls would have a Statement of SEN at primary school and at secondary school they would be three times more likely to have a Statement. Pupils who were entitled to free school meals and from certain cultural and ethnic backgrounds were also more likely to have a Statement of SEN.

Data (DfE, 2013a: 3) show that in January 2013, 30.6 per cent of children with SEN in state-funded primary schools had speech, language and communication needs, and that this was the most common need experienced in this phase of education. The most common need experienced in secondary schools was that of behavioural, emotional and social difficulties. Pupils educated in a special school were most likely to experience severe learning difficulties (24.7 per cent).

- A mainstream school is one that provides an education for all pupils, including those with SEN.

- A special school is normally one that provides an education for children who have an EHCP.

Summary statistics for schools in Scotland: www.gov.scot/Publications/2012/12/2355/15.

Summary statistics for schools in Wales: http://wales.gov.uk/topics/statistics/headlines/schools2013/pupils-statements-special-educational-needs-january-2013/?lang=en.

Summary statistics for schools in Northern Ireland: www.deni.gov.uk/index/facts-and-figures-new/education-statistics/32_statistics_and_research-numbersofschoolsandpupils_pg/32_education_and_library_board_level/statistics_and_research_elb_data_1213-2.htm.

SEN: a contested concept

In relation to individual children and the implementation of government legislation, deciding what is or is not a learning difficulty and what counts or does not count as a SEN can be difficult. For example, Terzi (2005) argues that the concept of SEN itself is difficult to specify and is in practice unworkable. Indeed, the Office for Standards in Education, Children's Services and Skills (Ofsted) in its review of special educational provision in 2010 found wide variations both within local authorities and within schools themselves in the number of children specified as having a SEN. It is also interesting to note that their investigations revealed an inconsistency as to how SEN were defined within schools in England. Moreover, Ofsted expressed a concern that some schools were employing the term SEN to refer to those children who simply needed better teaching or pastoral support. It seems apparent that for some schools SEN are not defined solely in relation to children who have a learning difficulty.

In recent years, it has become apparent that educational professionals have been subject to difficulties and confusion in establishing the differences between disability/special needs and the definition of SEN itself (see Education and Skills Committee, 2006). A child, for example, may have a special need but might not actually have a SEN in terms of the Children and Families Act 2014. Many people do confuse SEN and special needs and this can result in serious consequences (Frederickson and Cline, 2002). For example, this form of confusion may lead to low expectations of achievement for all children whose first language is not English. In addition, difficulties in defining special needs and SEN may lead to confusion in planning support; for example, expecting the same staff to have an expertise in teaching English as a second language as well as teaching children with reading difficulties (Frederickson and Cline, 2009).

Special needs or SEN?

A child has a special need if they 'come from a social group whose circumstances or background are different from most of the school population' (Frederickson and Cline, 2002: 36). A special need may relate to any child, at any time, during their school career. So, for example, a child could have a special need if they have emotional or physical challenges not normally experienced by their peers; or if they have a history of physical abuse; or if they are a member of a religious or cultural group. The key difference between this concept and that of SEN is that a special need does not necessarily manifest itself as a barrier to learning. As such, a child with a special need would not normally need access to SEN provision as detailed within the Children and Families Act 2014.

READER REFLECTION

Using the information given in each of the case studies below and the detail offered above in relation to special provision, decide if each child has a SEN, special need or both.

CASE STUDY 1.4

Pamela

Pamela (aged 15) employs a walking frame to aid her mobility around her school. She really enjoys geography and swimming, but does not like having to learn her spellings for the English test that she has to take on a weekly basis.

CASE STUDY 1.5

Paulo

Paulo (aged eight) migrated to England with his family three months ago. He has a hearing impairment and has had difficulty in learning English during the time he has been in school.

In examining the case studies above you may have found that defining special needs and SEN can be a difficult thing to do. In the first case study, Pamela might be considered as having a special need because of her reduced mobility. Yet, while she might not enjoy having to learn her 'spellings', this would not be classified as being a barrier to her ability to learn. In the second case study, Paulo presents quite a different and rather interesting case, as he perhaps could have a special need as a result of being from a minority cultural group. In terms of the Children and Families Act 2014, though, Paulo's employment of English as a second language would not constitute a SEN. What is interesting here is that Paulo's inability to learn English is being complicated by his hearing impairment. If you examine the categories box on pages 5 and 6, it is clear that a hearing impairment would indeed be considered to be a SEN.

A further issue with the employment of the term SEN is that it has been argued that the definition itself is negatively linked with a medical view of disability. In addition, Frederickson and Cline (2009) believe that SEN is a problematic term because it is associated with negative conceptualisations and difficulties in decision making such as those denoted in the case studies above. Terzi (2005) suggests that the concept of SEN, rather than moving away from the notion of categorising children as Warnock (DES, 1978) envisaged, in reality does nothing more than introduce a new category – that of SEN! As such, any difficulty a child may have with learning may be seen by the professionals involved as resulting from personal deficit and difference, and not from the barriers created by such things as inaccessible buildings, inflexible curricula, inappropriate teaching and learning approaches, and school organisation and policies (we will discuss these ideas more fully in Chapter 2). This form of labelling is not only disrespectful and hurtful to the individual child but also has repercussions for the manner in which their learning is supported (CSIE, 2005). Despite these arguments, we must remember that the term SEN has, within the context of the English educational system, a legal status, and that it is a term that is commonly employed in the vast majority of state and independent schools.

medical model – [handwritten annotation]

Conclusion

Within this chapter, the definition of SEN was considered in terms of the legislation that governs England, Scotland, Northern Ireland and Wales. Recent data were detailed that determined how many children in England were considered to have a SEN and these figures showed that males have a greater prevalence of SEN than do females. The final section of this chapter demonstrated the difficulties that professionals sometimes have in deciding whether a child has a special need or a SEN.

The student activities and further reading detailed below will help you to develop a much deeper understanding of the terminology and operation of SEN in our schools. They are also designed to make you question whether SEN is still a term that has use for children being educated in the twenty-first century.

STUDENT ACTIVITIES

1 With another student, discuss the definition of SEN as outlined in this chapter. Use the internet to contrast the definition of SEN in England with the definition of additional needs employed in Scotland.

2 Read Ofsted's (2010) *The Special Educational Needs and Disability Review – A Statement is Not Enough*, which is available at: www.gov.uk/ government/publications/special-educational-needs-and-disability-review. Make a list of the problems that this review found with the employment of the term SEN.

3 Download the Nasen (2009) policy option paper *Special Educational Needs Has Outlived its Usefulness: A Debate*, which is available at: www. sen-policyforum.org.uk/ckeditor/plugins/doksoft_uploader/userfiles/2_ SEN%20debate%20policy%20paper%20final%20March%2009.pdf. With other students, consider what the benefits and drawbacks are of the continued employment of the term SEN within an educational system. You may wish to use your reading and discussion to plan for a debate in one of your seminar sessions.

Further reading

Florian, L. (2013) *The Sage Handbook of Special Education* (vol. 1). London: Sage.
Chapters 1, 2 and 4 of this text provide an expansive explanation and examination of the history and current developments of special education and SEN as well as an overview of its categories of need.

Galloway, D., Armstrong, D. and Tomlinson, S. (1994/2014) *The Assessment of Special Educational Needs: Whose Problem?*. London: Routledge.
Although somewhat dated, Chapter 1 of this text provides a fascinating read into the origin and meaning of the terminology of SEN.

Terzi, L. (ed.) (2010) *Special Educational Needs – A New Look. Mary Warnock and Brahm Norwich*. London: Continuum.
This text offers a critical examination of the principles and practices of SEN. The interest in this text lies in the fact that one of its main contributors is Baroness Warnock, who was a key architect of the SEN system we observe in operation in schools today.

2

PRINCIPLES OF SEN: THEORETICAL PERSPECTIVES

CHAPTER OBJECTIVES

- To introduce the major models of disability.

- To compare and contrast the models enabling you to develop a theoretical toolbox, and to enable examination of the sometimes difficult and complex concepts contained in the following chapters.

Introduction

This chapter examines the manner in which our perceptions, experiences and conceptualisations of SEN, disability and inclusion are shaped by ideological frameworks. The chapter will provide you with a theoretical toolbox, which will help you to critically examine, interpret and gain an understanding of some of the difficult and complex concepts that are employed within the field of SEN.

SEN provision is governed in England by the Code of Practice (DfE, 2014b); similar codes operate in Scotland, Northern Ireland and Wales. The Code, which came into force in September 2014, details the principles for the organisation and management of SEN provision.

The Code differs from the previous one in that:

- it covers children and young adults in the 0–25 age range

- it has a clearer focus on the views of children in the decision-making process

(Continued)

(Continued)

- for children with more complex needs, a coordinated assessment process and the new 0–25 EHCP replaced statements and learning difficulty assessments
- there is new guidance on the support that pupils should receive in education and training settings.

(DfE, 2014b)

Clause 19 of the Children and Families Act (DfE, 2014a) sets out the principles underpinning the Code. These principles are designed to support:

- the involvement of children, parents and young people in decision making
- the identification of children and young people's needs
- collaboration between education, health and social care services to provide support
- high-quality provision to meet the needs of children and young people with SEN
- greater choice and control for young people and parents over their support
- successful preparation for adulthood, including independent living and employment.

The principles underpinning the Code also operate alongside the statement of inclusion that exists in the national curriculum, which came into force in September 2014.

This inclusion statement maintains that teachers should:

1 Set suitable challenges

- Teachers should set high expectations for every pupil. They should plan stretching work for pupils whose attainment is significantly above the expected standard. They have an even greater obligation to plan lessons for pupils who have low levels of prior attainment or come from disadvantaged backgrounds. Teachers should use appropriate assessment to set targets that are deliberately ambitious.

2 Respond to pupils' needs and overcome potential barriers for individuals and groups of children

- Teachers should take account of their duties under equal opportunities legislation that covers race, disability, sex, religion or belief, sexual orientation, pregnancy and maternity, and gender reassignment.

- A wide range of pupils have SEN, many of whom also have disabilities. Lessons should be planned to ensure that there are no barriers to every pupil achieving. In many cases, such planning will mean that these pupils will be able to study the full national curriculum. A minority of pupils will need access to specialist equipment and different approaches.

- With the right teaching, which recognises their individual needs, many disabled pupils may have little need for additional resources beyond the aids that they use as part of their daily lives. Teachers must plan lessons so that these pupils can study every national curriculum subject. Potential areas of difficulty should be identified and addressed at the outset of work.

- Teachers must also take account of the needs of pupils whose first language is not English. Monitoring of progress should take account of the pupil's age, length of time in this country, previous educational experience and ability in other languages.

- The ability of pupils for whom English is an additional language to take part in the national curriculum may be in advance of their communication skills in English. Teachers should plan teaching opportunities to help pupils develop their English and should aim to provide the support pupils need to take part in all subjects.

(DfE, 2014a: 4.1–4.6)

Reading the Code together with the national curriculum inclusion statement reveals that, in part, the documents conflict with each other. For example, whilst the Code makes plain how factors internal to the child should be considered as the prime focus, the national curriculum places great importance on external factors such as the learning environment and the ability of teachers to be able to set suitable learning targets. What is made clear by reading these two documents together with the statements made by the Prime Minister, David Cameron (see Chapter 3), is that the provision of special education and inclusive education is an area that is subject to a number of differing ideologies as to how, and indeed where, children with SEN should be educated. In the following chapters we will trace the history and development of these competing ideologies in detail. However, for the moment we will concentrate on determining what these differing ideological frameworks are and how these lead to the implementation of different forms of educational practice and provision.

The influence of ideological frameworks

Special and inclusive education are viewed by society and the individuals within it from a number of differing perspectives (Slee, 1998). Basically, three major ideological frameworks may be distinguished (Skidmore, 1996: see also Figure 2.1). These are the:

- **Psycho-medical model** – this model locates children's disabilities and needs within an individual's impairment or the restrictions in activity caused by that impairment (Thomas, 2014). In essence the psycho-medical model focuses upon the 'person with disability as the problem and looks for cures' (Harpur, 2012: 2). This model is also sometimes called the individual tragedy, deficit or medical model.

- **Social model** – this model rejects the categorisation of disabled people on the basis of their impairment (Goodley, 2014) and presents disability and SEN as being the result of society's actions, values and beliefs, which seek to enforce social marginalisation upon minority groups (Slee, 1998).
- **Disability movement perspectives** – by which disabled people have sought to assert their human rights to be included within society through the employment of politics, the legal system and the disability arts movement.

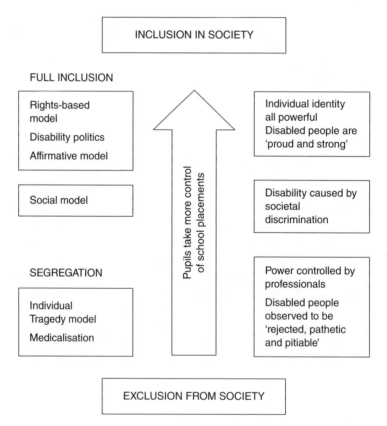

Figure 2.1   From segregation to inclusion: a continuum of models

Each of these theoretical frameworks operates by using different theories of:

- focus
- causation
- intervention methods
- education.

The psycho-medical model

Focus:	Individual child's difficulties.
Causation:	Individual pathology, impairments and disability.
Intervention:	Medical, health and educational professionals.
Education:	Segregation – special schools or units.

The individual tragedy model, or psycho-medical model as it has become known, has had a long and influential history (see Chapter 3). It is the traditional ideology through which Western society has conceptualised SEN and disabilities. These conceptualisations are embedded within the consciousness of society and reveal themselves through such things as the media, school textbooks, internet images, children's storybooks, language, beliefs, research, policy and the operation of professional practice. Within this ideological framework, special needs are understood to arise from the psychological, neurological or physiological limitations displayed by an individual (Skidmore, 1996). This model employs terminology and practices borrowed from the medical profession to judge children's limitations against what are called 'developmental' and 'functional' norms.

Developmental and functional norms are employed as a process of identification within the medical model. This identification requires developmental screening and assessment of a child suspected of having a SEN. By comparing a child's performance to the typical performance of other children of a similar age across a range of areas such as cognition, speech and language, fine and gross motor skills, and social and emotional functioning, the scope and severity of a child's SEN might be determined (see Dykeman, 2006).

The premise of the psycho-medical model is that a child's limitations will equate to a deficit in functioning that will need to be treated or indeed cured by professionals (Harpur, 2012). Through a process of screening, assessment and identification, children's limitations are labelled and described using clinical terminology, such as the 'aetiology of the syndrome' or 'the pathology of impairment' (Skidmore, 1996). In keeping with this model, the 'symptoms' displayed by a child are diagnosed and treatments, such as drug therapy or therapeutic/educational interventions, are employed in an attempt to cure or remediate the condition (Skidmore, 1996).

So the psycho-medical model:

- assesses what symptoms a child presents with
- diagnoses and labels the condition or syndrome
- attempts to fix the child's disability or syndrome (Harpur, 2012).

The psycho-medical model's preoccupation with the need to diagnose, label and treat a person, and the consequences of doing so, are highlighted in the case studies below.

CASE STUDY 2.1

Sara's story

Sara was born on 8th September 1999 in what was a difficult birth. When Sara was one year old, the doctors told me that her growth and mental functions were significantly delayed and that we should not expect her to achieve much in life. When she was two, the health care worker told me that she had special needs and that she had a significant learning difficulty that meant mainstream schooling would simply be impossible. At four, Sara was deemed to have a mental impairment and I was told that she would never be able to speak. When Sara went to school for the first time I was informed that she had a SEN and she would need special teaching in a special school. By the age of six, Sara was diagnosed with asthma, had autism, and complex and multiple learning difficulties. When Sara should have gone to secondary school she had to go into special care as she had multiple, severe and complex learning difficulties and had significant mental health issues. When Sara was 12, we removed her from the special school system and once again she became a person with a name not a syndrome or an issue. She was Sara – a beautiful girl who is full of fun, who has a mischievous laugh and a smile that lights up the room.

CASE STUDY 2.2

Peter's story

I always knew from the first day I went to school that I was different. The other children and the teachers constantly informed me of this. Other children were so hurtful they labelled me a 'nutcase' and a 'geek' and laughed at me when I twitched my head. One teacher said that I was an emotional cripple and that I was badly behaved. Another just used to call me vulgar and foul because I did swear a lot. To be perfectly honest, I prefer the label the doctors eventually gave me of Tourette syndrome. Some people do now understand that I cannot help what I do, it's just who I am.

READER REFLECTION

After reading Sara's and Peter's stories, reflect on the benefits and drawbacks of having a system of SEN that relies so heavily on diagnoses and labels.

The psycho-medical model and education

Since the earliest days of education there has been a strong link between educational provision for children with SEN and the medical profession. The employment of medical ideas has formed a significant part of the identification and placement of children within the schooling system. The result of this is to perpetuate educational goals in the narrow confines of remediation, diagnosis and prescription. Therefore, children who do not conform to learning environments are labelled and often removed from mainstream classrooms. Indeed, when state provision for special education was formulated in the nineteenth century, medical officers were involved in the process of identifying and placing children with special needs within a separate segregated system (see Chapter 3). Carrier (1986) contends that special education has employed the medical model to cloak itself in an aura of respectability in order to justify the interventions made by doctors, paediatricians and psychologists in the teaching of children with special needs. In reality, many people question this model's accuracy and its links to medicine, science and health (Elkins, 2009).

CASE STUDY 2.3

Ben's story

Ben is 11 and has a long history of behaviour problems, which have resulted in him being excluded from school for the day. He can be aggressive to his peers and is sometimes rude to members of staff. In class, he is easily distracted and has difficulty in sustaining his attention. He often fidgets and struggles to remain in his seat during lessons. Ben's teachers estimate that his literacy and numeracy skills are two years behind those of the other members of the class. As a result of the difficulties he has experienced, Ben was referred to an educational psychologist for an assessment. The psychologist saw Ben in school and administered the Wechsler intelligence test. She also gave Ben's teachers and parents a rating scale questionnaire to assess his behaviour both at home and at school. As a result of these assessments, Ben's parents were told that their son had ADHD. Ben's doctor prescribed a drug called methylphenidate (Ritalin), which he now takes twice a day.

READER REFLECTION

Ben's story shows how the application of the medical model seeks to assess, diagnose and cure the child. Having read Ben's story, reflect upon what other methods could have been employed rather than medication to help Ben progress with his learning and consider if Ritalin is the best answer to

(Continued)

(Continued)

Ben's learning difficulties. To help you further with your reflections on this issue, you may wish to read and watch:

- 'Does medication turn me into a different person?' This is part of the film *ADHD and Me*, which is available at: www.youtube.com/watch?v= Y8jqxZrjZII.

- 'Ritalin gone wrong', *The New York Times*, which is available at: www. nytimes.com/2012/01/29/opinion/sunday/childrens-add-drugs-dont- work-long-term.html?_r=0.

Criticisms of the psycho-medical model

One of the criticisms directed at the psycho-medical model is that it is theoretically weak. This is because it locates the causation of disability with the individual and their 'medical' problems. In this model there is a high degree of professional power over children and there is little coordination or collaboration between the professionals themselves. Indeed, for many writers in disability studies, this model is a 'patchwork quilt' of an approach 'whereby different and, sometimes contrasting information, is integrated' into a care plan 'but not necessarily with a unified outcome' that always benefits the child and their family (Gargiulo and Kilgo, 2014: 132). This model's application of pseudo-medical taxonomies and therapeutic treatments, which aim to cure disability, is undermined because the treatments offered invariably fail to take into account the society in which disabled people live. Many writers believe that a failure to view disability holistically means that the model denies disabled people their human rights and also fails to take into account their experiences of living in a disabling society (Swain and French, 2000).

In addition, this model relies heavily on professional judgements and it is because of this that it has become subject to challenge. As this model centres on the employment of scientific positivist methods of measurement, disabled people's lives are controlled by professionals and not by themselves. It is this, many argue, that leads disabled people to be objectified and dehumanised by medical and educational professionals (Lewis, 1991). The negative aspects of the medical model are clearly highlighted by Linda in her personal account of living with disability.

CASE STUDY 2.4

Linda's story

Hello, I'm Linda, a 66-year-old artist living in London. I know I am supposed to say at this point what my condition is and then tell you the words that the doctors use to label me – but hey I am a person, I am not a number and you can save your labels for your jam jars! My life though has been dominated by doctors who have told me since I was three that I had a problem they just had to fix. When I went to school I was told that I had to change, I had to fit in and that I should thank the doctors and the teachers who took control of my life. Note, here, that it's me that should change not **them**, the professionals or society. I was not prepared to change so they shut me away in an institution – 'out of sight and so out of mind'. The medical model teaches people to see me as different – not normal – to have suffered a tragedy. Through this model I am stereotyped, I become the pathetic victim and people should either fear me, or worse, pity me and my plight. From the time I was born doctors and their assessments have been used to say where I should live, where I should go to school and what type of education I should be allowed. Nobody listened to me and what I wanted. In my late 30s I broke away from all of this medicalisation and its professionals and became me again – Linda – a woman who just loves to paint!

It has also been suggested that these so-called scientific assessments are based upon vague symptoms, which professionals artificially construct into unitary medical conditions (Lewis, 1991). Many people argue that disabled people cannot, and moreover should not, be seen to be a single homogeneous group. Therefore, as they do not conform to particular types or behaviour, how can they be labelled using specific unitary taxonomies of sickness and illness (see Johnstone, 2001)?

The premise that there is one homogeneous group of disabled people is clearly undermined by this personal account.

Well, I must admit that I have real difficulties interacting with people with autism or worse, those who have Down's syndrome. I might use a wheelchair but I am not weird or thick like some of those people who have mental handicaps. I just cannot stand to be near those people. But there is the problem; I am always campaigning to stop people looking down on me; treating me as different and deficient but I do it to other people with disabilities.

As Johnstone (2001: 17) states, 'the creation of taxonomy of categories does little to adequately represent the sheer diversity and range that makes up the population of people with disabilities'. Furthermore, when this model is applied to special education it is observed to be nothing more than a mechanistic process whereby children's symptoms are identified and diagnosed and the condition or syndrome is treated within a specialised segregated system of education. As Skidmore (1996: 35) accounts, children within this system arrive 'at one end of a conveyor belt and are issued from the other end neatly allocated to their appropriate track in a smooth uninterrupted stream'. During the late 1970s, this mechanistic process, amongst other things, led to the medical model falling out of favour. However, in recent years, especially because of an 'explosion' of diagnosed cases of dyslexia and ADHD, it has experienced something of a renaissance (Lewis, 1991). For many disabled people the application of this model to education is simply wrong, because it leads to professionals focusing solely on what the child cannot do rather than on what he or she can learn (Corbett and Norwich, 2005). Many disabled people would point out that to employ the medical model to learning and behavioural difficulties effectively lets schools and educational institutions 'off the hook', because the causation of a pupil's 'problem' firmly resides with the pupil and not with the learning context (Lewis, 1991).

READER REFLECTION

Rieser (2014) discusses how the medical model observes the disabled person as the problem that needs to be fixed. He believes that within this model the person has to be adapted to fit into the world of normal people and that, if this is not possible, then disabled people should be segregated in specialised institutions or isolated at home. Rieser believes that the medical model puts power in the hands of the medical profession, which seeks to change the bodies in which disabled people live. He believes it is these professionals that have the power and they talk only of cures, normalisation and treatment.

Read the account above based upon the work of Rieser (2014), a campaigner on disability issues. Do you agree with the medical model's central tenet that it is the child's fault that they are unable to learn and not the teacher's or the doctor's? Is it possible or desirable to 'fix' all impairments and what does this say about society's view of disabilities?

The social model

Focus:	Societal attitudes, built environment.
Causation:	Barriers placed in the way of inclusion by society.
Intervention:	Non-disabled and disabled people working cooperatively to overcome the barriers.
Education:	Education evolves to make schooling inclusive.

The social model was built upon a number of guiding principles:

- It is the attitudes, values and beliefs operating within society that cause disability, not medical impairments.

- It is society that needs to be treated and cured, not individual people with impairments.

- Power over the lives of people with impairments should be held by those individuals, not professionals.

- Society, through its political apparatus, legislation and government, denies people with impairments their civil rights.

- Solutions to these issues cannot be effectively imposed from above or from outside, but can only be resolved by disabled people and non-disabled people working together.

(See Johnstone, 2001; Oliver, 1996)

This model was born out of the work of the Union of the Physically Impaired Against Segregation (UPIAS) and their document *Fundamental Principles of Disability* (UPIAS, 1976). This document argued that disability was not created by impairments but rather by disabling barriers created by society itself. As Oliver, a key architect of this document, stated:

> this was no amazing new insight on my part dreamed up in some ivory tower but was really an attempt to enable me to make sense of the world for my social work students and other professionals whom I taught. (Oliver, 1990a: 2)

So, the aim of the social model is to undermine the idea that disability is caused by bodily impairment. Within this ideological framework, it is society and the environment that disables people because it restricts their movements and their ability to communicate and function as effectively as people without impairments (Morgan, 2012). This model's central tenet is that society actually causes disability by placing barriers to accessibility in the way of people with impairments (Goering, 2010).

After years of experiencing segregation and medicalisation many disabled people found the social model revelatory. For example in Morgan's (2012) work, he recounts how many people saw the explanation offered by the social model as radical and an explanation for the difficulties they had been experiencing for years. Having been told that *they* were the problem, the focus now began to shift away from individuals with disabilities to external factors and the manner in which society created barriers that restricted access. Morgan accounts that the social model was also important as, for the first time, the attitudes and values of non-disabled people became subject to examination. For the disabled community then, Morgan accounts that this model was simply revolutionary.

Most built environments, for example, are designed by non-disabled people who have little or no understanding of the needs of people with impairments. A person who is a wheelchair user only becomes 'disabled' by the environments they operate within if these are not designed with accessibility in mind. If, for instance, a building lacks lifts, ramps and wide doorways, as well as accessible light switches, door handles, toilets and motorised doors, then a wheelchair user will be unable to function unaided within that building (Brainhe, 2007). This central tenet of the social model is brought into sharp focus by the following case study of an 18-year-old student who was 'disabled' by the actions of her local council.

CASE STUDY 2.5

The creation of 'disability': Lynette's story

I had been using my local library, which is located on the corner of my road, since I was five. During the past two years I have been studying for my A levels and so have used the library a lot, indeed, I was in there virtually every night. I enjoyed going to the library, although it was sometimes difficult to get into the building as it had been designed in the 1900s. The ramps that had been installed in the 1990s were, to say the least, difficult to use, and the narrow corridors made it tricky to move about especially when the library was full of people.

A few months ago I got a letter from the council informing me that the library was closing down and its resources were to be amalgamated with others into a new learning centre, which was to be on the site of a secondary school two miles away from where I live. Although this learning centre would not be as handy as the old library, I was so excited and looked forward to using it because the letter informed me it had up-to-date computer equipment and was in a building that had been specifically designed for people with impairments.

Last week, I decided to go to the new learning centre; I don't drive so I carefully planned my journey and found the best way to get there was by going on the bus. Luckily, the 'kneeling' bus service stopped at the end of my street and I knew that this bus could accommodate wheelchair users because the driver could lower the bus's floor so that I could gain access. I waited at the bus stop for about 15 minutes before the bus arrived and the door duly swung open. However, the bus did not 'kneel down' and so I could not get from the pavement onto the bus as the step was just too high up. I asked the driver to lower the step. He just shouted back, 'I am sorry I have not been trained in how to make the bus lower, only Trevor can do that and he's not on duty till tomorrow'. In that moment, I went from being happy and excited about my visit to the learning centre, to being a disabled person whose life was limited and controlled by the actions of others.

READER REFLECTION

Think about what could, or indeed should, have been done when the learning centre was opened to ensure that it was fully accessible to every person.

The social model and education

It is often claimed that disabled children are among the poorest and the most disadvantaged in their communities, and that they have been systematically excluded from education (Miles and Singal, 2010). A core component of the social model therefore is that education is a vitally important means of overcoming the prejudices shown by society towards people with impairments. Many people argue that our schooling system teaches children to observe disabled people as different from themselves, and sadly, how to discriminate against them. The social model is clear in its advocacy for school transformation (Norwich, 2014) and how education should evolve to make all schooling inclusive (Davis, 2014). Within a social model approach, then, the provision of education would be constituted very differently to that provided within the medical model. Indeed, the application of the principles of the social model to current educational systems would engender a major change in provision for children with SEN. A full application of this model would ensure that the segregated system of special schooling would end and be replaced with local accessible schools for all. Schools that adopted this ideological framework would also review their curriculum approaches, classroom management and organisations, as well as the expectations of teachers, assistants and their general ethos in order to ensure the stereotypical and discriminating attitudes that society holds in relation to disability and people with impairments would be broken down. (Chapter 4 provides further analysis of the move from segregated to inclusive approaches.)

Criticisms of the social model

The social model has now become recognised as being central to any debate relating to disability issues and the development of inclusive education (Terzi, 2005). As an ideological framework, it has also become embedded within the consciousness of many elements of British society. Furthermore, this model has helped to shift individuals and the collective understanding of disability (Johnstone, 2001), as well as transforming the attitudes that disabled people experience on a daily basis (Swain and French, 2000). However, from the outset this model was subject to criticism from disability charities, professional organisations as well as from disabled people themselves (Oliver, 2013). These criticisms, Oliver (2013) argues, have two main foci. The first is that the social model does not account for an individual's impairment. For example, Morris argued that:

> there is a tendency within the social model of disability to deny the experience of our own bodies, insisting that our physical differences and restrictions are entirely socially created.

> While environmental and social attitudes are a crucial part of our experience of disability – and do indeed disable us – to suggest that this is all there is, is to deny the personal experience of physical and intellectual restrictions, of illness, of the fear of dying. (Morris, 1991: 10)

The second area of critique is that this model fails to account for difference and presents disabled people as one homogenous group rather than a complex group of individuals who differ in terms of gender, sexuality, race, age and impairment (Oliver, 2013). For some people, this model's only real achievement is that it has led to a redefinition of the 'problem' of impairment and disability and although it works in theory it fails in practice (Morgan, 2012). For example, Swain and French (2000: 575) argued that the social model does nothing to challenge the 'erroneous idea that disabled people cannot be happy or enjoy an adequate quality of life'. As such, they contend that it allows the continuance of the notion that disability is a personal tragedy, which persons with impairments are forced to endure. Morgan (2012) also accounts that there is considerable evidence that many practitioners have struggled with the social model's premise that power and control should be shared with disabled people.

CASE STUDY 2.6

Becky's story

Becky is a student who has a hearing impairment. She is training to become a playworker. As part of this training Becky undergoes training in nursery and hospital settings. Becky's tutors carefully select the nursery settings and hospital wards that she visits. However, on her present placement the nursery refused to allow Becky to continue her work as they felt that her impairment created a risk. The headteacher of the nursery felt that Becky would not be able to successfully control the children or facilitate their learning, as she could not hear them talking and that Becky's speech was sometimes difficult to understand.

Do you think that this headteacher is acting reasonably? With a fellow student, provide your reasoning for and against supporting this headteacher's position.

For Terzi (2010), whilst the social model has made a fundamental contribution to knowledge, it has, by overlooking the concept of normality, presented only a partial view of the relationship between impairment, disability and society. Terzi suggests that, although this model provides a corrective to those based upon medical deficit, it still needs to clarify and extend its ideological framework if it is to be employed to understand the important and fundamental issues relating to the development of inclusive education.

An examination of Table 2.1 should leave you in no doubt that the differences in the ideological standpoints between the medical and social models are substantial. For those who subscribe to the medical model, then, the individual is the problem and the causation of the problem is the limitations in physical or psychological functioning (Oliver, 1990a). However, for those who accept the social model, it is society itself that is the problem and therefore the causation of disability stems from the barriers that society places in the way of inclusion for all its citizens.

Table 2.1   Contrasting the medical and social models

Medical model	Social model
Disability is an individual problem	Disability is a societal problem
Disabled people need care	Disabled people have rights
The agent of change is the professional	The agent of change is the individual, advocate or anybody who affects the arrangements between the individual and society
Segregation	Social integration
The remedy for disability and its related issues is cure or normalisation of the individual	The remedy for disablism is in the interactions between the individual and society
Disabled people can never be equal to non-disabled people	Disabled people have the same rights to full equality in society and education as all citizens
Personal adjustment	Environmental manipulation

As Oliver (1996: 41–2) famously stated, 'disability is wholly and exclusively social . . . disablement has nothing to do with the body'. This view is brought to the fore in the following, somewhat whimsical, account of the giraffe and elephant.

A giraffe and an elephant consider themselves friends, but when the giraffe invited the elephant into his home to join him in a business venture, problems ensued. The house was designed to meet the giraffe's needs, with tall ceilings and narrow doorways, and when the elephant attempted to manoeuvre, doorways buckled, stairs cracked and the walls began to crumble. Analysing the chaos, the giraffe saw that the problem with the door was that it was too narrow. He suggested that the elephant take aerobic classes to get him 'down to size'. The problem with the stairs, he said, was that they were too weak. He suggested the elephant take ballet lessons to get him 'light on his feet'. But the elephant was unconvinced of this approach. To him the house was the problem. (Glen Thomas, *Teaching Students with Mental Retardation* [1996]. Reprinted by permission of Pearson Education Inc., New York: p. 26.)

The affirmative model of disability

Focus:	societal attitudes and individual attitudes.
Causation:	impairment isn't the problem, learnt stereotypical attitudes are.
Intervention:	disabled people take control over their own bodies.
Education:	inclusive education.

Within the UK, the examination of the contrasting and contradictory explanations of causation and the interventions of disability, as outlined by the medical and social models, has led to the development of a more positive model of disability (Johnstone, 2001). This model emerged during the late twentieth century due to the work of the disability arts movement and disabled people's organisations (see Chapter 3). The affirmation model was first introduced by Swain and French in 2000 as a development to those underlying principles of the social model (Cameron, 2013).

The principles of this model, according to Swain and French (2000), are that it promotes a non-tragic view of disability and impairment, which includes positive social identities for disabled people. In addition, it makes plain that people with disabilities can, and do, lead rich and fulfilling lives. Swain and French believe that in affirming this positive identity, people with disabilities seek to undermine the systems of normality that dominate society.

READER REFLECTION

It is argued that the medical model is based upon negative conceptualisations of disabled people. How would the model that Swain and French (2000) present lead to the creation of positive identities for disabled people?

The affirmative model developed in direct opposition to the personal tragedy view of disability and impairment that had dominated societal thinking in the twentieth century. The model's theoretical significance is that it seeks to extend the social model by incorporating the lived experiences of disabled people (Johnstone, 2001). Swain and French (2004) identified what the affirmation model is and is not about (see Cameron, 2013).

The affirmation model is about:

- being different and thinking differently, both individually and collectively
- the affirmation of unique ways of being situated in society
- disabled people challenging presumptions about themselves and their lives in terms of not only how they differ from what is average or normal, but also about the assertion, on their own terms, of human embodiment, lifestyles, quality of life and identity
- ways of being that embrace difference.

(Swain and French, 2000: 185)

The aim of the affirmation model is to challenge the assumption that disabled people want to be cured, as well as to encourage the undermining of societal presumptions of what it means to be 'normal' and what constitutes a happy and fulfilling life (Swain and French, 2000; 2004). Deeply rooted beliefs about what it means to be 'normal' are illustrated in the three case studies detailed below.

CASE STUDY 2.7

What does it mean to be 'normal'? Paula's story

I attended a special school during the 1950s that was miles away from where I lived. One day I became really upset because the school nurse had told me that I should never give up hope – that one day medical science would find a cure for my illness. 'Wouldn't that be great?' she said if I could run around and play like the other little normal children. Well, I became really angry and shouted at the nurse. I told her that I just loved the way I was and did not want to be cured or fixed. My mates fell about laughing when I said this. The nurse though was not very pleased and told me that I really did not understand my condition and that I was 'wrong in the head' to believe that my disability was a good thing. She sent me to the headteacher and I was kept in detention for two nights for showing a bad attitude to the nurse.

CASE STUDY 2.8

What can happen if we strive for normality? Ismail's story of having a visual impairment

Well I do not have extraordinary hearing, I cannot navigate well in foggy conditions and, no, I would not be good at tuning pianos. These are all things that 'normal' people have said that I should be good at. What I am is visually impaired and this means I can only 'see' light and dark and nothing else. It is a condition I have had from birth. Before I was born, my parents were advised to have a termination because my impairment also has learning difficulties connected to it. The doctors told my mum that my life would not be worth living. Since the age of one, through various operations and filling me full of tablets, they have been trying to fix my impairment and remediate what they say is my poor behaviour. I do not want to be fixed or cured. I am happy as I am and I think it is disgraceful that my parents were told to terminate my life before I was born. The doctors never ask what I want, if they did I would tell them that I have a happy and fulfilling life, and that I just want to be left alone.

CASE STUDY 2.9

A personal blog: why do people feel that creating normality is important to all disabled people? Lynette's story

My name is Lynette, I am 15 and I am a wheelchair user. I like my wheelchair – it is the latest model. It is fully powered and I can beat my friends in races because it goes so fast. However, despite this new wheelchair, I still find life difficult. Many buildings are inaccessible to me and exploring around my local area is difficult, as all the pavements are uneven and full of pot holes. This means that my wheelchair constantly gets broken, or worse, it sometimes even tips over. When I travel about I am often told that I get in the way. On buses I often cannot get on because the accessible space is taken up with people's bags or pushchairs and I am told that I will have to wait for the next bus.

In the social model my impairment is recognised but it states that the disability I face on a daily basis comes from people's attitudes and the barriers that society places in my way. In my view, all buses and buildings should be accessible and people should be taught in school to have a better attitude towards people with impairments. No medical operation or new tablet will cure an inaccessible building or a bad attitude. We need to move away from this simple notion that a medical cure can fix everything that gets in the way of the daily trials and tribulations I have when I travel around in my wheelchair.

Swain and French (2004) argue that it is the premise of normality created by the medical model that has caused the formulation of stereotypical attitudes towards disability. They state it is these attitudes which act as a catalyst to the continuance of disability and the view that disabled people endure a tragic and pathetic state. This model, therefore, is built upon the premise that disabled people should have control of their lives and not medical or educational professionals. The model is based firstly upon identifying how society excludes people and, secondly, it seeks to develop an image of disabled people that is 'strong, angry and proud'. For Johnstone (2001: 22) the affirmative model's real significance is its 'potential for moving on the practical and academic understanding of disablement to a new level of inclusive and individual understanding'.

Disability politics and the rights-based model of disability – 'nothing about us without us'

Focus:	political/full inclusion.
Causation:	societal structures, values and beliefs.

Intervention:	radical interventions, use of the law to end discrimination against disabled people.
Education:	fully inclusive, with no tolerance being given to a separate segregated system of education.

Within the rights-based approach, people with disabilities would have the same rights and access to employment, health care and to education. This approach is about removing physical, attitudinal and social barriers that blight the lives of disabled people. The rights-based model seeks to take on employers, educational and health care professionals as well as policy makers to ensure our rights as people are upheld. This means that people would employ universal building design, coordinated public services and accessible technology, and that government would ensure that these are well resourced through the services we use. It also means though that those who do not do this would face the penalties that are enshrined in the laws that govern our land.

> 'Nothing about us without us' was the slogan promoted in 1981 by Disabled Peoples' International. This slogan's power derives from its opposition to oppression and resonates with the philosophy and history of the disability rights movement (Charlton, 2000).

According to Johnstone (2001: 22), both the social and the affirmative models are based upon 'liberal rather than radical conceptions of equal opportunities'. Critics of these models therefore suggest that what is actually required is a framework where the politicisation of disabled people (Johnstone, 2001) challenges the 'hegemony of disablism' (Allan, 2003: 31). This framework, then, should actively challenge the exclusion of disabled people from governance structures of businesses and education, and challenge the general perception of disabled people as helpless and defined by impairment (Vanhala, 2010). Disability politics seeks, therefore, by the employment of the political and social arena, to confront the non-disabled 'oppressors who perpetuate the exclusion of disabled people' (Allen, 2003: 31). Disability politics as a movement aims to liberate the silent voices of disabled people in an attempt to undermine societal values, beliefs and conventions, which are based upon the ideology of the medical model of disability (Allen, 2005). Proponents of this model argue that through direct action new affiliations and identifications for disabled people can be constructed. They maintain that it is through such new identities that people with impairments will emerge into mainstream politics to campaign for better provision for their minority group and for the removal of all barriers to inclusion in society (Shakespeare, 2006). In recent years, the growing impetus of the disability movement has moved the discussion of disability into encompassing legislation that governs human rights (Johnstone, 2001). Through the application of disability politics a more radical ideology has now emerged, one whose core principles follow a rights-based approach to the explanation of the provision received by disabled people. This model, through the application of equal opportunity theory, seeks to expand the social model of disability to include those dimensions of disablement caused by civil, political, economic, social, cultural and environmental factors (Johnstone, 2001).

The rights-based model and education

The rights-based model's central principle is that all children should attend a mainstream school that is based within their local community (Kenworthy and Whittaker, 2000). This model of disability seeks to challenge the widely held societal belief regarding the legitimacy of segregated education and the premise that it is simply impossible to include all children in mainstream education (CSIE, 2005). Based upon the principles encompassed by the rights-based model, the Centre for Studies on Inclusive Education (CSIE) has outlined ten reasons why inclusive education should become the norm and not the exception within British schools.

---

1 **HUMAN RIGHTS**   All children have the right to learn together.

2 Children should not be devalued or discriminated against by being excluded or sent away because of their disability or learning difficulty.

3 Disabled adults, describing themselves as 'special school survivors', are demanding an end to segregation.

4 There are no legitimate reasons to separate children for their education. Children belong together – with advantages and benefits for everyone. They do not need to be protected from each other.

5 **GOOD EDUCATION**   Research shows children do better, both academically and socially, in inclusive settings.

6 There is no specific teaching or care in a segregated school that cannot take place in an ordinary school.

7 Given commitment and support, inclusive education is a more efficient use of educational resources.

8 **SOCIAL SENSE**   Segregation teaches children to be fearful and ignorant and breeds prejudice.

9 All children need an education that will help them develop relationships and prepare them for life in the mainstream.

10 Only inclusion has the potential to reduce fear and to build friendship, respect and understanding.

(CSIE, 2008)

CASE STUDY 2.10

Mechanisms for claiming rights and holding governments accountable

Access to the courts can be an effective means of challenging the failure of the state to make adequate provision for education, achieve equality of opportunity or protect children whose rights are violated in the education system. A successful illustration of the use of legal redress is provided by a small disability organisation in Nepal that took the government to court to argue that the failure to provide additional time in public examinations for 'blind children' denied them the right to equality of opportunity in education, given that braille takes longer to read and write. The court decreed that blind children should be entitled to extra time in examinations to reflect this difference.

Legal mechanisms are not the only means of achieving accountability. Others include:

- **Transparency** – ensuring that people understand how and what decisions are being made, what resources are being provided to support the right to education and establishing public processes for regular reporting on progress.

- **Information** – rights are meaningless unless people are aware that they exist and that governments have obligations with regard to their implementation.

- **Participation** – creating effective consultative processes that offer meaningful opportunities for marginalised groups, including children, to contribute their experience and expertise to the development of education policy and provision.

- **Parliamentary accountability** – establishing all-party parliamentary committees to scrutinise government action and hold it accountable for its obligations to respect the right to education. (See UNICEF, 2007: 42)

Conclusion

This chapter introduced you to the major ideological models that affect people's knowledge and understanding of disability, impairment and inclusive schooling. Within the chapter we analysed the different ways in which each model identifies what the causation of disability is and how the effects of such might be ameliorated. This analysis revealed huge ideological differences – differences that affect the contemporary values and beliefs about the way schooling for children with SEN should be organised. Analysis of these ideological frameworks highlighted the inherent limitations in each model.

We observed, for example, how within the psycho-medical model pupils can be objectified and dehumanised, whereas within the social model the problem of disablism is placed firmly with society and pupils' impairments are in some way diminished. For Skidmore (1996), however, the fault of many of the ideological models is their tendency to reduce complex personal and societal issues to single unitary solutions. As such, the medical and social models do not provide a complete or satisfactory explanation of the way in which disability and SEN are conceptualised within our society. Oliver (1990a) believes that spending too much time on a consideration of what is meant by the medical or social models should actually be viewed as dangerous. He believes this to be the case because such discussions are based upon nothing more than semantics and as such they obscure the real issues of disability – those of oppression, discrimination and inequality.

In Chapters 3 and 4 we will examine how these ideological frameworks have developed over time and critically analyse their effect upon the development of education for children with SEN. Furthermore, in Chapter 5 we will look carefully at how the development of the social model was influential in the emergence and evolution of inclusive education.

The student activities and further reading detailed below are designed to provide you with a clearer understanding of the major ideological models of disability considered in the chapter. Throughout these activities, consider the question: is it possible, or even desirable, to have a system of fully inclusive education?

STUDENT ACTIVITIES

1 Carefully consider the CSIE inclusion statement. By using internet and journal sources, provide the evidence to support its view that fully inclusive education is the only way to organise educational provision for children with SEN.

2 Think carefully about the models of disability that you have been introduced to in this chapter. What are the inherent difficulties and benefits with each of these models for children who have impairments and disabilities?

3 Think carefully about what inclusive education is. Prepare an information pack for parents and children that introduces them to the models of disability presented above.

Further reading

Cameron, C. (2013) 'The affirmation model', in C. Cameron (ed.), *Disability Studies: A Student's Guide*. London: Sage.
Chapter 2 of this book provides an expansive discussion of the history and development of the affirmative model of disability.

Patton, S. (2011) *Don't Fix Me; I'm Not Broken: Changing our Minds About Ourselves and our Children*. Alresford: O Books.
In this book, Sally Patton brings a rather different perspective to how parents feel about their children with SEN. Rather than trying to 'fix them', the book presents a powerful message in relation to how we as a society must move past the labelling of our children.

Terzi, L. (2010) *Justice and Equality in Education: A Capability Perspective on Disability and Special Educational Needs*. London: Continuum.
This is a solid text that adds much detail to the basic ideas that have been introduced in this chapter. Chapter 2 (pp. 15–41) of this text provides a particularly good philosophical critique of the social model.

Wearmouth, J. (2012) *Special Educational Needs – the Basics*. London: Routledge.
This text provides a very useful guide to how SEN labels have developed over time. It also provides a very good overview of some of the more common 'conditions, syndromes and impairments'. The introductory chapter contains a detailed examination of the label of SEN and how some see such terminology as 'weasel words' that are intertwined with perceptions of helplessness and inadequacy.

3
DISABILITY: EXPLANATORY BEGINNINGS

CHAPTER OBJECTIVES

- To introduce how people with disabilities have been perceived by society from the time of the Stone Age through to the twentieth century.

- To explore how definitions of disability have developed in government legislation from the 1990s onwards.

- To examine the image of disability created by the media, children's textbooks and storybooks as well as internet technology.

- To consider how societal attitudes towards disability can influence educational policy.

Introduction

This chapter provides an introduction to disability by tracing the way in which perceptions of disability and impairment have changed over time. It examines how disability was understood in the ancient world and how developments in 'scientific thinking' led to the creation of theoretical frameworks that still dominate current educational thinking and practice today. In addition, it examines how the concept of disability evolved within government legislation from the 1990s to the present day. The final section of the chapter discusses how societal conceptions of disability are formed through such things as the media, children's textbooks and storybooks as well as internet technology. The chapter ends by considering how societal attitudes operating within the educational environment have the propensity to influence the evolution of the policies of inclusive and segregative education.

READER REFLECTION

Before you begin reading this chapter, make a note of your understanding of disability. You may also wish to consider what have been the major influences on the development of your knowledge of disability.

From 1997 until 2010, educational policy indicated that the placement of disabled children into mainstream schools, so called 'inclusive education', coupled with successful learning experiences, would lead to non-disabled children's attitudes and conceptions of disability becoming more positive (Hodkinson, 2007a). Whilst some argued that this policy initiative was based upon 'idealistic assumptions', as in reality some pupils with impairments were 'socially ostracised' (Spaling, 2002: 91), it did, at face value, indicate that for the New Labour government a social model of disability was of importance. Interestingly, David Cameron, who in 2010 became Prime Minister of a coalition government of Conservatives and Liberal Democrats, stated:

> We believe the most vulnerable children deserve the very highest quality of care. We will improve diagnostic assessment for schoolchildren, prevent the unnecessary closure of special schools, and remove the bias towards inclusion. (Cabinet Office, 2010)

An examination of the language contained in Cameron's statement, for example, phrases such as, 'vulnerable children', 'highest quality of care', 'improve diagnostic assessment' and 'remove the bias towards inclusion', suggests that for this government a different model of disability was perhaps dominating policy decisions. Whatever may be said about the Coalition government's educational policy, it would seem important to gain a knowledge, understanding and appreciation of how society views disability and disablism. This is because at the end of the day governments are influenced by the attitudes that dominate societal thinking.

READER REFLECTION

Think carefully about the language employed by David Cameron in the statement above. What model of disability do you believe is influencing this government's policy decisions in SEN?

Historical conceptions of disability

Disability, as conceptualised in history, is a difficult area to study as the terminology employed in ancient texts is often 'slippery' and viewed through the lens of modern times (Goodey and Rose, 2013: 17). However, in many Western societies disability is grounded within superstitions, myths and beliefs about people with impairments. These perceptions dominate societal thinking despite archaeological evidence from 1.6 million years ago, which suggests that Neanderthal peoples incorporated disability and impairment as part of a common good within society (Spikins, 2014). Moreover, in Roman times, whilst some impairments such as a 'hunched back' or 'dwarfism' were seen as sources of humour, skeletal remains from Gloucester and Dorchester show that during this period some people with severe impairments did survive into adulthood. Indeed, documentary evidence suggests that some individuals with impairments prospered (Wright-Southwell, 2013).

READER REFLECTION

Read the statement by Pliny the Younger (61AD–113AD), a magistrate in ancient Rome. What might this evidence tell us of the attitudes of some ancient Romans towards disability and impairment?

> Crippled and deformed in every limb, he could only enjoy his vast wealth by contemplating it and could not even turn in bed without assistance. He also had to have his teeth cleaned and brushed for him. ... Yet he went on living, and kept his will to live, helped chiefly by his wife. (Source: Wright-Southwell, 2013)

Present-day conceptions of disability, however, have their roots in classical Greek theatre and culture. Here, from the earliest times, the 'image of impairment' was linked with people's 'judgements about social acceptance' (Johnstone, 2001: vii) and society was grounded upon 'the idealisation of the body shape' (Barnes and Mercer, 2003: 23). Throughout the religious cultures of ancient Greece, ancient Rome and in the literature and art of Renaissance Europe, mainly negative conceptions of people with impairments were perpetuated (Borsay, 2005).

Disability: early religious conceptions

Throughout the history of our society, then, disability has been viewed as a contentious issue where the role of cultural values in the development of attitudes has been crucial. From the distant past, societal conceptions of impairments and disabilities have been influenced by Judaeo-Christian theology. The Bible contains many examples that serve to reinforce people's dread of impairment and this fear was further enforced by the Church's determination that people with impairments were afflicted with the soul of Satan as punishment for their past ancestral transgressions (Shakespeare, 1994).

In Leviticus, Chapter 21, verses 17–20, the Bible calls for people with visual and physical impairments to be excluded from offering bread in the temple. In Deuteronomy, Jones (2003) believes there is a clear reference that people with mental impairments should be regarded as 'beasts' and therefore should be treated as less than human.

In Leviticus, God instructs Moses to tell Aaron that He will not permit Aaron's disabled descendants to serve as priests:

No one of your offspring throughout their generations who has a blemish may approach to offer the food of his God. For no one who has a blemish shall draw near, one who is blind or lame, or one who has a mutilated face or a limb too long, or one who has a broken foot or a broken hand, or a hunchback, or a dwarf, or a man with a blemish in his eyes or an itching disease or scabs or crushed testicles. ... He may eat the food of his God. ... But he shall not come near the curtain or approach the altar, because he has a blemish, that he may not profane my sanctuaries. (www. kingjamesbibleonline.org; see Parry, 2013: 22 for a detailed account of disability and early Christian traditions)

It is apparent, then, that the development of religious conceptions of impairment and disability was inextricably linked to impurity and sin.

READER REFLECTION

Carefully read these passages from the King James Bible. What message do they offer in relation to how people with impairments should be treated?

John 9: 1–3

Now as Jesus passed by, He saw a man who was blind from birth. And His disciples asked Him, saying, 'Rabbi, who sinned, this man or his parents, that he was born blind?'. Jesus answered, 'Neither this man nor his parents sinned, but that the works of God should be revealed in him.' (www.kingjamesbibleonline.org)

Samuel 25: 8

Wherefore they said the blind and the lame shall not come into the house. (www.kingjamesbibleonline.org)

Now consider this statement by St. Augustine (354–430AD), a theologian who was significant in the growth of Western Christianity. What does this statement tell us about early Christian conceptions of disability?

[why did you] ... place in this oh so beautiful world the blind, the one-eyed, the cross-eyed, the deaf, the mute, the lame, the deformed, the distorted, the wormy, the leprous, the paralysed, the epileptic and those who are deficient in various other ways – some even look monstrous to us, because of their extreme ugliness and the horrible strangeness of their limbs ... some of slow mind, and others of mind so foolish that a human being, would rather live with cattle than with that sort of human being. (See Laes et al., 2013)

Noteworthy, in this respect, is that the founders of the Western church, Luther and Calvin, both '"dammed as emissaries of Satan" people who today we would label as having mental impairments' (Manion and Bersani, 1987: 235). Furthermore, Martin Luther proclaimed that he had seen Satan in a visually impaired child (Haffter, 1969). Indeed, during this period children with visual impairments were labelled as 'changelings' and were offered up by the Church as living proof of Satan's power on Earth. In the *Malleus Maleficarum*, a late fifteenth-century treatise sanctioned by the Pope, children with visual impairments were classified as being born from a liaison between their mother, witches and sorcery (Oliver and Barnes, 1998). These views are of course dated, however, it is perhaps relevant to note the alleged comments of one England football manager who seemed to openly subscribe to these forms of religious prejudices (see www.theguardian.com/football/1999/jan/30/newsstory.sport7).

Whatever may be said about such comments, it seems apparent that throughout history society has held that people with impairments, 'were possessed by the devil and therefore the common treatment was to beat the devil out of them' (Shakespeare, 1994: 284). While we may argue as to the modern relevance of these theological conceptions, it is perhaps more relevant here to examine how this concept has been transformed within our society with the passage of history.

Conceptions of disability: transformations through time

In tracing the historical development of societal attitudes to, and the conceptualisation of, disability it is helpful to employ the organising construct proposed by Finkelstein (1980). Within this construct there are three distinct periods in the development of the concept of disability. Later in the chapter, we will consider Finkelstein's third period of development, that of the post-industrial society (this will be countenanced through a critical examination of the employment of disability within both government legislation and the theoretical frameworks of impairment developed during the twentieth century). For now, though, let us turn to Finkelstein's first phase, that of the feudal period.

The feudal period

During the pre-industrial phase, which operated during the seventeenth to early nineteenth century in Western Europe, most people with impairments were routinely integrated within their villages and local communities. During this feudal period existence for many people was mainly based within agrarian economies, and for some, small cottage-based industries provided a livelihood (Barnes and Mercer, 2003). Indeed, conceptions of being 'able bodied' did not at this time relate to physical attributes *per se*, but rather in the capacity of an individual for farm labouring.

As societal relations and interactions during this period focused on subsistence rather than on wealth accumulation, many people with impairments were able to survive as part of their local community, albeit, with the majority existing at the bottom of the economic ladder. So while people with impairments might be observed to be individually unfortunate, they were not, as a rule, explicitly excluded from society (Oliver, 1990b). On occasion, though, people with impairments did experience a form of segregation, which was directly due to economic and familial circumstances. For example, for those people who were rejected by their families or whose economic performance was curtailed by impairment, begging or a reliance on charity alms could become the norm (Barnes and Mercer, 2003). In addition, for those with severe impairments who had managed to survive the high infant mortality rate their existence might become framed alongside the sick and bedridden in the small religious hospitals (Oliver and Barnes, 1998).

During the feudal period, then, although categories of disability were observable, and this did create a stigma around some individual disabilities (Parry, 2013), people with physical and mental impairments were regularly included, although they mainly occupied the lowest echelons of their society. It is also important to recognise that throughout this period disability was not solely conceptualised within the realms of bodily impairment, but rather was correlated to economic performance. As Gleeson writes, 'whilst impairment was probably a prosaic feature of feudal England, disablement was not' (1997: 194).

READER REFLECTION

Carefully consider the concept of disability that operated during the feudal period. What did society observe to be the causation of disability during this time?

The industrial capitalism period

Towards the end of the eighteenth century, Britain, Europe and North America witnessed an 'intensification of the commercialisation of land and agriculture' (Oliver and Barnes, 1998: 29). For Finkelstein, this period of industrial capitalism is most important as it transformed society's concept of disability. The rapid spread of market economics led to changes in working and living conditions as 'Westernised' countries changed to absorb the new mechanised systems of production. Increasingly, however, the Industrial Revolution introduced limitations upon the employment of people with impairments. As Ryan and Thomas (1980: 101) explain, 'The speed of factory work, the enforced discipline, the time keeping and production norms all these were highly unfavourable changes from the slower, more self determined and flexible methods of work into which many handicapped people had been integrated'.

'Handicapped' may be defined as a physical or mental impairment that renders a person unable to perform certain functions. It is a term that was used extensively in the original World Health Organization (WHO) classifications' system (1980) of disability, but it has now been replaced with the term 'participation'. This reflects the social model of disability, which considers what a person 'can do' in a particular environment when given the appropriate resources and support rather than focusing upon what a person can't do.

Gradually, the new social and economic order, with its expanding cities and towns, forced the decline of local and family-based support systems. Ultimately, this led to some people with impairments becoming disadvantaged and excluded from employment and society. Both Finkelstein (1980) and Oliver (1990b) have argued that it was the spread of this 'liberal utilitarianism' (Oliver and Barnes, 1998: 26) that forced society to consider that 'defective bodies and minds were . . . dangerous and threatening' (Barnes and Mercer, 2003: 32). These negative conceptions were further reinforced during this period by the spread of Darwinism and its theory of the survival of the fittest. With the passage of time and the development of the principles of eugenics, people with impairments were increasingly identified as being a threat to social progress.

> *Eugenics* was a term first employed by Sir Francis Galton (1822–1911) in relation to the study of selective breeding to improve the quality of the human race.

Finkelstein (1980) contends here that the birth of industrial capitalism was significant because it established society's modern-day concepts of disability. He suggests that as a direct result of these transformed conceptions, people with impairments routinely became segregated from the rest of society.

READER REFLECTION

Using the knowledge and understanding gained in Chapter 2, consider which concept of disability would best describe that in operation during the industrial capitalist phase of history.

The rise of industrial capitalism, then, created a new ideological framework, one in which 'able bodied' normality 'became the yardstick' for 'judging people with impairments as less than whole' (Oliver, 1990b: 89). The transformation of society's conception of disability led to the birth of large institutions as a method of controlling these societal 'misfits'. In turn, the individualistic medical approach to disability emerged as the new conceptual orthodoxy. From this time forward, Finkelstein comments, Western societies equated disability with 'flawed' minds and bodies. People with impairments were observed to have 'suffered' a 'personal tragedy', and thus they became both a social problem and a burden to the rest of society. Therefore, the nineteenth and twentieth centuries witnessed the approaches to dealing with people with impairments becoming more and more dominated by this conception of disability within education, medicine and charitable endeavours.

The post-industrial period

In his third phase, Finkelstein (1980) proposed that the post-industrial society brought forth more positive opportunities for the inclusion of people with impairments. He suggests that within this period in society disability will become reconceptualised, moving away from the notion of 'individual tragedy' and replacing it with the premise that disability is nothing more than a form of oppression (see Chapter 2 for a fuller discussion). However, before we proceed in employing this schema to trace the transformation of the concept of disability, it is important to note that Finkelstein's construct has been subject to criticism.

Firstly, it is still apparent even within the twenty-first century that the concept of disability as an individual medical tragedy is one that has maintained a powerful influence on societal attitudes. This is because the work of professionals in our society is still very important for the management of some people's medical conditions. Secondly, Finkelstein's analysis assumes a simple correlation between the development of industry and changing conceptions of impairment and disability. For some, this model is subject to a theoretical naivety in its premise that technological development and professional involvement will bring a new wave of integrative sentiment into society. Thirdly, the organising construct is further criticised because it fails to acknowledge that negative constructs of impairment existed before the advent of the Industrial Revolution. Indeed, as we will observe later, even today they still exert a powerful influence over societal conceptions of disability through such enterprises as the media.

Leaving all this critique aside, though, it is still useful to trace how the concept of disability was transformed during the late twentieth and early twenty-first century through the work of the disabled people's movement, international organisations and also via government legislation.

A reconceptualisation from within

The latter part of the twentieth century witnessed societal conceptions of disability slowly transforming and this was in no small part due to the work of people with impairments themselves. The 1970s and 1980s were a period when disabled people collectively emerged from the shadows and moved 'from acquiescence [to government policy] to uncertainty, discontent and finally to outright anger' (Davis, 1996: 124), becoming united in their condemnation of the way society was treating them as second-class citizens. Within the next section we will examine how, through the work of disabled people, society's understanding of disability has moved from observing it to be a tragic individual problem to one that observes it to be a 'situation of collective institutional discrimination and social oppression' (Oliver and Barnes, 1998: 3).

During the mid to late 1970s, the first politically orientated groups of disabled people were founded in the UK. In 1974 the Disability Alliance group was founded and 1976 saw the emergence of the UPIAS. UPIAS's aim was to replace separate segregated institutions for people with impairments with a right for all people to be able to engage fully in society and to live independent lives (Shakespeare, 2006).

These groups, through the employment of their shared experiences, re-examined the orthodoxy of the individual tragedy model of disability. In turn, this examination led to the transformation of the concept of disability into what we know today as the social model. Crucially, within this transformation the UPIAS drew an important distinction between impairment and disability (Barnes, 1997). For the UPIAS, people with impairments became disabled not because of their individual medical pathology but rather as a result of isolation and being prevented from participating fully in economic, social and political life (Johnstone, 2001).

In the UPIAS's (1976: 3) terms then:

disability is a situation, caused by social conditions, which requires for its elimination, (a) that no one aspect such as incomes, mobility or institutions is treated in isolation, (b) that disabled people should, with the advice and help of others, assume control over their lives, and (c) that professionals, experts and others who seek to help must be committed to promote such control by disabled people.

The UPIAS (1976: 3) went further and articulated a radically new conception of disability, stating that:

In our view, it is society which disables physically impaired people. Disability is something imposed on top of our impairments; by the way we are unnecessarily isolated and excluded from full participation in society. Disabled people are therefore an oppressed group in society.

A new era in the history of disability had begun, an era that was to be dominated by a reconceptualisation of the nature of society's understanding of the link between impairment and disability. This new social contextualisation of the concept of disability led directly to the birth of the social model, a model in which radical new reconstructions were forwarded and the distinction between impairment and disability was further, and specifically, separated (Shakespeare, 2006).

Oliver (1996), who was a key architect of the social model, has argued that impairment related to a missing or defective limb or a mechanism of the body that was compromised. However, for Oliver disability related to a disadvantage or restriction in a person's life that was caused by a social institution or a process that directly excluded people with impairments from mainstream social activities.

READER REFLECTION

What are the key distinctions that Oliver makes in his definition of disability from those that are outlined in the medical model?

The 'umbrella' organisation, the British Council of Disabled People, later expanded this defining statement to include many other impairments such as those which were sensory and intellectual. Six years later a new group – the Disabled People's International – further developed the UPIAS's definition by adding that disability was created by the imposition of barriers to inclusion that were erected by society against people with impairments. In the decades that followed, further initiatives such as the disabled arts movement and the affirmative rights and international models of disability were born. These in turn brought about a substantial and permanent reconceptualisation of the nature of disability in the hearts and minds of some elements of British society.

Legislative frameworks

Government policies during the past decades of the twentieth century had been constructed upon conceptions of disability and impairment formulated by the WHO. During the late 1970s the WHO commissioned Phillip Wood, Elizabeth Bradley and Mike Bury to extend an existing classification of disease to include the consequences of long-term illness (Barnes et al., 2002). The resultant International Classification of Impairment, Disability and Handicap (ICIDH) (Wood, 1980) introduced a triad of definitions into British society.

READER REFLECTION

Note the definitions detailed below by the ICIDH and those provided by the Disabled People's International. Compare and contrast these definitions, and with other students, discuss how differing models of disability lead to such variance in definitions of disability and impairment.

Firstly then, the ICIDH defines impairment as a deviation from a biomedical norm and a handicap, as 'a disadvantage for a given individual resulting from impairment or disability of a role that is normal (depending on age, sex and social and cultural factors) for the individual' (Wood, 1980: 291). Furthermore, it defines disability as a restriction of a lack of ability to perform an activity in a 'normal manner' because of impairment (Shakespeare, 2006).

In contrast, the Disabled People's International would define impairment as the functional limitation within the individual caused by physical, mental or sensory impairment. Disability though would equate to the loss or limitation of opportunities to take part in the normal life of the community on an equal level with others due to physical and social barriers (Goodley, 2011).

While the ICIDH's triad of definitions found favour with many social scientists and was observed to be useful in the accurate description of some dimensions of disabled people's experiences (Shakespeare, 2006), it was, however, subject to sustained attack and criticism from disabled people's organisations. This powerful criticism levelled at the classification system contended that the ICIDH had correlated impairment with disability and handicap. Thus, through this schema disability was caused by medical impairment, and not as the UPIAS observed, by societal barriers. As Johnstone (2001: 10) pointed out:

> the construct of 'disability' ... is seen to be a function of a hierarchy of practices and perceptions linked to certain, bodily, mental or behavioural states. ... The associations with disability and illness are clear.

A further criticism was that the schema employed the guiding principle of 'normality' as *the* concept against which to classify a person with impairment. Oliver and Barnes (1998) question how one judges the normality of psychological and physiological processes. They have contended that normality, as articulated within the ICIDH, reflects a narrow eurocentric view of society that is firmly predicated upon the values of healthy, male, middle-class professionals.

READER REFLECTION

Normality is an interesting concept. Watch the first three and a half minutes of the video, *What is Normal? Societal Perceptions on Disability*, which is available at: www.youtube.com/watch?v=yfjzoGfrzfE and has been created by graduate students in America.

Now reflect on what it actually means to be 'normal'. Indeed, you might also consider whether such a phenomenon as the normal person exists.

In 1997, the WHO began to revise the ICIDH in light of the criticisms that had been levelled against it by disabled people's organisations and by some medical professionals. Within the ICIDH2, as it became known, 'disability' was replaced by 'disablement' and 'handicap' was reconceptualised in terms of 'participation'. Disablement, within the new schema, operated on two levels: one incorporating environmental extrinsic factors, and the other incorporating intrinsic personal factors such as fitness, health, gender, age or psychological well-being. However, impairment within the new schema remained unchanged.

For many people, the WHO's new schema represented a step forward. However, for disabled people's organisations the ICIDH2 has remained problematic because it still advantaged individual medical pathology over and above celebrating what people with impairments can actually do (Johnstone, 2001).

Government perspectives

Interestingly, and despite the radical reconception of disability by the UPIAS and the WHO's more socially orientated employment, governments in Westminster, unlike governments in other European countries, have stubbornly chosen not to move forward in their own conceptualisation of disability. Indeed, within policy and legislative initiatives from the 1990s to the present day they have rigidly employed the original ICIDH's classification system (see Chapter 8 for a further comparative analysis).

This has meant that the distinctions between impairment, handicap and disability have persistently remained as the universal benchmark not only for how society conceptualises, but, moreover, for how it measures disability (Johnstone, 2001).

1990s and the Disability Discrimination Act(s)

In 1995, the then Conservative government finally introduced legislation that made it illegal to discriminate against people with impairments in terms of employment and service provision (Borsay, 2005). The Disability Discrimination Act (DDA) 1995 marked the end of a long period of activism by disabled people's organisations (Pearson and Watson, 2007). After 14 previous unsuccessful attempts to push through legislation, disabled people's organisations had finally hoped that 'a comprehensive anti-discrimination civil rights bill for disabled people' would be enacted (Evans, 1996: 1). Many had anticipated that this new legislation would provide a radical reconceptualisation of disability, one that would be based upon the social model developed by the disabled people's movement. However, and for many, disappointingly, the legislative framework empowered by the Act adopted the construct of disability put forward within the ICIDH.

Disability, within the DDA, was defined as:

A person has a disability if he has a physical or mental impairment which has a substantial long-term adverse effect on his ability to carry out normal day-to-day activities. (DDA, 1995: 1)

While the Act went on to provide a further elaboration of disability, it was quite clear to observers that the operational definition employed by it was based solely upon the discredited individual medicalised model (Evans, 1996).

The DDA, then, rather than heralding a new era in society's conceptualisation of disability actually reinforced the causal link between impairment and disability. Indeed, it could be argued that this legislation further promoted the medicalisation of disability within the UK. This was because it defined disability by the employment of medicalised forms of measurements within specific individualised parameters.

The DDA's employment of disability has since been roundly criticised, amongst others by the disabled people's movement, The Disability Rights Task Force and the Disability Rights Commission.

Influence of the New Labour government

In 1997 the Blair government was elected, amongst other things, upon a commitment to review the DDA. It was hoped by many that this government would take the opportunity to amend disability legislation to emphasise a 'more social construct ... where disability is [seen to be] a product of ... external environmental factors (Keil et al., 2006: 169). However, its first piece of disability legislation, the Special Educational Needs and Disability Act (DfES, 2001b), did nothing more than alter

Part 4 of the DDA in order to bring the educational provision into line with other discrimination legislation. As such, this legislation's definition of disability was based upon the medical model rather than the social model.

In 2005, new legislation was again enacted. However, as with previous legislation the government again chose not to expand its conceptualisation of disability. This DDA only amended Part III of the previous DDA and thereby placed a general duty on public institutions to promote disability equality. More than a decade after the enactment of the DDA it was clear that government's conceptualisation and articulation of disability was, despite the activism and development of the social model by disabled people's organisations, stubbornly unchanged. As a consequence, the Labour government still observed disability as an individual medical tragedy that was grounded upon personal impairment.

Equality Act 2010

In 2010 an Act was introduced into statute that replaced the DDA, this being the Equality Act. This Act was formulated to offer legal protection not just to those who had an impairment or disability, but also to those who possessed 'protected characteristics' (Brown, 2014: 129).

The Equality Act 2010 outlaws distinct forms of discrimination:

- direct discrimination

- associative discrimination

- indirect discrimination

- harassment

- third-party harassment

- victimisation.

You may wish to examine the guidance to this Act, which relates how discrimination might operate in relation to disability (see Chapter 7 for further analysis). The guidance is available at: http://webarchive.nationalarchives.gov.uk/20130703133823/http://odi.dwp.gov.uk/docs/wor/new/ea-guide.pdf.

The Equality Act 2010 states that a person has a disability if:

(a) The person has a physical or mental impairment, and
(b) The impairment has a substantial and long-term adverse effect on the person's ability to carry out normal day-to-day activities.

According to Brown (2014) this Act is problematic because instead of increasing an individual's protection, in law, it may actually dilute the rights of disabled people by grouping, so-called 'at risk' individuals into one piece of legislation. Furthermore,

Brown (2014) believes that this Act is still based upon the individual medical model of disability as it focuses upon an individual's impairment and ability to carry out 'normal' day-to-day activities.

READER REFLECTION

Trace the definition of disability that has existed since the 1990s in government legislation. Has the categorisation of disabled people actually changed?

Disability: conceptions and barriers to inclusion

Moving away from the examination of the history of disability we now turn to examine how society's conception of disability has been influenced by the 'picture' of disability created by the media. The media has a very powerful influence on people's lives and has an important function in determining an individual's sense of reality (Orbe, 2013). The literature base is replete with references as to how stereotypical assumptions are inherent in our culture and how the images reproduced within such media as books, films, television, newspapers, the internet and advertising have come to dominate people's conceptions of disability.

READER REFLECTION

An overview by Huws and Jones (2010) of the various research studies that have examined the portrayal of disability in the media, for example, television, radio, newspapers, advertising and the internet, suggests that these are an important source for the development of people's attitudes towards people with disability. They report that some studies have been critical of news reports about mental impairments because they are either too positive or employ storylines that reinforce negative and inaccurate portrayal of people with disabilities.

Think about how disability culture is represented in one particular television series that you have recently watched. Which model of disability would prove to be the most valuable in understanding how the show might impact on its viewers' understanding of disabled people?

The picture portrayed in books and newspapers

The influence of the media upon conceptions of disability has a long and pernicious history (Hodkinson, 2007b). The media have for a long time stigmatised people with impairments by focusing upon the medical model's outlook that disability is a 'personal misfortune' (Shakespeare, 1994: 284). Over the past two centuries classic plays, novels and newspapers have presented people with impairments as pathetic, passive victims or ugly and depraved, such as in Charles Dickens's *A Christmas Carol* and *Nicholas Nickleby*. In the first text, two characters with impairments, Tiny Tim and a man with a visual impairment, are portrayed as pitiable and in need of society's help (Swain and French, 2000).

READER REFLECTION

Read the following critique of Dickens's portrayal of disability. Do you agree with Stothers (2008) that the portrayal of Tiny Tim should be seen as offensive?

I hate Tiny Tim

Tiny Tim is on the ropes in Charles Dickens's Christmas Carol. Sickly and dependent, Tiny Tim is getting shakier and shakier on that home-made little crutch. But he is saved from death by old Ebenezer Scrooge, who sees the light in the nick of time.

Now, before you go apoplectic at my assault on wee Tim, think about how he helps shape some of society's most cherished attitudes – charity, pity (for poor little Tiny Tim), for example. Tiny Tim, plucky, sweet and inspirational, tugs at the public heart…

I hate it. I hate it because this Tiny Tim sentimentality stereotypes people with disabilities and contributes to our oppression. When you think about a person with a disability as someone to feel sorry for, as someone to be taken care of and looked after, it is difficult to think about hiring them as a teacher, an architect or an accountant. (Stothers, 2008)

Now read this extract from *Nicholas Nickleby*. What might this extract tell us of societal conceptions of disability at this time?

Pale and haggard faces, lank and bony figures, children with the countenances of old men, deformities with irons upon their limbs, boys of stunted growth, and others whose long meagre legs would hardly bear their stooping bodies, all crowded on the view together; there were the bleared eye, the hare-lip, the crooked foot, and every ugliness or distortion that told of unnatural aversion conceived by parents for their offsprings. (Dickens, [1838] 1985: 97)

(See Marchbanks (2006) for an in-depth analysis of the intellectual impairments in the work of Charles Dickens.)

In addition, some famous storybooks have used their villains to demonstrate how disability has twisted and rendered as evil a person with impairment (think, for instance, of Captain Ahab, Captain Hook or Long John Silver). In general, books from the Victorian era ensured that disability was employed to purvey emotive messages of courage, forgiveness and generosity (Shakespeare, 1994). Through such messages the literature of the nineteenth and twentieth centuries guaranteed that people with impairments were conceptualised as 'different' or as the 'other', an outsider trapped by their disability.

Newspaper reports and stories within the British press have attracted similar criticisms to those outlined above. The construction of the image of disability within the news industry is based upon the language used, the employment of image and the manner in which disabled people are 'framed' in news 'stories' (Findlay-Williams, 2014). Within this medium the employment of disablist language is common, both in the tabloid and the so-called quality papers. Reports about people with impairments are usually featured for their sensation value, and stories of individuals who 'bravely manage' to achieve despite their impairment are commonplace (Contact, 1991). Stereotypical constructs such as these, however, only serve to reinforce the belief that disabled people have 'something wrong with them', devaluing the contribution to society made by people with impairments and thereby helping to exclude them from fully participating in mainstream social and economic life (Oliver and Barnes, 1998).

READER REFLECTION

The majority of representations of disabled people in the news media reflect the manner in which disability is viewed from dominant societal perspectives. This does not however necessarily portray how disabled people see themselves (Findlay-Williams, 2014).

By employing your developing knowledge and understanding of disability, consider how the tabloid newspapers represent disability. You may also wish to have a look at the 'Disability now' website (available at: www.disabilitynow. org.uk/article/red-tops-cheats-crusade-fuels-hate) to examine how such media portrayal of disability has very real consequences for disabled people themselves.

The picture portrayed in films and television

Portrayals of impairment and disability in film and television have been the subject of research. Apart from specific specialist programming (of which there is very little), people with impairments have been under-represented in British television scheduling and film productions (Contact, 1991), and when a disabled character does appear, for example, in crime thrillers, they are often pictured as either the 'wicked' criminal or as the powerless and pathetic victim of a crime (Oliver and Barnes, 1998). In reality, television makes disabled people invisible and some observe this to be a form of social oppression (Barnes and Mercer, 2010).

If we examine films, we can observe that many villains are subject to an impairment, for example, in the *Batman* films – here the Joker, the Penguin and Two Face come to mind (Oliver and Barnes, 1998). And in the film *A Wonderful Life* a principle character, Mr Potter, is portrayed as evil, twisted and frustrated – and this status is linked to that character's confinement to a wheelchair (Swain and French, 2000).

An extensive content analysis of films and television has shown that the most con-sistently employed picture of disability within this medium is that of the maladjusted disabled person (Longmore, 1987). Research by Cumberbatch and Negrine (1992) further revealed that disabled people represented less than 1 per cent of characters in fictional programmes (see Barnes and Mercer, 2010). Furthermore, and despite recent positive constructions of disability in British soaps, it seems clear that the 'history of physical disability images in the movies has mostly been a history of distortion in the name of maintaining an ableist society' (Norden, 1994: 314).

The picture portrayed in advertising

At the most rudimentary level we may observe that people with impairments suffer from a lack of exposure within the advertising campaigns that appear in Britain (COI, 2001). It is also apparent that the negative conceptualisation of disability evidenced in films, television programmes, stories and newspapers is further enforced with the campaigns employed by the advertising industry (Oliver and Barnes, 1998). Early charity advertising was formulated upon images of people with physical flaws. The purpose of these campaigns was to 'evoke fear and sympa-thy in the viewer' (Barnes and Mercer, 2003: 93) and to establish a 'dependent, impairment active charity dynamic' (Hervey, 1992: 35–6). Indeed, charities gener-ally have presented a distorted image of disability in order to recruit volunteers and publicise their cause, but most importantly so that they can raise money. Many charities employ heart-rending images of loss, tragedy or bravery to ensure contin-ued government and public support for their work.

The picture of disability created by such advertising has been a major cause of concern for the disabled people's movement. This is because charity advertising, in particular, has continued to emphasise abnormality and the perceived inade-quacy of people with impairments. Positively, though, in recent years some charities have shifted the focus of their campaigns to concentrate upon ability and not disability, as well as to depict the prejudice and discrimination that people with impairments experience in everyday life (Barnes and Mercer, 2010). However, these developments, while recognised as a step in the right direction, have also faced criticism because they do nothing to empower people with impairments and still rely, in part, on the premise that disability is an individual personal tragedy. A review of the advertising campaigns over the past few decades has revealed that, while some campaigns have shown people with impairments in a more positive light (for example, the Co-op Bank and Coca-Cola in the 1990s, and Euro 1996: see COI, 2001), it is still apparent that advertising, especially when constructed by charity organisations, attempts to conceptualise disability by accentuating society's pity for people with impairments and their general dependence and helplessness.

The picture portrayed on the internet and schools' intranet

During the late 1990s, third-wave technologies, those of computers, the internet, multimedia and hypertexts began to dominate pedagogical materials in schools (Hodkinson, 2012a). Although many teachers, parents and children observe these digital technologies as positive, others believe that they should be treated with caution. Luke (1996: 1) believes these digital cultures teach children, 'how to become consumers and how to become boys and girls, lessons about skills and values and gender and social power'. In a recent study of digital technologies employed by schools, Hodkinson (2012a) found that the portrayal of disability was extremely limited and was bounded by medical deficit.

READER REFLECTION

A major finding from my own research details that in the wealth of school-orientated images that were analysed, such as playgrounds, classrooms, swimming lessons and school sports days, no picture of disability was observable (Hodkinson, 2012a).

Read the statement above. Consider what the effect of the 'invisibility of disability' in digital technologies employed in schools might have upon disabled children themselves?

Although, digital technologies have many positive aspects, there has been a growing issue in the employment of this medium over the past decade; that of cyber bullying (Slonje et al., 2013). Disabled children are some of the most frequent targets of such bullying. For example, it is suggested that around 65 per cent of pupils with Aspergers have been subject to bullying (Subramanian, 2014). Social media platforms are not free of such harassment but operate by employing the cultural and economic values replete in the wider society (Karppi, 2013).

Flaming is having an online fight that includes an exchange of insults and, at times, inappropriate language.

Trolling is starting a fight between two people online.

Cyber stalking is persistently sending intimidating or harassing messages through online platforms. (Subramanian, 2014).

It would appear that trolling, flaming and cyber stalking are going to be growing issues in relation to disability bullying and hate crime in the future. Subramanian (2014) discusses the extremes that such bullying can take in a story about a teenager called Kevin Kaneta who, because of his cerebral palsy, was forced to eat dog food and had pictures of this bullying placed on Facebook. According to Subramanian, many victims believe that this form of bullying happens because their disability makes them an easy target.

Conceptions of disability in society: a summary

Within our society it would appear, then, that the media in all its forms exerts a powerful stimulus for the formulation and maintenance of disabling stereotypes. It may be seen as forming the bedrock upon which attitudes towards, assumptions about and expectations of disabled people are based, by using the disabling images demonstrated in the books, films, television, the internet and in advertising campaigns that people come into contact with throughout their daily life. Barnes's (1992: 39) research concluded that it was these disabling stereotypes that were fundamental to the 'discrimination and exploitation ... [that] ... contribute significantly to the systematic exclusion from mainstream community life', which people with impairments experience. Shakespeare (1994) offers support for this viewpoint, arguing that the media, as well as everyday interacting, charity imaging and popular assumptions, acts as an attitude stimulus that places people with impairments who enter mainstream society into a subordinate position to their non-disabled peers. It is salient to note that some research studies may not have fully explored how the wealth of disablist messages received from the media are inculcated by society. A perhaps more cautious stance to adopt, then, is that the media has a pivotal role in the dissemination of images and opinions, but in its relation to the formulation of society's conceptions of disability its role remains unclear (Hodkinson, 2012a).

This chapter has thus far outlined a number of stimuli, both historical and current, that it has been argued have the potential to influence society's conception of disability. It now turns towards a specific critical examination of how the concept of disability is operationalised within the context of schools. In addition, it offers an outline of how these conceptions might affect teachers' implementation of inclusive educational policies. What is problematic, however, to this analysis is that it draws upon a small if growing research base and one that is mainly related to specific impairments. Furthermore, some of the research here is dated, as well as being subject to methodological weaknesses, and is located outside of the English educational system. Despite this, within the past 30 years there has been a growing interest in researching what attitudes are displayed towards individuals with disabilities (Wilson and Scior, 2014). While we need to exercise caution in using this information, it does provide an insight into the barriers that might exist to the inclusion of children with impairments within modern-day classrooms.

Conceptions within school communities

Deal (2003) has contended that educational communities are regulated by attitudinal systems constructed upon the premise of the 'normally' developing child. In addition, it would seem that pupils' conceptions of disability and impairments are being regulated by their interactions with older siblings and parents. Research suggests that conceptions of disability formulated through interactions within the home environment are translated and mediated within school communities by powerful processes of socialisation (Hodkinson, 2012a). The catalyst to this mediation appears to be 'playful interactions', such as singing songs, telling jokes and participating in the games that occur through pupils' daily participation in school life (Shakespeare, 1994: 294). Through this mediation process, children and young people agree 'commonly held sets of norms for the physical body which they employ when interacting with people they consider to be different from themselves' (Shakespeare, 1994: 294). The difficulty lies, however, in the evolution of a successful inclusive education for people with impairments, in that they 'are often at the mercy of the other's construction of what it means to have a disability' (Lenney and Sercombe, 2002: 6).

A positive view

Research conducted over the past few decades has produced contradictory conclusions in relation to non-disabled pupils' conceptualisation of disability and people with impairments. Some studies (see, for example, Harasymiw et al., 1976; Hodkinson, 2007a; Jacques et al., 1998; Siperstein and Gottlieb, 1997; Townsend et al., 1993) indicate that pupils, especially females, can and do display positive attitudes towards people with impairments and that in general children hold a more positive view than their adult counterparts.

In one research study a number of children articulated positive views about the inclusion of disabled children who were wheelchair users. Two children's views are outlined below.

> Yes, they should come into our class, because they are only humans with a wheelchair, and a wheelchair is like a bike, so it's a person with a bike.

> Yes, because children come to school to learn and a wheelchair does not stop them learning. (Hodkinson, 2007a: 71)

While these findings are interesting, they are subject to limitation and it is important to recognise this when interpreting them. For instance, while Jacques et al. (1998) found that positive attitudes existed, these were based upon the implementation of cooperative learning programmes, the like of which are not normally available in the UK. Furthermore, Hodkinson's (2007a) research, while revealing the existence of positive attitudes toward the inclusion of children with impairments, also found that these were based upon narrow conceptualisations of disability that were generally located within the realms of medical deficit. Moreover, both Hodkinson (2007a) and Laat et al. (2013) revealed that children have more positive attitudes towards some disabilities than others. An important caveat, then, to the maintenance of these research findings is that, as Harasymiw et al. (1976), Huckstadt and Shutts (2014), Hodkinson (2007a) and, to a lesser extent, Townsend et al. (1993) determined, generally positive attitudes exist only for those children whose impairments most closely conform to the 'norms set by society' (Deal, 2003: 899).

Despite these limitations, it is still pertinent to note that Jacques et al. (1998: 30) contend that the inclusion of pupils with sensory, physical or intellectual impairments can lead to significant gains in societal acceptance of disability. Furthermore, and despite some rather pessimistic findings, Hodkinson (2007a) concluded that the vast majority of non-disabled children participants in his study had one of the major ingredients for successful inclusive education – that is, in one form or another, they appeared to be strongly committed to the ideal of equality in educational opportunity. This is a finding supported by Beckett (2014), who details that children can and do make reference to disability in terms of 'human rights,' 'fairness' and 'equality of opportunity'.

A negative view

These positive attitudinal findings however remain undermined by a body of research that actually suggests it is negative conceptualisations of disability that dominate classroom environments (Beckett, 2014; Huckstadt and Shutts, 2014; Nowicki and Sandieson, 2002). Research conducted during the past 30 years suggests that children with impairments are at risk of increased levels of bullying and teasing (see, for example, Gray, 2002; Martlew and Hodson, 1991; Mencap, 2007; Thomas, 1996), lower sociometric positioning in class (Jacques et al., 1998; Siperstein and Gottlieb, 1997; Zic and Igri, 2001), that young non-disabled children may be less interested in interacting with them (Huckstadt and Shutts, 2014) and that these individuals also experience social distancing (Guralnick, 2002; Hodkinson, 2007a; Nazar and Nikoli, 1991; Weiserbs and Gottlieb, 2000; Zic and Igri, 2001).

A survey by Mencap (2007) found that some 82 per cent of children with an intellectual impairment had been bullied, of which 58 per cent had been physically assaulted. Additionally, the survey revealed that 79 per cent of the participants were frightened to go out because of the threat of bullying. Hodkinson's (2007a) study also found that non-disabled children, even those who had had no interaction with a person with impairment, held negative attitudes towards disability, observing children with impairments to be more unintelligent, ugly, boring, cowardly and poorer than their non-disabled peers.

READER REFLECTION

Read the following case studies. How do these make you feel? Can inclusive education ever become a reality without tackling non-disabled children's views?

CASE STUDY 3.1

Amy's story

When I was nine years old the girls in my class began to call me names and push me about. This used to happen every day but especially before we had PE lessons. I have Prader-Willi syndrome, which means that I have constant hunger pains and I cannot stop eating. Last year the bullying became really bad and a group of girls pulled off my shirt in the PE lesson and shouted to everybody, 'here comes the fat girl, look at her wobble'. I could not stop crying and I was so embarrassed as everybody just stared at me and laughed. I don't do PE now, I am just too scared.

Amy's advice to people who bully

Just think about what you do and the words you use. You can have a massive impact on somebody's life. If you had a broken leg, you would not be bullied for not being able to run fast – would you? I cannot help being overweight, please everybody don't laugh at me, why don't you try to be my friend instead?

Having read this case study, what would your advice be to the children that bullied Amy?

What is more worrying here, for both children with impairments and educators alike, are the findings from studies such as Weinberg's (1978), which illustrate that negative conceptualisations of disability develop early, with children as young as four preferring non-disabled individuals to those who they perceive to be 'disabled'. These findings, however, should be tempered by the findings of Jackson (1983), who suggests that, while people may express negative views, they do not always turn these into actions such as bullying or discriminating against disabled people. Furthermore, although the discovery of negative attitudes towards people with impairments is disturbing, it is perhaps relevant to note Davis and Watson's (2001: 673) statement 'that disabled children encounter discriminating notions of "normality" and difference both in "special" and mainstream schools'.

READER REFLECTION

Read and consider the responses of the non-disabled primary school children below to questions about disabled people. How might educators break the chain of poor understanding and bullying that exists in our schools today?

Interviewer: Do you think disabled people sometimes have children and families of their own?

Boy 1: No, no, no, no, no!

(Continued)

(Continued)

Girl 1:	No!
Interviewer:	Why is that?
Boy 1:	Because they're disabled, they won't ever look after them because …
Boy 2:	[Interrupts] They can't look after themselves!
Boy 1:	Most of them can't [get a girlfriend/boyfriend].
	[...]
Boy 2:	And people probably think that they're ugly.

(Source: Beckett, 2014)

A summary of the evidence outlined above, does not, it seems, provide an argument that undermines the premise that all children can be successfully educated within mainstream school settings. However, what the review does make clear is that inclusive education is closely linked to how society at large conceptualises disability and the number of barriers it places in the path of inclusion for people with impairments into mainstream schools.

Conclusion

In this chapter we employed Finkelstein's (1980) construct to outline the history of the development of the concept of disability. We discovered that, to some extent, the concept of disability did not exist before the advent of the Industrial Revolution. Indeed, it was contended that it was the social engineering and educational system formulated as a result of the Industrial Revolution that created 'misfits' who were segregated and excluded by society. Later in the chapter, we observed how the media influences society's concepts of disability and how the attitudes that children develop at home can be mediated and transformed by the powerful socialising influence of their school environment. Finally, we examined specific research that outlined the experiences of children with impairments who had been 'included' into mainstream schools.

In the following chapters we will analyse how schooling for children with SEN has developed and we shall critically examine whether new legislation and government initiatives have enabled these children to become more fully included within their local schools and communities.

The student activities and further reading detailed below are designed to make you think carefully about your own conceptions of disability and those that have dominated society over the past few hundred years. The aim of these readings and activities is to enable you to critically examine the media that you encounter on a daily basis so as to ascertain the image of disability that dominates the everyday experiences of people in the UK.

STUDENT ACTIVITIES

1 At the start of this chapter you were asked to make a note of your understanding of disability and consider how you have arrived at such an understanding. Having read this chapter, has your understanding changed?

2 You might like to locate early definitions of disability contained in government legislation during the 1950s, 1960s and 1970s. Consider how these definitions are similar or different to those that exist in the Equality Act 2010.

3 Using the resources available in most university education libraries, examine the picture of disability employed in ten textbooks commonly presented to children in either primary schools or secondary schools. How do your findings compare with those presented by Hodkinson in 2007 (see Hodkinson, 2007b)?

Further reading

Barnes, C. and Mercer, G. (2010) *Exploring Disability*. Cambridge: Polity Press.
This is a very readable book that provides the background to the issues and concepts discussed in this chapter.

English Heritage (2012) *Mental Illness in the 16th and 17th Centuries*. Available at: https://historicengland.org.uk/research/inclusive-heritage/disability-history/1485-1660/mental-illness-in-the-16th-and-17th-centuries/.
This is a very useful website that provides a basic introduction to the history of specific impairments.

Turner, D.M. (2012) *Disability in Eighteenth-Century England. Imagining Physical Impairment*. London: Routledge.
Chapter 1 provides an interesting account of the development of terminology such as 'impairment' and 'disability' in eighteenth-century England.

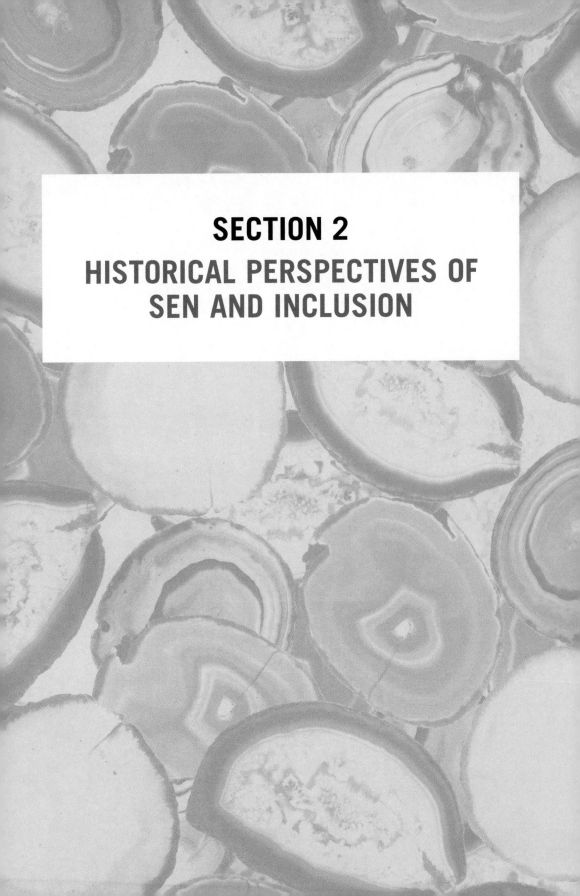

SECTION 2
HISTORICAL PERSPECTIVES OF SEN AND INCLUSION

4

THE DEVELOPMENT OF SEN: FROM BENEVOLENT HUMANITARIANISM TO THE HALFWAY HOUSE OF INTEGRATION

CHAPTER OBJECTIVES

- To provide an overview of the development and expansion of special educational provision from the late 1800s to the early 1980s through an examination of the legislation that governs education.

- To introduce and examine the concept of the categorisation of SEN.

- To introduce and critically examine the concept of integrative education and explore how special educational provision was formulated by the Warnock Report and subsequent 1981 Education Act.

Introduction

This chapter provides an outline of the development of special educational provision from its embryonic beginnings in the late eighteenth century through to the birth of integrative practice in the late 1970s and early 1980s. During this period the legislation and service provision for children with SEN were subject to radical change. The chapter considers how modern-day special educational provision is a result of its own history – a history that was shaped by the dominant societal values, beliefs and ideologies of the time. In addition, the chapter examines how government legislation and reports, combined with the prevailing societal attitudes, led to changes in the policies and services that governed the provision of education for children with SEN.

In Chapter 3 we observed that in Britain, before the advent of an industrialised and mechanised society, SEN as a concept did not exist, nor for that matter was there a need for it to exist. Children with SEN were normally 'looked after' by their families or by the Church, and for those from the lowest echelons of society education was not needed to facilitate inclusion in Britain, as it was a largely agrarian-based society. However, by the late 1700s and early 1800s Britain was subject to radical change as the Industrial Revolution ravaged society. Although rapid industrialisation meant that Britain became the powerhouse of the world, a side effect of this development was the creation of societal 'misfits' whose additional needs became barriers to inclusion within this new industrial age.

This period created an underclass of citizens who were cared for with 'benevolent humanitarianism' (Allan, 2003: 176). The nineteenth century bore witness to a phenomenal growth in charitable provision as the wealthier members of society felt a civic responsibility to provide aid for people whom they observed to be less fortunate than themselves (Lees and Ralph, 2004). This form of humanitarianism, combined with a good dose of Methodism and Evangelicalism (Pritchard, 1963), led to the establishment of workshops and asylums for children who had sensory impairments that were not being catered for by 'ordinary' schools (Frederickson and Cline, 2002). By the mid-1800s, special institutions had been created for virtually 'every human ill, individual or social, moral or physical' (Lees and Ralph, 2004: 149). The provision for children with SEN had, in a relatively short space of time, become firmly rooted in the ideology of the medical model.

The first special 'schools': a singularly voluntary enterprise

As with education in general, education for children with SEN began through the enterprise of individuals and charities (DES, 1978). The first 'school' for children with visual impairments was opened, in Edinburgh, in 1760 by Thomas Braidwood. He was followed in 1791 by Henry Dannett, who opened a school for the indigent blind in Liverpool. Then in 1841 the first Church-controlled special school, The Catholic Blind Asylum, was established also in Liverpool. In 1851, there followed a school for children with physical impairments, The Cripples Home for Girls, which was established in Marylebone, London.

The following quote refers to the first few years of the operation of the Liverpool School for the Indigent Blind. It paints a rosy picture of the educational provision provided by the school.

> At the opening of the present school ... the number of pupils was increased to seventy: in 1809 to one hundred: and the number at present in the school is one hundred and twenty. They are all of them usefully employed, and they exhibit a picture of cheerfulness and comfort which can scarcely be paralleled by an equal number of individuals of any description whatever collected under one roof. (Williams, 2005)

These early schools, however, were nothing like those we have today. Far from it. They were protective places available to a few where children, mainly from wealthy families, had little or no contact with the outside world (DES, 1978). As societal attitudes during the nineteenth century moved away from caring for children to sheltering them from society (Safford and Safford, 1996), this embryonic segregated education system was subject to further development as 'for personal and ideological reasons' segregated provision, based upon the medical model, prevailed and came to dominate the future system of education for children with SEN (Copeland, 2001: abstract).

The philosophy of special educational provision at this time was driven by a doctrine that strongly emphasised self-help (Lees and Ralph, 2004). A contemporary belief was that work with children and adults with SEN could yield positive economic results (Johnstone, 2001).

This account from the 1860s clearly indicates the nature of education provided within special schools:

[In] ... many of the schemes for the improvements of idiots, a most important object was to enable those capable of reaping, the highest advantage, to become adept in some useful branch of industry, and to make their work remunerative, exchanging their solitary and idle habits for social industrious and productive occupation. (*Edinburgh Review*, 1865: 56)

The curricula of many of these special schools were founded upon vocational education, including 'subjects' such as weaving, spinning, basket making and music. Put simply, children were taught to earn a living.

Below is an outline of how special education developed in Britain. It provides an overview of the important legislation and events that helped shaped the development of special education from 1760, with the introduction of special schools through to the policy of integrating pupils into mainstream classrooms in the early 1980s.

KEY EVENTS IN THE DEVELOPMENT OF SPECIAL EDUCATIONAL NEEDS

1700s–1890s: benevolent humanitarianism

1760   First school for children with visual impairments opened.

1851   First Church school for children with physical impairments opened.

1870   Forster Education Act – introduced compulsory state schooling.

1872   Elementary Education (Scotland) Act – introduced compulsory state schooling in Scotland.

1874   London School Board establishes a class for children with hearing impairments, which is attached to a state school.

(Continued)

(Continued)

1890   Education of Blind and Deaf Mute Children Act compels school boards to provide education for children with sensory impairments in Scotland.

1893   James Kerr is appointed as a medical officer to the Bradford School Board 1893. Elementary Education (Blind and Deaf Children) Act – provides education in England and Wales for children with sensory impairments.

1899   Egerton Commission reports upon the provision for children with sensory impairments.

1899   Education (Defective and Epileptic Children) Act – requires school boards to provide education for children who have disabilities other than sensory impairments.

1902–1944: the zenith of categorisation

1902   Education Act creates local education authorities.

1913   Cyril Burt appointed as London's first educational psychologist.

1921   Education Act constitutes five categories for the assessment of children with SEN and disabilities.

1923   Hadow Report accepts intelligence testing as a legitimate method of diagnosing mental deficiency.

1944   Butler Education Act requires all local education to meet the needs of 'handicapped' children.

1945   The Handicapped Pupils and School Health Service Regulations establish 11 categories for the assessment of disabilities.

1960s–1980s: challenging the orthodoxy of segregation

1970   Education (Handicapped Children) Act – all children become subjects of local education authorities.

1978   Warnock Report – introduces the term 'special educational needs'.

1981   Education Act – introduces the statement of SEN and an integrative educational approach to the placement of children with SEN.

(For further and more detailed information on the Forster Act and the development of compulsory schooling, see Bartlett and Burton, 2012.)

The 1870 Forster Act: education for all?

With the introduction of the 1870 Elementary Education Act (Education Scotland Act 1872), compulsory state schooling for all was developed 'to produce skilled workers who could compete in an era of growing industrial productivity'

(Wood, 2004: 91). Through this legislation, school boards were created to provide education where an insufficient capacity existed within the local charitable and voluntary provision (DES, 1978). Whilst the Act did not specifically include provision for children with SEN it did nonetheless create a basic right for all children to be educated within local schools. However, it was only after its implementation when large numbers of children with SEN who had previously been 'educated' at home entered mainstream education that their 'difficulties' became subject to national recognition. It became obvious that many of these children were experiencing difficulties in making progress within ordinary schools, as elementary classes then contained large numbers of pupils who were taught by teachers with no specific special educational training. Both educationalists and society at large came to the same conclusion that children with SEN were hindering normal teaching activities. Moreover, they firmly believed that these children were limiting the educational progress of the other 'normal' pupils. The prevailing societal attitude, therefore, became one that was based upon a premise that children with SEN were unfit to be included in normal mainstream educational provision (Coune, 2003).

State-controlled special education: the first tentative steps

Shortly after the implementation of the Forster Act 1870 charity organisations began campaigning for the rights of children with visual and hearing impairments to be fully educated, and for the school boards to ensure that educational provision was fit to include all children. In the mid-1870s a few school boards, of their own volition, did indeed begin to make tentative moves towards catering for such children (DES, 1978). In 1874, for example, the London School Board established a class for children with hearing impairments at one of its state elementary schools. By 1888, 14 such centres had come into existence, catering for some 373 children. In 1893, James Kerr was appointed as a medical officer to the Bradford School Board. His specific role was to assess children's mental processes and identify those children who were not suitable for education in ordinary schools (Farrell, 2004). However, as progressive as these initiatives might have been, they remained limited because special education incurred a higher cost than ordinary provision. Therefore, in practice very few boards were willing or able to provide specialised education. Indeed, in many areas children with SEN were either isolated in ordinary schools or received no schooling whatsoever. This isolation in turn often led to these children being segregated from their peers and denied access to the normal opportunities and activities afforded by local schools and the wider community (Coune, 2003).

The 1890s: the formalisation of the categories of SEN

On 20th January 1886 a Royal Commission was established to investigate and report upon the condition of the blind in the UK and to similarly report on the condition and education of the 'deaf and dumb'. The commission was tasked with the examination of the problem of uneducable children and to establish how widespread this problem actually was (Gibson and Blandford, 2005). The Egerton Commission, as it became known, reported back in 1889. It recommended that all school boards should provide an education for children with visual impairments from the age of five and that children with hearing impairments should be taught by specialist teachers who should be paid more than mainstream teachers. The commission also recommended that each school board should appoint a medical officer to distinguish between children who were named as 'feeble-minded', 'imbeciles' or 'idiots'.

Feeble derives from the Latin word *flebilis*, meaning doleful, sad and melancholy. It was used as early as 1611 in the Bible: 'Now we exhort you, brethren, warn them that are unruly, comfort the feebleminded, support the weak, be patient toward all'. (Thessalonians, 5: 14; www.kingjamesbibleonline.org/1-Thessalonians-5-14/)

During the early days of the twentieth century a child would be determined as having a 'feeble mind' if they scored 25 or below on an intelligence test. Other terminology employed at this time also related to an assessment of children's intelligence. Children were considered to be 'normal' if they scored 100 or above in an intelligence test, or were labelled as:

- morons, if they scored 50 to 75

- imbeciles, if they scored 25 to 50

- idiots, if they scored below 25.

For further and more detailed information on the language employed to categorise children and adults with SEN, see the paper by Marsh and Clarke (2002), 'Patriarchy in the UK: the language of disability', which is available online at the Disability Archive UK (www.leeds.ac.uk/disability-studies/archiveuk).

The commission felt that 'imbeciles' should not remain in asylums but should, wherever possible, enter formal schooling. For children designated as 'feeble-minded' they argued that education should be provided in auxiliary schools, which were to be separate from the mainstream (DES, 1978).

The report from the Egerton Commission was followed in 1890 by legislation in Scotland (Education of Blind and Deaf Mute Children Act), and three years later, England and Wales followed suit with the 1893 Elementary Education (Blind and Deaf Children) Act. These acts required school boards to provide education for children with sensory impairments. In the years after their implementation, pressure from teachers and medical officers over the plight of children with physical impairments led the government to establish the Sharpe Committee. Its major recommendation was that special schools should be established to make mandatory and effective provision for pupils who had disabilities other than sensory impairments (Gibson and Blandford, 2005). The subsequent Education Act of 1899 incorporated many of this committee's recommendations and so formalised the categorisation and segregation of children with SEN within a two-tier education system. The Act stated that:

> A school authority ... may ... make such arrangements ... for ascertaining what children in their district, not being imbecile, and not being merely dull or backward, are defective, that is to say, what children by reason of mental or physical defect are incapable of receiving proper benefit from ... instruction in the ordinary ... schools. (Roberts, 2007)

In summary, then, the development of mass schooling within the late nineteenth century ushered in the rapid expansion of a segregated special school system where 'children [with] particular difficulties were put together with other children who had similar needs' (Frederickson and Cline, 2002: 63). The provision of segregated schooling was reinforced because a system of payment by results designated that there was no benefit, for ordinary schools, in adopting inclusive practices. Indeed, the emergence of the special school system was firmly built upon the foundation that children with SEN were different and could be 'categorised according to their difficulties' (Thomas et al., 2005: 3).

1902–1944: the zenith of categorisation

The Education Act of 1902 abolished the existing school boards created by the Forster Act of 1870 and replaced them with local education authorities. Educational provision was formally separated into two phases – elementary and secondary education. While major developments were observable within mainstream education, the provision of education for children with SEN remained largely unchanged until 1944. The development of special educational provision that was observed during this period was strongly influenced by Victorian notions of child deficit.

The dominant societal ideology of the early twentieth century, therefore, was that a child with SEN was simply different to the normal child and so it was no more than simple common sense to educate such children outside of the normal school system (Frederickson and Cline, 2002). As a result, this period witnessed the evolution of a large variety of special school provisions. For example, there were open air schools for 'weak' children, day and boarding schools for children with physical impairments, and schools in hospitals and convalescent homes (DES, 1978).

The early part of the twentieth century also witnessed the beginnings of educational provision for children deemed to have behavioural difficulties. For instance, the Education Act 1921 formally constituted five categories for use in the assessment of children who were judged to have mental 'handicaps' that would inhibit them from attending mainstream schools. Other children, adjudged to be uneducable, were to be removed from ordinary schools and accommodated in specialist wards and hospitals (Gibson and Blandford, 2005). To enable the assessment of children's mental processes required by this, local education authorities began to rely more heavily on the advice of doctors, medical officers and the developing field of psychological assessment.

CASE STUDY 4.1

Bob's story

Read the case study below. What does Bob's story tell us about the state of special education during the period of the categorisation of children?

Hello my name is Bob and I attended a special school in a sunny seaside town in the north of England during the mid-1950s. I have a hearing impairment and my dad, who was hearing impaired too, taught me to sign when I was four. I loved to sign because I found it very difficult to speak and often people could not understand me. However, when I six I was sent to this special school where I was told that I could not sign and that I must always speak when spoken too. The school simply thought that signing was wrong and that we should communicate like 'normal' people. One day I was caught signing when I was in the playground. The teacher was very angry with me and told me that I had let myself down and that I had to try much harder to talk to people. He sent me to the headteacher who made me wear huge boxing gloves for a week. This meant that I could not sign at all and I felt very sad and very lonely. I wanted to talk to my dad about this as I knew he would understand, but I had no way of getting in touch with him. He lived 70 miles away and there was no phone and my writing was not that good then so I could not send him a letter. When he was allowed to visit two weeks later I told him what had happened and he confronted the headteacher, but the school did not listen to my dad. They said to him if I signed again that I would be expelled and I would get no education at all. I spent six years in that school. I hated it.

Cyril Burt and the rise of psychometrics and eugenics

In 1913, at the age of 30, a young lecturer from the University of Liverpool was appointed, on a part-time basis, to be London's first educational psychologist. Cyril Burt's remit was to be concerned with the 'backward, delinquent and maladjusted' children who had been referred for assessment by their teachers, school doctors, magistrates, care workers and parents (DES, 1978). This appointment was highly significant for the development of special educational provision because it added momentum to the 'burgeoning science' of psychometrics and eugenics (Thomas et al., 2005: 3).

> *Psychometrics* is the measurement of knowledge, abilities and aptitudes through tests such as the intelligence quotient (IQ).

Burt advocated the employment of the developing technology of intelligence testing, which he amongst others strongly believed could provide statistical evidence to identify a child's intellectual deficit, which would hinder their educational progress (Corbett and Norwich, 2005). Burt believed strongly that:

> no grindstone can make a good blade out of bad metal; and no amount of coaching will ever transform the inborn dullard into a normal child. The pupil who is merely backward forms a different problem. He is a knife without edge – good steel that has never been sharpened. He hacks away at his daily loaf; but will never cut true or smooth until he has been sent off to the repair shop to be whetted and sharpened. (Burt, 1937: 9)

READER REFLECTION

Carefully read the quote above from Cyril Burt in 1937 about children with SEN. Make a note of the problematic language employed. What are your thoughts on the language that Burt employs? Do you believe it is the case that some children simply cannot be educated?

Throughout the period of the drafting of the 1921 Education Act, Burt and others such as Schonell (1924) exerted their influence on policies affecting the educational provision for children with SEN. Burt detailed that his psychometric testing revealed that some 15 per cent of children 'suffered' an 'intellectual deficit' that would render them unsuitable for mainstream education. In addition, he contended that this group, consisting of three separate categories of children (those of 'sub-normal intelligence, mentally dull and inferior intelligence'; Burt, 1917: 38–39), would only benefit from specialised curriculum and schooling. Burt maintained that:

> The ideal arrangement [for these children], therefore, would be a series of classes where promotion was slower or the increasing difficulty was less. Since backwardness affects scholastic and abstract work more than practical or concrete the curriculum would include a large proportion of concrete and manual work. (Burt, 1917: 38–9)

CASE STUDY 4.2

Andrew

Andrew is a ten-year-old boy who is struggling with all aspects of the formal curriculum, notably, maths, English and science. His teachers want to alter his curriculum so that it is based mainly on art, PE and games. What do you think about the teachers' proposals? Should all children be entitled to a broad and balanced curriculum?

Burt's growing reputation within the field of psychology in general and psychometrics in particular was a catalyst to the expansion of a separate, segregated education system based upon the categorisation of deficit (Thomas and Loxley, 2001).

In 1923, the Hadow Report accepted the principle that intelligence tests were a useful tool for the diagnosis of mental deficiency. The report did however contain a warning that no child should ever be treated as 'mentally deficient' based solely on the information gained from an intelligence test (infed.org, 2007). Despite this warning, Burt's contention that children with SEN 'suffered' from reduced cognition, coupled with the notion of psychometrics and eugenics, provided the legitimisation needed for the segregated special school system to be further expanded.

1944 and the Butler Education Act: the orthodoxy of segregation

In 1944, as the Second World War reached its climax, significant reforms were proposed to the education system in Britain. The 1944 Education Act established a general duty upon local education authorities to provide education within primary, secondary and further education based on each pupil's age, aptitude and abilities. Sections 33 and 34 of the Act replaced Part 5 of the 1921 Education Act and required that all local education authorities should meet the needs of handicapped children within their area. The Education (Scotland) Act of 1945 made similar provision in Scottish schools.

The 1944 Act detailed that local authorities must:

> secure that provision is made for pupils who suffer from any disability of mind or body, by providing either in special schools, or otherwise, special educational treatment, that is to say education by special methods to persons suffering from that disability. (Roberts, 2007)

A further duty placed on local authorities was to ascertain which children would require this special educational 'treatment'. In pursuit of this, local authorities were empowered to compel parents to submit their children to medical officers and psychologists for the purposes of an examination of their mental capabilities (DES, 1978).

The 1944 Act, coupled with the Handicapped Pupils and School Health Service Regulations (1945), established 11 categories of handicap that children would be separated into. These medical and quasi-medical categories (in part created by Burt) were:

- blind
- partially sighted
- deaf
- partially deaf
- delicate
- diabetic

- educationally sub-normal
- epileptic
- maladjusted
- physically handicapped
- children with speech defects.

The system of categorisation, based upon the ideology of the medical model, ensured that the causation of a child's learning difficulties was firmly located within the individual and not in the system of education they experienced. From this time forward then, after the requisite examination, any child who was deemed to be educable was afforded the right of access to state schooling. However, children who were judged to be 'severely sub-normal' were to be reported under the provision of the Mental Deficiency Act of 1913 as uneducable and sent to National Health Service (NHS) training centres. The 1944 Act developed for all pupils, and not just those with SEN, a hierarchy of educational provision. Moreover, this hierarchical approach was observed to be an equitable method of service delivery because all children were seemingly enabled to reach a level of education that matched their level of aptitude and ability. Furthermore, the system of assessment used to categorise and segregate children was deemed to be stable, reliable and valid because it was based upon the 'science' of psychometric testing (Wearmouth, 2001).

During the decades that followed the 1944 Act, children with SEN became excluded from ordinary schools because of their perceived differences. Those with illnesses were deemed delicate and so were sent to open-air schools; those with hearing impairments went to schools for the deaf; children with visual impairments attended schools for the blind, and so on. Children were labelled, categorised and dispatched to special school placements with many never having the opportunity to discover if they could make progress in ordinary schools. Furthermore, this period witnessed the birth of a new language of special education, which substantiated the 'science' of segregation and pupils thus stopped being children and were pigeon-holed as 'educationally sub-normal, maladjusted or disturbed'. Moreover, and seemingly worse, was the fact that society formulated other distasteful terminology that reinforced the nature of some children's differences. Within the segregated special school system, children developed a clear idea of how they were viewed by their peers in ordinary schools and saw themselves as 'spastics', 'loonies' and 'cripples'. The system of segregated provision and, for those who were uneducable, the NHS training centres, led to children being stigmatised and denied access to the full range of educational opportunities afforded by ordinary schools (Frederickson and Cline, 2002). The delivery of education through a system of segregated special provision became the orthodox policy for the next three decades, one that was to become 'embedded in the individual and institutional consciousness' for generations to come (Thomas et al., 2005: 4). (For further, and more detailed, information on the Butler Act and the development of the tripartite system of education, see Bartlett and Burton, 2012.)

READER REFLECTION

The overview of the history of the development of SEN up to the present clearly identifies that special education was formulated upon the employment of categories, which relied upon the premise that SEN was something an individual suffered from.

1 List what you consider to be the main points and issues related to special education thinking during the period of the formalisation of the categories of SEN.

2 Why is this type of thinking problematic for the formulation of educational provision for children with SEN?

3 What are the positives and negatives of employing labels for SEN?

The 1960s–1980s: challenging the orthodoxy of segregation

The orthodoxy of segregation created by the 1944 Act was not subject to serious challenge until the late 1960s. Indeed, it was not until the Education (Handicapped Children) Act of 1970 (DoE, 1970) that all children finally became legally entitled to a 'full and broad' education when the responsibility for children deemed to be severely 'educationally sub-normal' was transferred from health to local education authorities (Wearmouth, 2001). Throughout the late 1960s and into the 1970s parents, disability rights groups and educators began to subject the policy of segregated special school provision to increasing criticism. They argued that 'continued segregation could no longer be justified from either a research or rights perspective' (Frederickson and Cline, 2002: 68). Demands were increasingly made, not only from the community at large, but also from those adults who had experienced segregated provision that argued the idea of special schools was unjust. In line with the comprehensive movement of the 1960s and 1970s, society in general actively sought to break down the stigmatising barriers created by the 1944 Education Act (Thomas and Loxley, 2001). It was clear that people's understanding of SEN was shifting from the medical model's ideology of individual causation to one of societal responsibility.

This period of concerted societal criticism coincided with new research that cast serious doubt on the reliability and validity of the psychometric testing, which had become the bedrock of the system of special school provision. The concern expressed by many researchers, educators and parents was that intelligence testing was based upon a model of child deficit, which was increasingly being seen as arbitrary and rigid. The prevailing argument was that psychometric testing was flawed because it failed to take into account the holistic nature of a child's education and how school environments could ameliorate or even add to a child's educational difficulties (Evans, 1995). It was clear, then, that a more social approach was needed for the provision of an education for those children with SEN, one where schools would become more responsive to their needs. Furthermore, many people at this time believed that segregated education did not benefit children with SEN, but rather negated the responsibilities of teachers in ordinary schools to devise and implement curricular for pupils who appeared unable to progress with their learning via normal instruction (Jenkinson, 1997). As the 1960s progressed, psychometric testing and the employment of categories of disability ultimately came to be seen as key factors that were limiting children's educational and life opportunities (Thomas and Loxley, 2001).

The end of the 1960s and the beginning of the 1970s also witnessed pioneering work by psychologists such as Klaus Wedell and Peter Mittler. Within hospital settings they helped determine that 'the child-deficit model [of additional needs] was reaching the end of its usefulness' (Clough and Corbett, 2000: 12). The developing ideology of the time was that the 'integration of children [into ordinary schools] would facilitate access and participation in society, both as adults and children' (Frederickson and Cline, 2002: 68). Society's emerging acceptance of this ideology heralded the birth of a new integrated system of educational provision, but as history would show, this change in societal attitude did not signal the death throes of the ideology nor the practice of segregation.

The Warnock Report

By the early 1970s educational professionals and parents had begun to step up pressure on the government to investigate the standards of national provision for children with additional needs (Gibson and Blandford, 2005). In 1973, Margaret Thatcher, the then Minister for Education, established a committee under the chair of Mary Warnock to:

> review educational provision in England, Scotland and Wales for children and young people handicapped by disabilities of body and mind. (Evans, 1995: 146)

The committee completed its work in 1978 and its final report made some 225 recommendations on the policy and organisation that governed the education of children with additional needs (Sturt, 2007).

The Warnock Report's major conclusions were that:

- Categories of handicap should be replaced by a continuum of special needs and a concept of SEN should be introduced (Gibson and Blandford, 2005).

- Children's educational needs should be judged on the basis of multi-professional assessments and formally recorded (Evans, 1995).

- New terminology should be employed to describe children's SEN and these needs would be located within speech and language disorders, visual and hearing difficulties, emotional and behavioural disorders and learning difficulties, which could be specific, mild or severe (Soan, 2005).

The recommendations contained in the Warnock Report criticised the orthodoxy of segregation and argued that the employment of handicap to categorise children was both damaging and irrelevant (Sturt, 2007). Warnock argued that the existing categories suggested nothing in the form of educational assistance and hence the provision that a child with SEN would require. Furthermore, the report recommended that rather than categorising children by deficit they should have their SEN identified and, where possible, these needs should be met within ordinary mainstream schools. The findings of the report's 'research' also indicated that as many as 20 per cent of children could experience a learning difficulty at some time during their school careers, and that for some 2 per cent of these children, their difficulties would be so 'distinct that they would require an official statement of need' (Clough and Corbett, 2000: 4). The report concluded by stating that a child's SEN should be met through a continuum of integrated provision that should be mainly delivered in ordinary schools.

The 1981 Education Act

The legitimisation of integrated educational provision

The Education Act of 1981 translated many of the recommendations in the Warnock Report into legislation. The term 'SEN' was specifically defined and afforded legal status, and with this, the employment of the categories of handicap (Gibson and Blandford, 2005) that had been in use since 1945 was ended. Furthermore, the Act clearly articulated how children with SEN should be assessed and how a Statement of SEN should be formulated.

> A Statement of SEN was a document that had legal status and was provided to parents, teachers and other professionals working with a child after a statutory assessment of a child's learning difficulties. It detailed a child's SEN and the educational provision that would be needed to address the barriers that a child was experiencing. A Statement was only prepared for those children with the most severe and/or complex needs.

More importantly, though, the Act affirmed the principles of integrative practice by stating that children with SEN should, wherever possible, be educated alongside their peers within mainstream educational settings. However, it also built upon the recommendations of the Warnock Report and the 1976 Education Act and so reinforced the principle that children should only be integrated into ordinary schools if their needs could be reasonably met; that this should be efficient in terms of resources; and that it should not be to the detriment of other children (Wearmouth, 2001). Despite these caveats, the 1981 Act can now be viewed as a highly significant piece of legislation – because it was to influence the attitudes held by a whole generation of teachers in mainstream schools. From this time on, it was to become abundantly clear that pupils with SEN would be every teacher's responsibility (Coune, 2003).

Integrative practice: why did it ultimately fail?

Problematic for the aspirations of the 1981 Act was that as the 1980s progressed the development of integrative educational provision became increasingly subject to a narrow conceptualisation. Warnock (1999: 31), relating back to the 1970s, explains that:

> looking back on those days of the committee, when everyone felt that a new world was opening for disadvantaged children, the most strikingly absurd fact is that the committee was forbidden to count social deprivation as in any way contributing to educational needs. The very idea of such separation now seems preposterous.

While the 1981 Act should have provided a continuum of educational provision, the lack of a strong lead from central government over placement policies for children with SEN (Dyson and Millward, 2000) instead created a system where enormous discretion over the development of integrative practice was placed in the hands of local education authorities (Jones, 2004). In addition, and despite Warnock and the 1981 Act championing the rights of parents, in practice they had no say over the educational placement of their children as the final decision always remained with the local education authority. Furthermore, the notion of the reasonableness of placement contained in the legislation, coupled with the lack of extra money to implement the Act, meant effective integration became subject to a postcode lottery (Farrell, 2004). This meant that, while some local education authorities enthusiastically developed integrative educational practices, others chose to retain the existing system of segregated special school provision (Dyson and Millward, 2000). In practice, then, integration policies did not lead to a radical shift in educational provision. Indeed, during the period 1983 to 1991 the proportion of children being educated in special schools only dropped by 12.5 per cent and in some local education authorities the number of children placed in segregated provision actually increased (Evans, 1995).

By the end of the 1980s, integration had increasingly become subject to poor delivery and practice and some would argue that this led to a system that failed to account for individual need (Ainscow, 1995). Ainscow contends that integration was reduced to 'making superficial changes [and] providing restricted provision for pupils ... in schools where the communities had changed very little in attitudes and values' (Judge, 2003: 158). However, this contention may be seen by those who implemented an integrated system of provision to be unnecessarily pessimistic as there were still many examples to be found of successful integrative practice within mainstream schools.

CASE STUDY 4.3

Nigel

Read the following teacher's account, which outlines how a child with Down's syndrome was eventually, and successfully, integrated into his local mainstream school.

Nigel was aged 11 when he arrived at our school in the September of 1992. We had little warning of his arrival or of his 'condition'. I must admit that I was a little worried about how I would cope with a boy who had Down's syndrome, as I had no training in how to teach these children.

Things got off to a bad start and Nigel had a bad first few days as the other children, especially the older boys, teased him terribly. I often found Nigel hiding in the cloakroom as he was scared to go out onto the yard. I also found it very difficult to plan work for Nigel because he was so far behind the other children with his reading and writing. However, as the months went by, things began to improve. I worked closely with Nigel's parents and the local Down's Association as well as spending many hours reading about his condition. However, in the playground things did not really get any better as many of the Year 6 boys still continued to tease Nigel and made rude remarks about him.

In the final week of the summer term, we held our annual sports day with all the usual races and events. Nigel asked if he could take part in the 100 metres sprint as all the Year 6 boys had been talking about it.

I must admit that both myself and Nigel's parents were concerned about this because he had a heart condition and so we tried to persuade him not to take part. Nigel though was adamant and so on a sunny morning in July he lined up with the other boys at the start line. The gun sounded and the Year 6 boys shot off at some pace. Nigel could only manage a slow walk and so by the time all the other boys had finished the race, he had barely started. At this point we expected the other boys to poke fun at Nigel for being so slow.

In fact they all crowded around Nigel, shouting lots of encouragement and they all walked with him to the end of the track. As he finished, a great cheer went up from the crowd and many of the Year 6 boys put their arms around Nigel. They had realised how much effort he had put into just taking part in the race. It was at that point I realised that Nigel had finally been accepted and that integrating him into our school had changed these children's perceptions of disability forever.

It does seem reasonable to suggest here that whilst integration heralded the establishment of a new level of individual and institutional consciousness, and that for some children with SEN it enabled access to mainstream education, this access was on the school's and not the child's terms. In respect of children's rights to a full and broad education, history has shown that integration was to become something of a halfway house between the policies of segregation and those of inclusive education.

Conclusion

This chapter has introduced you to major legislation, key reports and the societal attitudes that influenced the development of special educational provision from the late eighteenth century to the end of the 1980s. This historical appraisal has revealed the seemingly dramatic shifts in the ideology governing the delivery of provision for children with SEN. We have observed how nineteenth-century benevolent humanitarianism began, in the 1960s and 1970s, to give way to a belief that children did not need to be looked after and sheltered from society but that they should have their educational needs assessed and, moreover, that these should be met within ordinary mainstream schools. While the 1981 Education Act is rightly observed as having been highly significant for the development of educational provision for children with SEN, it did nonetheless create a legacy of ad hoc service delivery as well as failing to bring about the end of the Victorian principles that still maintained segregated educational practice.

However, despite the problems associated with the 1981 Act, we may conclude that from the 1960s onwards very real progress was made in the provision of education for children with SEN. By the end of the 1980s, it was clear to all that the education of children with SEN had developed more in line with the ideologies of social democracy and equity. But as the next chapter will show, the real historical significance of integration was that it paved the way for the new policies and practices of inclusive education to flourish.

The activities and further reading that are detailed below ask you to carefully consider how the terminology of SEN and disability has been employed during the past century and in the first decade of the twenty-first century. In your consideration of SEN you might ask yourself the question: have only the labels attached to disability changed and not the attitudes?

STUDENT ACTIVITIES

1 Discuss, with others, the following statement made by Oliver (1988: 20):

   From the introduction of categories such as 'idiots and imbeciles' in early legislation through the medical categories of 1944 to SEN in 1981, it could be argued that only the labels have changed; the underlying reality of an education system unable or willing to meet the needs of all children remains the same.

2 Do you agree or disagree with these sentiments? Has the delivery of special educational provision actually changed?

3 With reference to the recommended reading outlined below, examine what the major achievements and failings of the Warnock Report were and what, if anything, is its lasting legacy?

4 Consider how the terminology of SEN changed during the period covered by this chapter.

Further reading

Gibson, S. and Blandford, S. (2005) *Managing Special Educational Needs: A Practical Guide for Primary and Secondary Schools.* London: Paul Chapman.
This text provides a very practical guide to how SEN processes might be operated in schools.

Serge, T. (2009) 'From integration to inclusive education: does changing the terms improve practice?', *International Journal of Inclusive Education*, 13(6): 553–63.
This article provides an expansive review of the evolution of inclusive education.

Winzer, M.A. (2013) 'Confronting difference: a brief history of special education', in L. Florian (ed.), *The Sage Handbook of Special Education.* London: Sage, pp. 23–38.
This book provides a useful and detailed overview of the history of SEN in England.

5

THE EMERGENCE OF INCLUSIVE EDUCATION: FROM HUMBLE BEGINNINGS

CHAPTER OBJECTIVES

- To explore the emergence of inclusive education in the 1990s.
- To critique the concept of inclusive education.
- To examine the barriers that stalled the development of inclusive education.

Introduction

The aim of this chapter is to critically analyse the development of inclusive education from the 1990s onwards. It begins by defining inclusion from a number of differing and competing standpoints and relates how in the twenty-first century some people have begun to believe that inclusion is an illusionary concept. In addition, the chapter considers how the implementation of inclusive education during the late 1990s and early twenty-first century has been stalled by the barriers created by local authorities, schools, competing educational policy initiatives and by government themselves.

At the start of this chapter, it would seem necessary to provide some contextual detail about the policy of inclusion. Whilst it may seem that the New Labour government of 1997 claimed ownership of inclusion, in reality it has a long history that lies outside the influence of current politicians.

The ideology of inclusion should not be viewed as a wholly new phenomenon; indeed, its origins go back to the late 1800s and those educational pioneers who believed in non-segregated schooling systems. However, in its current form, inclusion may be observed as the beginning of the end of a journey that began in the late 1950s when segregated institutions were subject to criticism by disabled people (Barnes and Mercer, 2010). Critics of 'special' education, with its 'systematic individualisation and medicalisation of the body and mind' (Barnes, 1997: 19) and employment of assessments of need as exercises of power (Oliver, 1996), began to argue that separating disabled children from their family, peers and local communities could only have negative effects (Morris, 1991; Morris, 2005). Morris (1991: 192) argues that it was this separation from 'common humanity' dictated by 'those who were not disabled' (1991: 71) that led to disabled people being seen as 'fundamentally different and alien' (Abberley, 1987: 14). During the late 1950s an opposing tradition was developed by disabled people (Barnes and Mercer, 2003), which was foregrounded by the premise that special schools lower expectations (Armstrong and Barton, 1999) and their continuance was nothing more than social oppression (Morris, 1991). In the 1960s, policies of educational segregation became subject to increasing critique within the disability community (see Chapter 4). This questioning of policy heralded the birth of a new integrated educational system that was seemingly legitimised by the Warnock Report and the subsequent 1981 Education Act. For some, these events began a journey towards inclusion; however, for others the last years of the 1980s witnessed integration being criticised as a policy that failed to account for individual need (Ainscow, 1995). An argument by Oliver (1990a), Barton (1997) and others was that, from the perspectives of the social model, educational exclusion was generated by policy makers' and professionals' 'practices, attitudes and policies' (Morina Diez, 2010), which when combined, led to the educational and social marginalisation of disabled people (Slee and Allan, 2005). The disability movement therefore proposed that 'the term inclusion ... as developed from the social model perspective should replace the term integration as developed by politicians' (Oliver, 1996: 15). A review of the literature base, whilst leaving no doubt that inclusion has gained status in schools, also suggests a tension in how it became to be defined and operationalised by government, educational practitioners and the disability movement (Armstrong et al., 2009; Benjamin, 2002; Hodkinson, 2012b; Hornby, 2001).

The emergence and evolution of inclusive education

The evolution of inclusive education within the English educational system began with the election of New Labour in 1997 (Hodkinson, 2005). Upon taking office, it acted swiftly and through the imposition of the Green Paper (DfEE, 1997) and the subsequent Programme of Action (DfEE, 1998) it set the tone for the central thrust of education reform throughout the last decade of the twentieth century. What became clear to observers was that the New Labour government had put inclusion firmly on the political agenda, as it stated:

> We want to develop an education system in which special provision is seen as an integral part of overall provision aiming wherever possible to return children to the mainstream and to increase the skills and resources available to mainstream schools, and to ensure that the LEA support services are used to support mainstream placement. (DfEE, 1997: 44)

New Labour's inclusion policy though, while radical in nature to some writers and researchers, was criticised by others for promoting a narrow vision of inclusion. Clough and Corbett (2000) suggest that this inclusive initiative did not go far enough because it only dealt with what might be termed 'locational inclusion'. They believe that this early form of inclusion implied:

> schools will promote inclusion in society as adults. However, this is clearly a naïve view since many other factors are involved, such as appropriate curriculum, adequate transition planning and available support services. (Clough and Corbett, 2000: 9)

The Labour government in its second term of office sought to address the apparent deficiencies of its SEN policy. In 2000 it introduced a revised curriculum that was designed to:

> secure for all pupils ... an entitlement to a number of areas of learning and to develop knowledge, understanding, skills and attitudes necessary for their self-fulfilment as active and responsible citizens. (DfES/QCA, 1999: 12)

Within the curriculum document itself, non-statutory guidance was offered on how inclusive practices could be fostered through the delivery of the core and foundation subjects. Thus, at face value it did appear that this government had fully committed itself to the ideology of inclusion.

Government inclusion in the twenty-first century

The beginning of the new millennium witnessed the evolution of a variety of inclusive practices, which were supported by a raft of government policies, initiatives and legislation. It appeared that these initiatives signalled New Labour's apparent acceptance of the ideology of inclusion by stating that 'the special educational needs of children will normally be met in mainstream schools or settings'. These initiatives impacted significantly upon educational provision in England and it would appear, at one level, that they clearly demonstrated New Labour's 'continuous drive to eradicate inequalities in our society' (Judge, 2003: 167). However, while New Labour's spin and political rhetoric intimated that inclusive education had become the bulwark of the English educational system, we will observe throughout this chapter that development of inclusive education was stalled by the problems of its definition and of governments' acceptance of this form of education.

Inclusion: the difficulties of definition

A review of the past two decades of literature relating to SEN leaves no one in any doubt that inclusion in general and inclusive education in particular have become the new orthodoxy of educational thinking (Allan, 1999). Inclusion is the 'buzz-word' (Evans and Lunt, 2005: 41) that has gained high status and acquired international currency within the UK's educational and social policy initiatives. The term 'inclusion' has become the common parlance that now permeates (see Chapters 6 and 7) government policy within the area of SEN (Rose and Howley, 2007). However, while this term might be widely employed, the question that dominates people's thinking is what exactly does inclusion mean? Within the literature base there is a plethora of definitions of inclusion and it is more than apparent that this is a concept that may be defined in a variety of ways.

READER REFLECTION

With another student, discuss how you would define inclusion.

- Does inclusion relate just to the children with SEN?

- Does, or indeed, should inclusion mean that all children must always be incorporated into mainstream schools?

- Consider your educational journey in schools. Have you witnessed aspects of inclusive education? Share your thoughts with another student about what you have witnessed.

Government's early definitions of inclusion

From the late 1990s onwards, government legislation promoted an educational ideology that seemingly placed the inclusion of children with SEN at the heart of the development of its educational practices and processes (Hodkinson, 2012b).

In 1997 the government defined inclusion as:

[seeing] more pupils with SEN included in mainstream primary and secondary schools. By inclusion we mean not only that pupils with SEN should wherever possible receive their education in a mainstream school, but also that they should join fully with their peers in the curriculum and the life of the school. For example, we believe, that ... children with SEN should generally take part in mainstream lessons rather than being isolated in separate units. (DfES, 1997: 44)

During the last decade of the twentieth century, then, educational policy promoted inclusive education as the teaching of disabled and non-disabled children within the same neighbourhood schools. Further definitions suggested that all pupils, regardless of their weaknesses, should become part of the school community (Judge, 2003). Firstly, these definitions are difficult to accept because they appear to relate to what may be called locational inclusion. This is where pupils being educated together is more important than the attitudes or environment that each child is subjected to. As Barton (2003: 9) comments, 'inclusion is not about the assimilation of individuals into an essentially unchanged system of educational provision and practice'.

A second flaw undermining these early government definitions is that they rely on categorisations and the language of medical deficit. Inevitably, definitions founded upon the medical model shackle an individual's inclusion to our entrenched societal views of disability. Moreover, the employment of the terminology of 'weakness' and 'disability' is observed by some to be both patronising and degrading. Definitions formulated in these terms do not promote inclusion but, conversely, encourage the return to integration, and thereby tolerance, not inclusion, of children with SEN.

To illustrate this point further, let us consider the word 'weakness' as employed within some government documentation. In particular, imagine if you will, that David Cameron was placed in a room with Professor Stephen Hawking and was then asked to discuss the relative merits of quantum physics, or say, quark theory – who would display a weakness then? Weakness, as utilised in this instance, is certainly different from how it is employed in government statements. This word, then, like 'disability', is subjective and bound within hierarchical societal notions of normality. By employing the language of deficit we do not instil pride, respect and value for all children, but rather refer to individuals who society feels are not able to be included because of impairment. Some people would argue that we must move away from this form of language and accept that recognition and a celebration of difference are the most important keystones of inclusion. This principle is supported by Barton (2003: 10), who contends that:

> Inclusive education is about the why, how, when, where and the consequences of educating all learners. It involves the politics of recognition and is concerned with the serious issue of who is included and who is excluded within education and society in general.

A third difficulty that early government definitions of inclusion encounter is that they are framed within confusing and sometimes contradictory language. This has led some to contend that such government definitions cannot be embraced by everyone (Rose, 2003). For example, in 1997 the New Labour government, through the Green Paper (DfEE, 1997) and its 1998 Programme of Action (DfEE, 1998), trumpeted their commitment to the principles and practice of inclusion (Barton, 2003). Through policy initiatives such as these you might conclude that such inclusion is employed to ensure that the educational provision offers an opportunity for all children to achieve their full potential. However, even within these early definitions there exist contradictions, confusions and even an ambivalence, which indicates that the New Labour government had not totally embraced an adequate definition of inclusion and that its commitment to this policy was qualified (Barton, 2003; Rose, 2003).

To be specific, within the 1997 Green Paper the government defined inclusion by using phrases such as 'wherever possible' and that it 'should generally take place in mainstream lessons' (DfEE, 1997: 44). This form of language places a qualification on the definition of inclusion. Furthermore, another contradictory statement employed is that 'children should be educated as far as possible with their peers' (DfEE, 1997: 4) and that the government would 'redefine the role of specialist schools to develop a specialist network of support' (DfEE, 1997: 4).

This form of qualification is again apparent in the government's Programme of Action (DfEE, 1998), where inclusion was promoted as 'when parents want it and where appropriate support can be provided'. Moreover, in the report of the Special Working Group, the commitment to special school education was reinforced, with comments such as, 'the future role of special schools within the overarching framework of inclusion is strongly advocated' and 'the special school section enjoys the government's full support' (DfES, 2003: 2).

In June 1994 representatives of 92 governments and 25 international organisations formed the World Conference on Special Needs Education, held in Salamanca, Spain. They agreed a dynamic new statement on the education of all disabled children, which called for inclusion to be the norm. In addition, the conference adopted a new Framework for Action, the guiding principle of which is that ordinary schools should accommodate all children, regardless of their physical, intellectual, social, emotional, linguistic or other conditions.

The Salamanca Statement of Inclusion also detailed that academic achievement should be observed as being secondary to the development of the self through individual choice.

(Source: CSIE, www.csie.org.uk/inclusion/unesco-salamanca.shtml)

Let us pause, though, to reconsider again the definitions of inclusion offered above and analyse how their mediation and representation of inclusion stand at some distance from that of the Salamanca Statement. If we examine the first definition and consider the government's employment of words, another more elusive and 'slippery' definition of inclusion materialises. The use of phrases such as 'seeing more pupils', 'wherever possible', 'that children should generally take part in', and a 'neighbourhood of schools' suggests that government intended to pursue a 'twin-track system' of SEN where the segregation of some pupils within the *loci* of special schools was acceptable (Barton, 2003). Pupils, then, were to be put there but not allowed here, present in an inclusive system but absent from a mainstream classroom.

It is apparent, then, that while the New Labour government documentation and legislation included a 'strong commitment to the principle of inclusion' (Croll and Moses, 2003: 747), it still observed inclusion defined in terms of a twin-track system that continued to promote the orthodoxy of segregation within special schools. While the New Labour government supposedly based its definitions on the rights of all children, this critical interrogation of its education policies and practices shows that it also acknowledged that its definition and operation of inclusion were subject to limits (Evans and Lunt, 2005).

Inclusion: can it be a twin track system?

READER REFLECTION

On the campaign trail on 27th April 2010, David Cameron was confronted by Jonathan Bartley, a parent of a child with SEN. In retrospect, this incident has become a pivotal moment for analysing how Prime Minister Cameron believes effective education should be formulated.

Read the conversation detailed below, watch the associated video and consider the view of special education put forward by Cameron and Bartley. What is your view on this issue? Should all special schools be closed and all children placed in mainstream education? Under New Labour, was there actually a bias towards inclusive education? You might like to conduct your own research on this issue.

Evidence to help you with your reflection:

Mr Bartley, who has a son with SEN, asked Mr Cameron in the full glare of the television cameras why his manifesto lacked a strong statement about the benefits of inclusive education. Mr Cameron replied that his manifesto did support the inclusion of children with disabilities into mainstream schools. However, later when people read the Conservative manifesto in detail, they found it contained a statement suggesting that vulnerable children should receive the highest quality of care and that what Cameron called the 'ideologically-driven closure of special schools' would end. It went on to say that the Conservatives would, 'end the bias towards the inclusion of children with special needs in mainstream schools' (Conservative Manifesto, 2010: 53). This statement about ending the bias towards inclusion is one that has become really important to parents, children, teachers and researchers in this area. Indeed, Mr Cameron went on to say that special schooling and inclusive education was an emotive issue and that under New Labour children were sometimes forced to go to mainstream schools even when they did not want to. He argued that special schools were an invaluable resource and that even New Labour's first Education Minister David Blunkett, who went to a special school, felt strongly about such schools.

For further information, see:

- http://blogs.channel4.com/factcheck/tory-manifesto-favours-special-needs-children-in-mainstream-schools/2204)

- www.theguardian.com/politics/2010/apr/27/david-cameron-schools-special-education)

(Continued)

(Continued)

- 'Special needs children "failed by mainstream schools"'. Available at: www.dailymail.co.uk/news/article-394206/Special-needs-children-failed-mainstream-schools.html

- the video of this event, which is available at: http://news.sky.com/story/775328/dads-fury-at-cameron-over-tory-schools-plan.

For some educational professionals though, the continuance of a separate system of segregated education creates a tension.

> This tension created by the continuance of a separate system of education is clearly indicated in the following statement by the Centre for Studies on Inclusive Education (CSIE, 2005):
>
> The central message from the ... Department and Ministers is that special schools should continue and that their role should be enhanced through a variety of changes. We strongly disagree with this position and reject entirely the idea that there will always be a need for special schools for some pupils. There is nothing taking place in special schools that isn't also taking place in ordinary schools, somewhere. Special schools no longer have the monopoly on educating pupils who experience barriers to learning and participation, including those categorised as having complex and severe needs.

The rights agenda and the ideology of full inclusion

For Glazzard (2014: 40):

> Inclusion represents a proactive stance. It challenges educational settings to make adaptations and adjustments to cater for the needs of diverse learners. The purpose of inclusion is to provide all learners with equality of educational opportunity and this right is guaranteed through equality legislation, which places a statutory duty on schools and other educational settings to make reasonable adjustments to break down barriers to participation and achievement.

Other educationalists though (Booth, 2000; Reynolds, 1989) would argue that inclusion is a concept far beyond any one single definition. For some people, inclusion should be a process inextricably linked to the 'goal of full inclusion'

(Hornby, 2002: 4). Within full inclusion, it is generally accepted that all children should be educated together in terms of location, need, curriculum and attitudes, with no tolerance of or justification for the maintenance of a separate segregated system of education.

The ideology of full inclusion was formed and moulded by the worldwide pressure for civil rights during the 1960s and 1970s. This movement offered people with disabilities an avenue to voice their frustration and anger over what many perceived as the stigmatising and degrading educational experiences they had endured during their passage through the system of segregated special schools (Clough and Corbett, 2000). These frustrations translated into a real desire to deconstruct segregation and to then reconstruct an educational system that was based upon a philosophy of fraternity and an equality of opportunity (Thomas et al., 2005).

Ideas such as these took hold during the development of the comprehensive system of education during the 1970s. During this period a strong moral case for full inclusion was advanced and many people argued that it was simply the right thing to do. This growing desire for a fairer education system was lent further support during the 1980s and 1990s when research evidence, albeit limited, suggested that differential outcomes for children with SEN in mainstream and special school placements were minimal (Clough and Corbett, 2000). Based upon this evidence it was also argued that the theoretical underpinning for the continuance of separate special educational provision was now redundant (Thomas and Loxley, 2001).

CASE STUDY 5.1

Enid's story

I am now in my early 90s and so schooling seems a dim and distance memory to me. However, sometimes at night the horror of what I went through in my special school still haunts my dreams. I started going to this residential special school when I was five and did not leave until my 16th birthday. At the start I thought my school was brilliant: I loved the uniform, especially the straw hat and satchel that I was given. However, this excitement did not last long. After a week I missed my family who lived over 200 miles away. They could only afford to come and see me every two months or so and then we had only a couple of hours together before they had to leave. I felt so lonely and isolated, and I missed all my brothers' and sisters' birthdays. I have felt throughout my life a stranger to my family and I still feel very sad about this. On the odd occasions I did manage to get home, the local children often spoilt the short time I had with my family. They would throw stones at me and call me a special kid or names that were worse than this. They did not know me and never bothered to find out why I was different.

(Continued)

(Continued)

Why would they? Society at the time shut us away so that they would not have to think about people with disabilities.

What was worse though in the school was that you had the same teachers for over 11 years. I fell out with the English teacher when I was ten, for the next six years he never let me forget it. Even in the evenings I could not get away from his constant ridicule. He hated me and I hated him. When I eventually left this school I realised that I had not got any qualifications, they never really bothered with them at the school. This lack of qualifications affected the rest of my life as I always had low-paid and boring jobs. I hated my special school and I hate the idea that they are still in existence today. I think they should all be closed, the sooner the better.

Despite such strong convictions and the moral stance taken by the full inclusionists, their conceptualisation of inclusion as a human rights issue has been the subject of criticism. For some, full inclusion is nothing more than a fervent campaign (Bailey, 1998), based upon an 'expressive zeal' (Low, 1997: 76), which fails to consider the practical realities of disability. It is thus contended that these practical realities make it difficult, if not impossible, to translate the theory of full inclusion into effective practice in mainstream schools. Croll and Moses's (2000) research supports this view: their work, with 38 education officers and headteachers across 11 local authorities, suggested full inclusion was an unrealistic expectation, especially for those children with complex and severe needs or for those who experienced emotional and behavioural difficulties. Farrell (2000: 10) suggests that full inclusion, based entirely upon the principles of human rights, is actually 'logically and conceptually naïve' because it fails to take into account mainstream children's right to receive a good education. It is arguments such as these that have led some to suggest that the ideology of full inclusion should be dropped in favour of responsible or cautious inclusion practices (Fuchs and Fuchs, 1994; Hornby, 2002).

In more recent times, however, research has begun to show the benefits that inclusion can have for children, schools and society. For example, Cairns and McClatchey (2013) detail that non-disabled children from inclusive schools did have more positive attitudes towards and a better understanding of disability because of their interactions with disabled children. This research finding is supported by numerous researches in Europe (de Boer et al., 2012; de Laat et al., 2013).

Should there be a choice?

As we have seen, the government's failure to promote full inclusion is viewed by some to be a positive step forward in the development of an effective inclusive educational system. This is because by not promoting full inclusion the government appears to be advocating that inclusion should be by choice and not compulsion (Smith, in Tod, 2002). Notably, Warnock subscribes to the premise of inclusion by choice. Indeed, for some this notion of choice is vitally important, especially as the research suggests that some children do not want to be forced into mainstream placements (Norwich and Kelly, 2004). Warnock believes that the special school sector, rather than being a place of last resort, should be regarded as offering a 'more productive and creative interpretation of the ideal of inclusive education for all' (Warnock, 2005: 1).

Warnock believes the single most effective way to improve educational provision for children who are 'fragile' and with 'learning difficulties' is through small, maintained schools. As she states:

> their right to learn we must defend, not their right to learn in the same environment as everyone else. For them we must emphasize their difference (i.e.) their needs as learners, not their similarities with all the rest. (See also Terzi, 2010.)

Barriers to inclusive education
Accountability and standards

In common with many other educational initiatives and policy development, inclusion has become defined and controlled by the government's agents of accountability, performativity and standards. Indeed, in their relentless drive to improve standards, new systems of accountability, policed by autocratic inspection regimes, have been created. It has been argued that it is this 'accountability noose' (Grainger and Todd, 2000) of 'driving up standards' that has pushed educational provision towards an 'increasing emphasis on narrow conceptualisations of performance' (Booth, 2000: 12).

Standards agenda – 'an approach to educational reforms which seeks to "drive up" standards of attainment, including workforce skill levels and ultimately national competitiveness in a globalized economy' (Ainscow et al., 2006: 296).

Performativity – 'refers to the emphasis on the use of outcome-related performance indicators. These are frequently expressed as quantitative measures of performance which drive the modern education system through the use of narrow performance indicators, which are then used to evaluate school effectiveness. School performance is ... made public through the use of league tables and the publishing of inspection ratings' (Glazzard, 2014: 40).

Indeed the inclusion agenda has not escaped the gaze of the operators of the regimes of accountability. As early as 2000, Ofsted defined inclusion in relation to a statement of principles that promoted all learners and as such its scope was broad (Ofsted, 2000). Furthermore, it (2000: 13) had observed that an inclusive school was one in which 'the teaching and learning achievements, attitudes and well-being of every person matter'. Moreover, Ofsted contended that 'effective schools were educationally inclusive schools' (2000: 7). To ensure that schools delivered effective inclusive education, Ofsted produced a checklist, which they now employ when inspecting schools. While we may observe that this checklist of principles is an improvement on government definitions that employed the language of deficit, we should still question whether inclusion can, or indeed should ever, be determined in relation to either the standards agenda or the metrics of accountability (Hodkinson, 2011).

CASE STUDY 5.2

Performativity and accountability

Carefully read the case study below. Consider the following questions:

- What are the purposes of education?
- Is education just about achieving high scores in examinations and, if this is the case, what happens to those children who cannot do this?

The standards agenda became a reality, a challenge and, for my school, a major concern.

I had been a deputy head for ten years and I used to work in a lovely small school based in a town in the Midlands. For years, we were known as a school that included all children and we won awards for the teaching of children with SEN and disabilities. Indeed, at one stage, we had 27 children who had a Statement of SEN. Our school then really reflected the rich diversity of life that is out there in society. However, this ideal job changed dramatically when a new headteacher descended on our school just at the same time that the Ofsted inspection regime began. Our new head was all about targets, how many children got level fours in their Standard Assessment Tests (SATs). She had no time for the children who would not achieve this. When we had our first Ofsted inspection, the report did not talk about the excellent work we did with children with SEN, rather it criticised us for not achieving national averages for English, maths and science. The children that were once seen as a real asset to our school became observed, by some, to be a burden and a drain on our resources.

Later, performance management came into being and my career became dependent upon examination success, indeed, my pay did too. I took early retirement a few years ago as I had become disillusioned with my job. I found myself asking what is education for? Surely every child is entitled to an education that best suits his/her needs. What do we do with those kids who are different; those who will never have exam success – are we saying they have no worth?

Some have observed that the issue of school accountability is the biggest challenge to the development of inclusive education. It has been argued that English schools have become a laboratory for educational reform and it is this, coupled with accountability and performativity, that has led to the progress of inclusion being 'painfully slow' (Ainscow et al., 2006: 296). For some, the standards agenda has led to a backlash from teachers against the inclusion of pupils with SEN (Ainscow et al., 2006: 296).

A school's effectiveness is mainly judged against children's attainment in SATs and examinations. For example, a primary school's success is judged by how many pupils achieve a level four in their SATs in numeracy and literacy. For some headteachers, but certainly not all, this level of accountability can cause a tension between on the one hand achieving academic success, and on the other, supporting pupils who may never achieve academic success as defined by the government. Such tension is illustrated by this headteacher, who is clearly struggling to develop effective inclusive education in her school.

> Now don't get me wrong, I fully support the principle of inclusive education, just not in my school and not when I am about to undergo an Ofsted inspection. I have a limited amount of resources and a limited amount of teachers. These children with SEN take up a lot of my teachers' time that would be better spent working with children who could, with a push, achieve a level four in their SATs.
>
> Whatever I or my teachers do, these children will never get to a level 2 let alone a level 4. So there is no way that I am going to put my best, most experienced teachers with them, it would be an inefficient use of my resources. It is the number of pupils I get to level 4 that I am judged on and mine and the teachers' jobs depend on this, not how happy the children are or how many we include. If I'm being honest, as long as I can keep these children quiet and occupied they won't affect the education of the other children. I know that's not a politically correct thing to say, but that is just the way it is. As far as I am concerned, I cannot meet the government standards and be a paid-up member of the inclusive education club, it just does not work.

As Hanko (2003: 126) relates 'the National Curriculum with its contentious league tables testing [and] ... an excessively competitive academic results centred teaching climate [has] led to academic failure and disaffection for some'. He continues, 'inflexible forms of assessment of pupils' progress and schools' academic results have become threats rather than an indication of the need for support'. In relation to inclusion the government's obsession with the metrics of accountability may be seen to have ensured schools, 'whose reputation and financial viability have become dependent on surface success' (Hanko, 2003: 126), have become 'wary of accepting children whose low attainment and discipline may affect others' learning by depressing examination and SAT scores' (Fredrickson and Cline, 2002: 67).

For some commentators, inclusion linked to standards is simply unworkable. As Allan (2003: 178) states, inclusion 'is not about figures, politics or ... dogma, it is, about beliefs, faith, caring and the creation of community. ... It is about human rights and human beings'. Ainscow (1995) has argued that the development of peer friendships and relationships between schools, as well as developing all children, are of paramount importance rather than the employment of inclusion within the confines of the national curriculum. Dyson and Slee (2001) have also cautioned against correlating inclusion with educational performance. They believe that the pressure of enforcement, from bodies such as Ofsted, presents a very real danger that inclusion policy will be 'steam-rolled by the stronger standards agenda' (Dyson and Slee, 2001: 17).

Arguments such as these are positive proof that for many writers and researchers inclusion is not, nor can it ever be, a summative, measurable entity as Ofsted would like to have us believe. Perhaps, then, inclusion is a concept that does not have a single definition. Indeed, it could be argued that, 'a definition is less important', but what actually is crucial is that schools achieve a 'meaningful understanding of the core values of inclusion' (Coles and Hancock, 2002: 9).

The barriers created by local authorities

Over the past decade or so, there have been significant developments in the role of the local authority within the system of English education (Ainscow et al., 2010). Whilst it has been argued above that government has a massive role in the standards agenda, we should not forget that the growing political commitment to raising standards has also led to a change in the way local authority education departments are now run (Ainscow et al., 2010). For some (Beveridge, 2004), the local authority is observed to be the guarantor of standards and the rights of children and parents. However, increasingly some schools are reporting that their planning is being deliberately skewed by local authority advisors in their attempts to deliver on the government's standard's agenda (Ainscow et al., 2006). There can be no doubt that local authority policy can exert a tremendous influence on the policy of inclusive schooling not just in terms of academic performance, but also in terms of its expectations of inclusive education and its views on representation of parents and children in the processes and practices of SEN (Beveridge, 2004). Indeed, most recently, while local authorities have continued with the pressure to increase standards, teachers remain uncertain as to what their role will be in terms of the new Code of Practice (DfE, 2014b) (see Pearson et al., 2014).

In respect to the development of inclusion, local authorities perform a number of functions; not only do they create local policy but they also decide, in the main, the level of funding for such education. These two functions are crucial to the successful implementation of inclusive education within local schools. However, in terms of special education, hindsight has revealed that local authorities have been accused of developing and maintaining a postcode lottery of provision for SEN. Regrettably, it would seem that inclusive education might be succumbing to the same difficulties that have already been witnessed in relation to the policy of integration.

For example, some local authorities' policies observe the building of new and more inclusive special schools; others develop inclusive provision by transferring monies from their SEN budgets to mainstream schools; some no longer provide special schools for certain categories of need (Coles and Hancock, 2002). This variety of policy approaches means that families are once again being faced with unacceptable variations in the level of service provision (Audit Commission, 2002). This means that for some children inclusion, like the policy of integration beforehand, will take the form of a school 'placement without adequate provision' for their individual needs (Corbett, 2001: 22). It would seem that while government rhetoric is advocating inclusion by choice, some families will be left with no option but the choice of inclusion.

A further barrier placed in the way of the provision of inclusive education is the 'complexity of funding arrangements' operating within local authorities (MacLeod, 2001: 191). Indeed, it might become the case that mainstream schools will not sign up to inclusion if they perceive there is insufficient funding for the support of individual children's needs.

In this respect, it is interesting to note that a national study has observed that 76 per cent of SENCos felt that their role was undermined by a lack of funding and 40 per cent believed that there was not sufficient support for pupils with SEN (NUT, 2004).

All mainstream schools must appoint a designated teacher, the SENCo, who is responsible for the day-to-day operation of a school's SEN policy. He or she will coordinate provision for pupils with SEN and liaise with parents, staff and external agencies.

In 2005 the CSIE conducted research that clearly highlighted the development of a postcode lottery of special educational provision. Its main findings were:

- statistics report for England shows very little progress towards inclusion nationally between 2002 and 2004

- one third of local authorities increased the segregation of disabled pupils over the three years

- disturbing local variations exist in placement across England: in 2004, pupils with Statements of SEN in South Tyneside were 24 times more likely to receive a segregated education than those in Newham, London (Rustemier and Vaughan, 2005).

The issue of funding here is vital to the successful implementation of inclusionary practices and is one that has undermined such policies in the past. However, it would be unfair to lay the blame for the creation of these barriers solely within the sphere of control operated by the local authority. Many authorities have been placed in an impossible position by the government, for while they have to continue funding special schools, they are also required to provide funding to support early intervention and inclusive educational strategies for all. The question to consider then is that if local authorities are not provided with adequate financial support, rather than being a catalyst to inclusion might they be left with no choice but to impose barriers that will inhibit the development of this educational initiative?

The barriers created by schools

READER REFLECTION

Read the text below and consider the following: what are the prerequisites for successful inclusive teaching?

The Council for the European Union believes that the successful inclusion of children with SEN is based upon:

- increased use of personalised approaches

- harnessing of assessment to support the learning process

- providing teachers with skills to manage and benefit from diversity

- use of cooperative teaching and learning, and in widening access and participation to education.

According to Forlin (2008), successful and effective inclusive teaching requires that teachers have high levels of ethics and morals that both inform and facilitate teaching and learning. Forlin also believes that teachers must act as role models and have a real commitment to making inclusion happen for all children.

Inclusion for some children is being stalled because the 'educational system is not fit to include' them, owing to the barriers of 'lack of knowledge, lack of will, lack of vision, lack of resources and (even) lack of morality' (Clough and Garner, 2003: 87). Successful inclusion, it could be argued, begins and ends with individuals and everyone involved has to consider how their own practices can create or remove barriers to inclusion (Allan, 2003). Frederickson and Cline (2009) contend that for schools to become more inclusive they must critically examine how they might increase participation for the diversity of pupils that they serve within the local community. This examination, however, is difficult as it requires all teachers and support staff to challenge their own anti-discriminatory practices.

A school's approach to inclusion depends upon its teachers' attitudes and professional competencies. Training for the teaching of pupils with diverse needs has been an issue that has inhibited the successful implementation of SEN strategies in the past (Hodkinson, 2009). As far back as the Warnock Report (DES, 1978), the distinct lack of specialist training has been raised as a potential barrier to the successful implementation of SEN strategies. Twenty years later, the Programme of Action (DfEE, 1998) again indicated the need for teachers to undertake specific training in relation to SEN, and the New Labour government indicated that successful practice was being inhibited by the same issue (DfES, 2004a). It seems reasonable to conclude then that despite continuing and widespread requests for the training of all teachers in the pedagogy of SEN, there remains a common feeling amongst educational professionals that the levels of training, to date, have been 'woefully inadequate' (Corbett, 2001: 22).

Key, it seems then, to the development of successful inclusive education is the development of positives attitudes towards this form of education. Problematically, although teachers and trainee teachers seemingly have more positive attitudes towards inclusion than a decade ago (Beacham and Rouse, 2011; Humphrey and Symes, 2013), research continues to demonstrate that such positive attitudes are based upon effective training and 'successful' interactions with children with SEN. The issue of training is a significant one as research studies (see, for example, Croll and Moses, 2000; Hodkinson, 2005, 2006, 2009; Scruggs and Mastropieri, 1996) have indicated that, whilst a majority of teachers would support the concept of inclusive education, they can only do so with some reservations. Teachers, it would seem, are willing to support inclusion policies *if* they relate to children with mild mobility or sensory difficulties (Corbett, 2001). There is however the suggestion that teachers do not have the same inclusive vision in relation to those children who exhibit extreme behavioural difficulties.

The belief that teachers find it difficult to include children with behavioural problems is clearly outlined by these two quotes from teaching staff.

I think there's an issue with violent behaviour. I think that's something that's coming up especially with current society, especially with recent things happening in schools around the country. There is violence and young people use violence. I think there's health and safety issues here that have to be looked at by educational authorities rather than teaching staff. You cannot include children who are going to be violent in their behaviour. You cannot put other children and staff in danger can you?

A normal mainstream school is a very boisterous place and it is just not the place for some children with emotional and behavioural difficulties and sadly that is the nature of the beast. It's not the best thing to say 'I know', but I just think that a secondary school is not the place for them. The vulnerability of some of these children and the stress that it puts them under means that they would misbehave or possibly, you know, I am trying to think of a good word to say ... they would misbehave and they would just be, they could be, violent or whatever. It is just not the place for them.

Research in this area demonstrates that for these children, teachers believe that exclusion is necessary purely on practical grounds (Corbett, 2001). If schools are to become more inclusive then it seems that support will be needed to develop a school ethos that not only enables all pupils to be supported, but also provides for the needs of teachers as well (Hanko, 2003; Hodkinson, 2007a, 2009).

Inclusion: a definition for the twenty-first century

While full inclusionists', Ofsted's and government's definitions of inclusion prove interesting, it has been demonstrated that they are nonetheless subject to criticism. This has been the case because they attempt to define inclusion within the limits of institutional and societal control (Hodkinson, 2010). It has been suggested that inclusion cannot be defined simply in terms of Ofsted's notions of academic achievement, nor can it be countenanced in relation to a process that forces inclusive education on every individual regardless of whether they want it or not. It would seem essential, therefore, that any definition of inclusion should be located firmly within the sphere of the individual and their right to choose. Furthermore, it would seem that any definitions should accept the sentiments of the Salamanca Statement where academic achievement is observed as being secondary to the development of the self through individual choice. From this perspective, then, it is perhaps more useful to define inclusion as a catalyst that requires both schools and society to identify and overcome the barriers that inhibit a child's choices and their ability to achieve their full potential. Within such a definition, the controlling power of the state, its institutions and its vested interests, as well as the accountability of academic metrics, are diminished and replaced by an understanding of individual value, respect and a commitment to the development of the self.

Conclusion

Within this chapter we have learnt that educational policy is at a crossroads in respect to how it deals with inclusive education. We examined how the New Labour government placed inclusive education at the heart of its educational policy. What was revealed during this chapter was that the Coalition government of 2014 did not appear to have the same inclusive ideals. We also explored how, since 1997, inclusive education has been stalled by various barriers created by schools, government and society. It was argued that if these barriers to inclusion are to be overcome, it would seem clear that, 'individual pupils ... must be at the core of all we do' (Coles and Hancock, 2002: 1) and that the power of government influence in the implementation of inclusive education should be reduced. Despite the influence of such barriers, we must though remember that many people now argue that the teaching and learning of children with SEN have improved substantially during the early part of the twenty-first century.

The future evolution of inclusive education however still holds many challenges for both teachers and pupils alike. It appears that we may not see more children with SEN being taught with their peers in local schools because of current government initiatives to 'end the bias towards inclusion'. This is a mistake and I believe that children, parents and professionals must continue to argue for the development of inclusive education. However, this by itself will not ensure successful inclusion. Politicians must also guarantee that the professional development of teachers and adequate funding for schools are given a high priority within any future policy developments. Furthermore, if any government is to meet the needs of all children in local schools, it must as a matter of urgency move away from the Victorian systems of accountability towards an education policy that allows local authorities, schools and families to work together in a partnership where mutual trust and respect, and not examination results, dominate.

Whatever happens during the next decade, you will through your reading of this chapter perhaps realise that Westminster needs to understand and take account of the mistakes of the past and employ this knowledge and understanding to inform its future planning. It must develop a clear vision for the education of children with SEN, one that is supported by straightforward, coordinated and fully resourced policies (Hodkinson, 2012b). This chapter should have helped to lead you to an understanding that if any government is to achieve an inclusive consciousness it must ensure that all children achieve their full potential and become a 'normal' part of society. This, it would seem, can only be realised by listening to children and their families and by ensuring that inclusion is by choice and not by compulsion.

In summary, then, this chapter set out to offer a critical overview of the emergence and evolution of inclusive education from the 1990s onwards whilst considering the barriers created by the government, local authorities and schools that have served to stall the development of SEN practice. Within the next section we will locate how SEN, equality and inclusion are operated within the English legislative system. In addition, we will analyse how SEN and inclusion are formulated and delivered within other countries' educational systems.

In completing the activities and readings detailed below, you should consider the question: what is the best way of defining inclusion and inclusive education? In addition, after completing these tasks and the readings, you might like to discuss with other students the following: who should hold control of the inclusion of children in mainstream schools? Should it be the local authority, the teachers, the parents or the children?

STUDENT ACTIVITIES

1 Read Lani Florian's, a professor of social and educational inclusion, views on the term 'inclusion'. Using the knowledge gained from this chapter and the previous ones you have read, decide whether the term 'inclusion' has become too broad or indeed is a concept that has just replaced the term 'special', and in reality, nothing in schools has actually changed over the course of the past 20 years.

(Continued)

(Continued)

There is uneasiness about the term 'inclusion'. On the one hand, it has been observed that narrow conceptualisations have resulted in simply replacing the word 'special' with 'inclusive' and nothing much has changed. On the other hand, there is a fear that the definition has become so broad that it is meaningless or, worse, that educationally important differences are being overlooked (Florian, 2008: 206).

2 With another student, discuss whether individual pupils with SEN should decide whether they want to be included in mainstream schools or whether government should ensure inclusive education by closing all of the special schools?

Further reading

Ainscow, M., Farrell, P. and Tweddle, D. (2010) 'Developing policies for inclusive education: a study of the role of local education authorities', *International Journal of Inclusive Education*, 4(3), pp. 211–29.
There is precious little research that has examined the role of the local authority in inclusive educational practice. This research, therefore, provides a useful window into this complex world.

Council of the European Union (2010) *Council Conclusions on the Social Dimension of Education and Training*, 3013th Education, Youth and Culture meeting, Brussels, 11th May 2010. Available at: www.european-agency.org/news/news-files/Council-Conclusions-May-2010-Social-Dimension.pdf.
This text provides a very detailed overview of inclusion and teacher training in Europe.

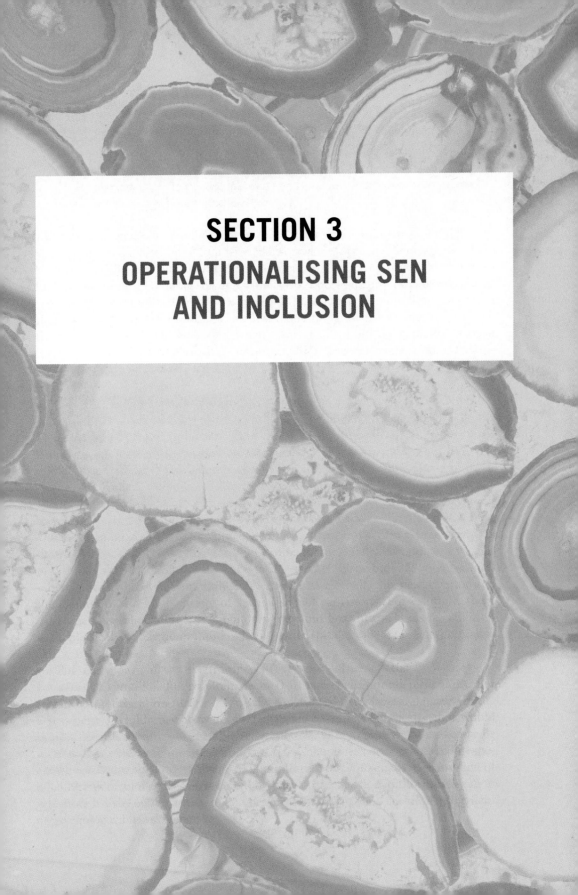

SECTION 3
OPERATIONALISING SEN AND INCLUSION

6

CURRENT LEGISLATION GOVERNING SEN AND INCLUSION

CHAPTER OBJECTIVES

- To explore changes in the legislation that governs SEN and disability.

- To introduce and provide a critical examination of the operation of SEN and disability legislation in schools in England.

Introduction

In Chapter 5 we considered the view that inclusive education and SEN practice were under threat because successive governments had introduced competing policy initiatives from the 1990s onwards. It was suggested that governments must put ideology to one side and take account of past mistakes to develop a clear framework of SEN and equality that is built upon straightforward and coordinated policies.

Chapter 6 examines how SEN and equality policy and legislation have changed in recent times. It provides a detailed overview of current legislation and educational policy and outlines the guiding principles that have informed these changes. The chapter therefore considers the key principles underpinning the legislation that influences current practices in schools. Below is an overview of some of the important pieces of legislation that govern SEN and equality provision and practice. It might be of some surprise to you that legislation from the 1970s still has a major part to play in the development of SEN and inclusive educational provision in the twenty-first century.

The important pieces of legislation that govern SEN and equality provision and practice are:

- Chronically Sick and Disabled Person Act 1970. Available at:

  www.legislation.gov.uk/ukpga/1970/44/contents
- Children Act 1989 (Section 17). Available at:

  www.legislation.gov.uk/ukpga/1989/41/section/17
- Children Act 2004. Available at:

  www.legislation.gov.uk/uksi/2005/1972/contents/made
- Mental Capacity Act 2005. Available at:

  www.legislation.gov.uk/ukpga/2005/9/contents
- The Equality Act 2010. Available at:

  www.legislation.gov.uk/ukpga/2010/15/contents
- Teachers' Standards 2012. Available at:

  www.gov.uk/government/collections/teachers-standards
- The National Curriculum for England and Wales 2014. Available at:

  www.gov.uk/government/collections/national-curriculum
- Children and Families Act 2014. Available at:

  www.legislation.gov.uk/ukpga/2014/6/contents/enacted
- SEN and Disability Regulations 2014. Available at:

  www.legislation.gov.uk/uksi/2014/1530/contents/made.

The Chronically Sick and Disabled Person Act 1970

The Chronically Sick and Disabled Person Act 1970 was introduced to parliament by Alf Morris, who was a Member of Parliament (MP) for Manchester Wythenshawe. This Act is observed as groundbreaking because it was the first in the world to provide rights and equal opportunities to people with disabilities (BBC, n.d.). This legislation, amongst other things, introduced a code of practice to ensure that public buildings were accessible. The Act stated:

> Any person undertaking the provision of a building ... shall, in the means of access both to and within the building, and in the parking facilities and sanitary conveniences to be available (if any), make provision, in so far as it is in the circumstances both practicable and reasonable, for the needs of persons using the building who are disabled. (Section 8.1)

READER REFLECTION

Consider the argument below, which defines how important access to services is for all children. Consider whether legislation alone is capable of ensuring equality of access. Mind map what other issues should be considered.

> The Council for Disabled Children (n.d.) believes that all disabled children are children first and therefore they should have equal access to all the services available to children. Such services should include nurseries, playgroups, playgrounds, leisure services, children's centres and mainstream schools.

This legislation also required local authorities to support disabled people in accessing travel and educational activities outside of the home. Section 2 of the Act has been denoted to be the 'finest community care statute' that exists because of the manner in which it brought forward enforceable rights for disabled people in relation to community care services (see Bowen, n.d.: 1).

READER REFLECTION

Watch the short video of Lord Morris discussing how he found out that he was able to take this legislation to be discussed in parliament. Consider why he felt it was so important to introduce this legislation at this time. The video is available at: http://news.bbc.co.uk/local/lancashire/hi/people_and_places/newsid_8697000/8697441.stm.

Lord Morris was a very interesting person. You might like to research his background in relation to disability rights, something he worked tirelessly to support.

The Children Act 1989

This Act, introduced in October 1991, is perhaps one of the most significant to reach the statute book, as for the first time it unified legislation that related to children into one legal framework (Allen, 2005). The major function of this Act was to deliver the 'legal tools' to those who held parental responsibility for children so that they could act in their best interest (Allen, 2005: 1). Under Part 2, local authorities are required to support contact between 'looked after children' and their families (Sen and Broadhurst, 2011). In addition, Section 3(5) provides that teachers, and other professionals, as well as the local authority have a duty of care towards children and that they must, 'do all that is reasonable in the circumstances for the purposes of safeguarding or promoting the welfare of the child' (NUT, 2013: 4).

The Children Act is a large piece of legislation made up 12 parts, containing some 100 different sections. This legislation has been subject to several amendments not least through the Adoption and Children Act 2002 and the Children Act 2004. This, and other legislation, has amended provision in terms of parental responsibility, special guardianship orders, care plans and local authority complaints procedures (Allen, 2005).

The Act provides that the following people have 'parental responsibility':

(i) The mother and father of a legitimate child (or the adoptive parents of a child who has been legally adopted).

(ii) The mother of an illegitimate child.

(iii) A guardian – the person appointed to act as the child's guardian – usually only when there is no one else who has parental responsibility.

(iv) A person with whom the child is to live under what is called a 'residence order' and a local authority in whose favour a care order has been made have parental responsibility.

(Children Act 1989)

According to the Council for Disabled Children (2014), the Children Act 1989 is the key piece of legislation that provides additional services to support disabled children. The Act creates a general duty on local authorities to provide children's services that safeguard as well promote the welfare of children in need within their areas. Sections 20 and 22 of the Children Act place a duty on local authorities to ensure that children are consulted about their needs and are consulted in respect to the services that are to be provided to them (Joseph Rowntree Foundation, 1999).

Section 17(10) of the Children Act 1989 defines a 'child in need' as:

(a) one who is unlikely to achieve or maintain, or to have the opportunity of achieving or maintaining, a reasonable standard of health or development without the provision for him of services by a local authority ... ; or

(b) his health or development is likely to be significantly impaired, or further impaired, without the provision for him of such services; or

(c) he is disabled.

This legislation though has been subject to criticism. For example, early research, conducted by the Joseph Rowntree Foundation (1999) suggested that in terms of disabled children, the Act:

- was not ensuring that they received adequate protection
- was not ensuring that children's feelings and wishes were being taken into consideration in relation to their placements in residential care
- did not provide information about how many children were spending time away from home and what form of service provision was involved in their care.

Furthermore, whilst Section 62 of the Act requires social worker input in terms of children placed into residential care, research by the Joseph Rowntree Foundation (1999) suggested that this form of support was not in evidence. In addition, it was noted that there was confusion as to how the regulations of the Children Act applied to children placed in respite care. Sen and Broadhurst (2011) also question how the Act defined family contact. They cite evidence that suggests this Act was ensuring that family contact was being maintained even when such contact was psychologically damaging for the children concerned.

The Children Act 1989 continued the tradition of ensuring that teachers had a duty of care towards their pupils; an idea that dates back to the nineteenth century. However, according to Hunt (2013) many teachers are unsure about where the line between caring for a child as a teacher and the work of a social worker is to be placed. Consider the following case studies and decide what a teacher should be reasonably expected to do in each given circumstance.

CASE STUDY 6.1

Paul

Paul, a six-year-old child, attends his local primary school. His teacher, Mrs Ajay notices that Paul is quite thin for his age. After talking with Paul, Mrs Ajay realises that Paul's parents do not always provide him with a breakfast each morning before he leaves for school. She decides to bring in a breakfast for Paul each morning to ensure that he is eating well.

CASE STUDY 6.2

Mrs Banks

Mrs Banks notices that Jemma often comes to school in dirty clothing, which in recent times has begun to smell. Mrs Banks decides that under her duty of care, she should provide Jemma with a replacement uniform and that she should wash Jemma's dirty clothes at least twice a week.

CASE STUDY 6.3

Mrs Kenon

Mrs Kenon has successfully run a school canoeing trip for the past ten years for her secondary school children. However, this year she has decided to cancel the trip as she is unsure about whether organising such an adventurous outing would be maintaining her duty of care towards the children in her class.

The Children Act 2004

This Act came into being as a response to the death of Victoria Climbié and other child abuse inquiries (Roche and Tucker, 2007). The Children Act 2004 came into statute on 1st September 2005 and was designed to strengthen the Children Act of 1989. This Act brought forward the biggest organisational change of children's services that had been observed in recent times (Reid, 2005). The legislation aimed to ensure that schools and their facilities were made available to be used by their local communities 365 days a year through the implementation of what was to be called the 'extended day' (Reid, 2005).

EXTENDED SCHOOLS

Extended schools provide a range of services and activities beyond the school day to help meet the needs of their pupils, families and the wider community.

These services, normally entitled 'wraparound care', are observed to have importance for dealing with social inclusion issues, such as poor attendance, persistent late arrival at school, and a single point of access for parents and carers so that they may return to work or access appropriate training (see Roche and Tucker, 2007).

This Act provided the central pillar to New Labour's attempts to improve services to 'vulnerable children" and to protect local communities' (Reid, 2005: 12). Parton (2011) notes that this legislation and the associated Every Child Matters agenda was the beginning of a journey towards the radical reform of services and policies that related to children (see Roche and Tucker, 2007). The Act had five aims in relation to children. That it:

- protected their physical and mental health, and emotional well-being
- protected them from harm and neglect
- provided education, training and recreation
- ensured that children made a positive contribution to society
- promoted children's social and economic well-being. (Section 25)

This legislation created the post of the Children's Commissioner and enabled the government to create an electronic record for every child in England, Scotland and

Wales. The purpose of these records was to ensure that when children moved across local authorities their well-being would continue to be monitored. In addition, the legislation also placed a duty on all service providers to work together to protect children and to ensure that no child 'fell between the gaps' of provision and monitoring. Moreover, it established Local Safeguarding Children's Boards who became responsible for child protection in their area (see *The Guardian*, 2009). The objectives of such safeguarding boards, defined in Section 32 of the Act, were to coordinate service provision and ensure the effectiveness of that provision.

The Children's Commissioner promotes and protects children's rights and ensures that children are taken seriously. Further information is available at:

- for England: www.childrenscommissioner.gov.uk
- for Wales: www.childcomwales.org.uk
- for Scotland: www.sccyp.org.uk
- for Northern Ireland: www.niccy.org.

To fulfil the requirements of this Act, every local authority had to appoint a Director of Children's Services (Lead Director in Wales) for children and young people whose role was to coordinate and oversee children's services. These Directors of Children's Services have three key roles. These being:

- responsibility for promoting partnership working both corporately across the local authority and, in recognition of its leadership role, between the authority and its partners
- providing leadership to drive change
- ensuring that the local authority implements the rights of children and young people.

The Children Act 2004 placed a statutory duty on all schools, including independent schools, non-maintained schools and further education institutions to exercise their functions, with a view to safeguarding and promoting the welfare of their pupils by:

- creating and maintaining a safe learning environment for children and young people;

- identifying where there are child welfare concerns and taking action to address them, where appropriate, in partnership with other agencies; and

- developing children's understanding, awareness, and resilience.

(Welsh Assembly Government, 2006: 54)

This legislation though brought forward considerable challenges for those working in educational services because it called for a radical change in the culture of schools themselves. From this time forward, schools were to become the centre of provision for the safeguarding and protection of all children (Roche and Tucker, 2007). Many teachers therefore found themselves undertaking different forms of work from those they had traditionally been used to. For example, teachers were asked to become lead professionals who were responsible for ensuring that families could access services and provision that were available on school premises (Roche and Tucker, 2007). Headteachers and senior management teams of schools were now to be observed as part of a complicated but totally integrated service for children and their families (Reid, 2005). Moreover, the roles of local authority behavioural support staff and education welfare officers were also significantly affected (Reid, 2005). One of the major criticisms of the Act though was that it was not backed up by extra resourcing. Many local authorities reported that they struggled to meet the cost of the increased level of children's services, especially that incurred by provision of residential accommodation for children (Batty, 2005). Furthermore, in 2005, during the introduction of these reforms, local authorities reported that they were having serious difficulties recruiting the necessary staff to ensure that the duties placed upon them by the Children Act were being met.

READER REFLECTION

By employing internet and library resources, examine whether the Children Act 2004 was viewed as a successful piece of legislation. Were the initial difficulties experienced overcome?

A good place to start this examination would be with the internet resource, www.theguardian.com/society/2005/may/18/childrensservices.

The Mental Capacity Act 2005

The Mental Capacity Act 2005 provides the legal framework to provide protection for people who cannot make decisions for themselves due to a learning disability, mental health condition or any other reason. The Act came into force on 1st October 2007 and is supported by its own Code of Practice. This legislation applies in England and Wales to anyone whose mental capacity is affected by 'an impairment of, or a disturbance in the functioning of, the mind or brain'. This act is based upon five key principles: These being:

- **Presumption of capacity**. Every adult has the right to make their own decisions if they have the capacity to do so.

- **Maximising decision making capacity**. People should receive support to help them make their own decisions.

- **Right to make unwise decisions**. People have the right to make decisions that others might think are unwise. A person who makes a decision that others think is unwise should not automatically be labelled as lacking the capacity to make a decision.

- **Best interests**. Any act, or any decision made on behalf of, someone who lacks capacity must be in their best interests.

- **Least restrictive option**. Any act, or any decision made on behalf of, someone who lacks capacity should be the least restrictive option possible.

(See Mind, 2005.)

This legislation also set up the Office of the Public Guardian, who is responsible for protecting people who lack the capacity to make choices for themselves. They work with service providers, individuals and families to supervise how decisions are being made for those people who cannot make such judgements for themselves.

READER REFLECTION

Watch the film *Three Stories*, which is about the Mental Capacity Act. List the benefits of this legislation for the individuals who are shown in the film. The film is available at: http://webarchive.nationalarchives.gov.uk/20080805 202309/direct.gov.uk/en/DisabledPeople/HealthAndSupport/YourRights InHealth/DG_10016888.

The Equality Act 2010

The development of legislation to prevent discrimination on the grounds of disability, laying the groundwork for the Equality Act 2010, began in 1995 with the introduction of the Disability Discrimination Act (DDA). This introduced the largest reform ever observed in terms of equality legislation (Hills, 2011). This Act introduced the legal concept of disability discrimination (Lockewood et al., 2012) as well as the premise that employees should make 'reasonable adjustment' for disabled employees.

Making reasonable adjustments

A term that can cause consternation to some is that of 'reasonable adjustments'. This relates to schools having to make some attempt to interpret the legislation when trying to meet the individual needs of children with SEN. Obviously, the dilemma for teachers and schools was what counts as 'reasonable' (Brothers et al., 2002) in relation both to access to buildings and the curriculum. It did in fact advocate that reasonable adjustments should be conceived as changes to the school layout, improved signage and information, relevant staff training and adaptation of the curriculum to ensure accessibility to education for children with SEN. Reasonable adjustments therefore were

(Continued)

(Continued)

about what was practicably achievable within educational institutions and individual situations based upon the resources available. Consequently, schools and teachers were not going to be required to make changes that were either impractical or beyond their means.

According to the Equality Act 2010 (see DfE, 2014c: 26) the school must make reasonable adjustments for disabled people:

- where something a school does places a disabled pupil at a disadvantage compared to other pupils

- where schools expect to provide an auxiliary aid or service when it would be reasonable to do so and if such an aid would alleviate any substantial disadvantage that the pupil faces in comparison to non-disabled pupils.

READER REFLECTION

Review the term 'reasonable adjustments' and make a list of what you consider to be appropriate to adapt and modify within educational settings. In analysing this, try to make justifications for why you think certain adaptations are reasonable, whilst others are more problematic to achieve.

Over the next ten years or so, the DDA was amended not least by the Special Educational Needs and Disability Act (SENDA) of 2001 (DfES, 2001b). SENDA brought education within the remit of the DDA (1995). As such, it suggested that:

- an education institution should not treat a disabled person 'less favourably' for a reason relating to their disability
- an institution is required to make 'reasonable adjustments' if a disabled person would otherwise be placed at a 'substantial disadvantage'
- adjustments should be 'anticipatory'
- the legislation applies to all admissions, enrolments and other 'student services', which includes assessment and teaching materials.

In examining this legislation, however, many of its key intentions were rather vague and open to interpretation. For example, what can be determined as 'less favourable treatment', 'reasonable adjustments' and 'substantial disadvantage' had to be tested in the courts. In commenting upon the introduction of the new legislation, Bert Massie, Chair of the Disability Rights Commission, suggested that we all want to live in communities where we can participate fully and equally. Furthermore, we want all children to do well at school, to take part in all areas of school life and to reach their full potential.

READER REFLECTION

Imagine you are a class teacher who regularly teaches children with SEN in mainstream settings. The headteacher has provided you with the report from the Equality and Human Rights Commission (2014) that showed children with SEN tend to do less well compared with their non-disabled peers both educationally and in employment. The headteacher wants you to make some recommendations to the senior management team of the school as part of introducing the new national curriculum, with the specific aim of raising aspirations and attainment for children with SEN.

Make a list of the strategies, actions and recommendations you would consider vital in raising attainment with such children in your school. When you have completed your list, you can review the Equality and Human Rights Commission's (2014) advice in relation to making adjustments so that educational provision can be made effective for all children. The advice is available at: www.equalityhumanrights.com/sites/default/files/uploads/documents/reasonable_adjustments_for_disabled_pupils_guidance_pdf.pdf.

In February 2005 the then Labour government commissioned a review of equality law and policy to, 'consider the fundamental principles of discrimination legislation ... and the opportunities for creating a clearer and more streamline, framework of equality legislation'. For Crowther (2007: 791), the decade from 1995–2005 witnessed a paradigm shift in equality legislation, moving it from 'grudging acceptance' of the rights of disabled people to that of the positive duty of enforceable civil rights.

The process of modernising discrimination legislation came to an end when on 24th April 2009 a new single Equality Bill was presented to the Houses of Commons. This Act harmonised discrimination legislation into one statute and further enshrined the duties set out in the DDA, 1995 (Porter et al., 2011). This legislation, then, details the legal duties that are placed on educational providers, employees and service providers to make reasonable adjustments so that disabled people can take part in education, use services and engage in work. It is a large piece of legislation covering some 200 sections and 28 schedules. Section 6 covers the protected characteristics of disability and establishes who is, and is not, disabled for the purposes of this act (Wadham et al., 2012: 7).

This legislation makes it unlawful for a school or educational provider to discriminate against, harass or victimise a pupil, or potential pupil, in relation to the way it admits a child to school and provides them with an education. For the first time, this legislation specifically covered the curriculum that pupils were introduced to. The Act also makes it unlawful to discriminate against pupils on the grounds of their:

- sex
- race
- disability
- religion or belief

- sexual orientation
- gender reassignment
- pregnancy or maternity.

In terms of the Equality Act 2010, there are four kinds of unlawful behaviour. These being: direct discrimination; indirect discrimination; harassment; and victimisation.

Direct discrimination – occurs when one person treats another less favourably because of one of the characteristics defined above.

Indirect discrimination – occurs when a provision, criterion or practice is applied generally, but affects people with a protected characteristic to a greater degree.

Harassment – is the unwanted conduct to a relevant protected characteristic, which has the purpose or effect of violating a person's dignity or creating an intimidating, hostile, degrading, humiliating or offensive environment for that person.

Victimisation – occurs when a person is treated less favourably than they otherwise would have been because of something they have done.

(See DfE, 2014c: 10)

READER REFLECTION

Consider the following case studies and decide whether the Equality Act was contravened and what, if any, of the four kinds of unlawful behaviour might apply.

CASE STUDY 6.4

Mr Jenkins

Mr Jenkins, the Head of Year, during a school assembly belittles a child because of 'ticks and noises' that are resultant to the child having a condition called Tourette syndrome.

CASE STUDY 6.5

James

A local school bans a pupil from taking part in sports day as it feels that, as James has Down's syndrome, he will not be able to run quickly enough. The headteacher is concerned that by James taking part in the event they will not be able to keep the sports day running to time.

CASE STUDY 6.6

Mrs Brown

Mrs Brown wants to send her four-year-old daughter, Anna, to the local state primary school. Her daughter, as a result of a disability, is not able to fully exercise control of her bowel movements. The school has told Mrs Brown that Anna cannot attend the school because the school's policy maintains that all children must be toilet trained. The school states that it is not refusing access to the school because Anna has a disability, but is applying its toilet training policy equally to all children.

In terms of the Equality Act, disability discrimination has a different status to that covered within the other protected characteristics (DfE, 2014c). In terms of disability, schools may treat disabled pupils more favourably than non-disabled pupils and in some cases through the implementation of 'reasonable adjustments' are actually required to do so by law. The application of reasonable adjustments is provided to ensure that disabled pupils are 'put on a more level footing' than those pupils who do not have disabilities (DfE, 2014c: 11). The Act defines a person as having a disability when a:

> person has a physical or mental impairment which has a substantial and long term adverse effect on that person's ability to carry out normal day to day activities. Some specified medical conditions, HIV, multiple sclerosis and cancer are all considered as disabilities, regardless of their effect. (DfE, 2014c: 25)

Public Sector Equality Duty (PSED)

The Equality Act 2010 also introduced a single PSED that applies to all maintained schools and academies. This duty, which came into force in April 2011, required public bodies such as schools, to have due regard to:

- eliminating discrimination and other conduct that is prohibited by the Act
- advancing equality of opportunity between people who share a protected characteristic and people who do not share it
- fostering good relations across all characteristics – between people who share a protected characteristic and people who do not share it.

Advancing equality of opportunity means:

(a) removing or minimising disadvantages suffered by people that are connected to a particular characteristic they have

(b) taking steps to meet the particular needs of people who have a particular need; and

(c) encouraging people who have a particular characteristic to participate fully in any activities.

(DfE, 2014c: 33–4)

For schools, then, having regard to the general duties of the PSED means that:

- decision makers in schools must have 'due regard' when making a decision or taking an action and must assess whether it may have particular implications for people with protected characteristics
- schools should consider equality implications before and at the time that they develop policy and take decisions, and they need to keep policies under review
- schools' functions need to be interrogated to ensure they are carrying out their equality duty seriously and rigorously
- schools can't delegate responsibility for carrying out the duty to anyone else.

(see DfE, 2014c: 29–30)

These duties therefore require all maintained primary, secondary and special schools as well as academies to take proactive steps to ensure their disabled pupils, staff, governors, parents and care givers, and other people using the school are treated equally. The duty is not necessarily about changing the physical infrastructure of buildings or making adjustments for individuals. It is about embedding equality for disabled children and adults within the culture of the whole school's ethos and through practical strategies that make a real difference to the opportunities and achievements that are available to them.

It is important therefore to recognise that the PSED is not about trying to jump through the right hoops quickly. Rather, it is about developing a whole-school approach to disability equality and working towards achieving this over a sustained period of time. As we know, schools offer a wide and diverse range of opportunities for interaction and engagement between different children, as well as employment opportunities for adults and the services they can provide to the wider community. Consequently, schools are potentially well placed to help challenge and overcome discrimination in society.

READER REFLECTION

In examining the PSED we can see that it requires schools to carry out three general duties. Reflect upon these three points and consider what strategies schools could consider addressing to meet these duties.

Discrimination tribunals

In relation to the Equality Act 2010, special tribunals that have experience and knowledge of disability issues were set up to hear cases of the educational provision that contravened the general duty in relation to disability. These 'First-Tier' tribunals hear cases brought by pupils or parents against a school. If a tribunal rules that there is a case to answer, it has the power to require a school to find a remedy, including putting in place the necessary measures to meet a child's needs and to help a child catch up with other pupils (DfE, 2014c).

In summary, the Equality Act 2010 is a significant piece of legislation that 'simplifies, streamlines and strengthens the law' (Equality and Human Rights Commission, 2014). It offers individuals, including those with disabilities, much greater protection from unfair discrimination and sets new standards for public services to ensure that everyone is treated with dignity and respect. The legislation is supported both by a Code of Practice, which outlines what exactly the legislation means and how it is to be applied, and the Equality and Human Rights Commission, which provides guidance and technical assistance.

These duties, then, represent a significant leap forward in legislative terms, with the emphasis moving away from minimum compliance towards an attempt to build a positive and sustained cultural change within schools. The Equality Act strengthens the educational rights of children with SEN and places a duty on schools to make reasonable adjustments. These duties require schools to eliminate discrimination and to 'develop proactive approaches to making a real and positive change to the lives of disabled people' (DfE, 2014c).

- The Code of Practice that supports the Equality Act 2010 is available at:

  www.equalityhumanrights.com/legal-and-policy/legislation/equality-act-2010/equality-act-codes-practice-and-technical-guidance.

- Information relating to the Equality and Human Rights Commission is available at: www.equalityhumanrights.com.

Teachers' Standards 2012

The Teachers' Standards define the minimum level of practice expected of teachers. These standards came into force in schools in September 2012 (DfE, 2013b). The Standards were developed to 'raise the bar for teaching and improve pupil performance and behaviour' in schools (Gove, in Sellgren, 2011). They lay out the key areas in which a teacher must be able to assess their own professional practice.

The Standards have minimal reference to SEN that teachers must take account of in terms of assessing their own level of professional practice. For example, they define children with SEN as:

> children who have a learning difficulty. This means that they either: have a significantly greater difficulty in learning than the majority of children of the same age; or have a disability which prevents or hinders them from making use of educational facilities of a kind generally provided for children of the same age in schools within the area of the local education authority. (DfE, 2013b: 9)

They also designate that teachers should promote equal opportunities and make reasonable adjustments for those with disabilities in line with the Equality Act 2010.

Whilst all of the Standards are relevant for children and young people with SEN, the following Standards would seem to have most relevance. That teachers:

5.2 have a secure understanding of how a range of factors can inhibit pupils' ability to learn, and how best to overcome these

5.3 – demonstrate an awareness of the physical, social and intellectual development of children, and know how to adapt teaching to support pupils' education at different stages of development

5.4 – have a clear understanding of the needs of all pupils, including those with SEN; those of high ability; those with English as an additional language; those with disabilities; and be able to use and evaluate distinctive teaching approaches to engage and support them. (DfE, 2013c.)

READER REFLECTION

Interestingly the Teachers' Standards do not mention inclusion or inclusive education specifically. Imagine that you have been asked to formulate two standards to support inclusive education – what would you deem to be the most important in terms of what teachers should be able to do?

These Standards, though, are there for accreditation purposes and do not include the development of evaluative skills nor the values that underpin practice in working with children with SEN. Allan (2003: 171) believes that earlier standards were just an 'official script', which was 'determinant and restrictive and which emphasised the discipline and control of children', not the support of children with complex and severe disabilities. It would appear that these new standards do not alter, in any way, the ability of teachers to feel more confident and be more competent in their ability to identify and address the personalised learning needs of all pupils.

The National Curriculum for England and Wales 2014

From 1989 curricula have changed significantly as successive governments have interfered directly in the teaching and learning of pupils in state-funded schools (Carpenter et al., 2001b). The national curriculum forced a major rethink in schools as to how education should be delivered (Carpenter et al., 2001b) not least for those children with SEN. On the whole, we may observe the national curriculum as a positive development in that for the first time it provided an entitlement for all children to access the same curriculum. However, the introduction of various national curricula since 1998 has led to tensions and some resistance from teachers of children with SEN. Many teachers feared that these curriculum initiatives would impede the learning of children with SEN because of the curriculum's reliance on subject-based teaching and its pernicious assessment regimes (see Carpenter et al., 2001a).

In 2014 a national curriculum was introduced to schools in England and Wales. This curriculum, according to the Department for Education (DfE) was designed to allow teachers to adapt their teaching to meet the needs of pupils in their classrooms. The DfE believed that this 'new freedom' would be particularly important in enabling teachers to meet the individual needs of pupils with SEN. To support SEN in this new curriculum, the DfE awarded specialists contracts to the Autism Trust, Communications Trust, Dyslexia SPLD Trust and the National Sensory Impairment Partnership. The role of these trusts was to provide support and guidance to ensure that all children would be afforded the opportunity to acquire the 'essential knowledge and skills that they needed to succeed in life'. The government, through the DfE, also revised the national curriculum inclusion statement to reaffirm schools' duties to provide equality of learning in terms of their learning and teaching (see Chapter 1). The national curriculum, then, determines the teaching interventions and support that schools must provide to enable all children to participate fully in all parts of school life and to have full access to all teaching and learning activities. To enable full access to the curriculum, teachers are enabled to make reasonable adjustment to the teaching and learning activities they provide (DfE, 2014d).

READER REFLECTION

Carpenter et al. (2001a: 6–7) details that whatever curriculum is in place in schools a learner has the right to ask their teachers, 'what do I get out of this?'. Amongst other things they state that pupils should:

- gain self-esteem

- increase independence

- develop knowledge

- make choices

- express preferences

- be active participants

- gain communicative skills.

With another student, add the knowledge, skills and understanding that you feel children should gain from their time in school.

Children and Families Act 2014

In 2010 the leader of the then opposition party, David Cameron, detailed his conviction that schools should, 'end the bias towards inclusive education' and that ideology should no longer be allowed to control the provision of education for children with SEN. This conviction was adopted by the new Conservative/Liberal

Coalition that took power after the general election. The government set to work to overhaul how SEN was to be managed in England. Initially, it launched a consultation document, *Special Educational Needs and Disability Green Paper. Support and Aspiration: A New Approach to Special Educational Needs and Disability – A Consultation*, with a view to initiate major legislative reform (Runswick-Cole, 2011). On 13th March 2014, the government received Royal Assent for its Children's and Families Bill.

Edward Timpson, Parliamentary Under-Secretary of State for Children and Families, commented that:

> Today's system for supporting children with SEN is based on a model introduced more than 30 years ago that is no longer fit for purpose. Enquiries and reviews of SEN provision ... have identified that the current system is complex, bewildering and adversarial. The evidence points to an assessment process which is inefficient, bureaucratic and costly, as well as insufficiently child-centred or user-friendly. Needs are sometimes identified late and interventions are not planned or implemented in a timely or effective way. Families tell us that they feel they have to battle at each stage of the system. (See Perry, 2014a.)

Key changes brought into effect by the Children and Families Act are it:

- replaces the Statements of SEN with a single assessment named as the Education, Health and Care Plan (EHCP)
- provides that children who have an EHCP have similar statutory protection to that afforded by the previous Statements of SEN
- replaces the system of School Action and School Action Plus with one graduated approach
- provides for parents and young people to manage their own personal budgets that relate to their support packages
- places a duty on health services and local authorities to jointly commission and plan services for children, young people and families
- provides that local authorities must make known to parents and children what services are available within the local area in a document that will be known as *The Local Offer*
- changes the manner in which adoption and foster services are to be provided.

The Conservative/Liberal Coalition government believed that this legislation would offer greater protection and support for children and that it would bring into being a new way of helping children with SEN. The legislation was supported by a capital investment of 30 million pounds to enable parents and children to access support from 1,800 trained supporters (Timpson, cited in Perry, 2014b). In addition, it introduced a new Code of Practice for children who had SEN. The Code sets out how the new assessment process for children with SEN is to be completed.

Independent supporters – these are individuals who will be trained by the voluntary, private and community sector, and whose task will be to provide guidance and support to parents of children with SEN during the processes of statutory assessment. The main function of these independent supporters is to help families build resilience and support the work of local authority parental partnership services (Council for Disabled Children, 2014). For more information, see: www.ncb.org.uk/media/1102886/independent_support_q_and_a.pdf.

The Special Educational Needs and Disability Regulations 2014

The revised Special Educational Needs and Disability Code provides the statutory guidance for how the duties, policies and procedures contained within Part 3 of the Children and Families Bill should be operationalised. It should be noted that children with disabilities who do not have a SEN are not covered either by the Children and Families Act or the Code. Statutory provision for these children is detailed within the Children Act 1989, the Equality Act 2010 and the Health and Social Care Act 2012 (Nasen, n.d.).

The Code is a lengthy document that runs to some 276 pages. Whilst it was broadly welcomed by MPs, the timescale for its implementation was regarded with unease by members of the Legislative Committee of the Houses of Parliament. This was because the Bill's passage through parliament left only a few months before schools were expected to implement the code and so no time was left to provide workforce training (Perry, 2014a). To support the introduction of the code, extra funding of £45.2 million was granted and a further £70 million was made available to local authorities through the Special Educational Needs Reform Grant (see Perry, 2014a).

The Code, then, sets out to provide practical advice to local authorities, maintained schools, early education settings (nurseries) and others as regards to undertaking their statutory duties to identify, assess and make provision for children's SEN. As such, it is informed by the guiding principles that:

- the views, wishes and feelings of the child or young person, and the child's parents are taken into consideration
- under the new Act, children, young people and parents must be provided with information, advice and support so that they can fully participate in the discussion and decisions in relation to their child's SEN
- it is important that the child or young person, and the child's parents, participate as fully as possible in decisions, and that they are provided with the information and support necessary to enable participation in those decisions.

the child or young person's needs, and those of the child's parents are supported, in order to facilitate the development of the child or young person and to help them achieve the best possible educational and other outcomes and to prepare them effectively for adulthood. (See DfE, 2014b: Section 1.1.)

The Children and Families Act provides significant new rights for children and young people, especially when they reach the end of compulsory schooling at 16. Chapter 8 of the Code details how decision-making rights transfer from the parent to young children at 16.

Speaking about the new measures, Edward Timpson said:

It's a radical overhaul that breaks down artificial barriers, and that champions children with SEN as never before from birth right through to adulthood. (See Perry, 2014a.)

READER REFLECTION

In relation to this legislation the Independent Parental Special Education Advice (IPSEA) service comments on its website: 'Don't panic! Much of the new law is still the same ...'.

The IPSEA website is available at: www.ipsea.org.uk/what-you-need-to-know/ frequently-asked-questions-by-topic/frequently-asked-questions/about-the-new-sen-legal-framework.

Whilst the Code of Practice is claimed to be a 'radical overhaul' of SEN policy, the question that remains is: is this really the case? Working with a peer, review the previous Code of Practice formulated under the New Labour government. Can you find any areas that still remain the same?

The Code maintains that mainstream schools must:

- use their best endeavours to make sure that a child with SEN gets the support they need
- ensure that children with SEN engage in the activities of the school alongside pupils who do not have SEN
- designate a teacher to be responsible for coordinating SEN provision – the SENCo
- inform parents when they are making special educational provision for a child
- prepare an SEN information report and their arrangements for the admission of disabled children, the steps being taken to prevent disabled children from being treated less favourably than others, the facilities provided to enable access to the school for disabled children and their accessibility plan showing how they plan to improve access progressively over time
- have a member of the governing body with specific responsibility for SEN
- observe their duty under the Equality Act 2010 towards individual disabled children and make reasonable anticipatory adjustments to prevent discrimination, and promote equality of opportunity.

Anticipatory provision for children with SEN – in practice, this means that schools should be making efforts to improve accessibility generally rather than waiting for a specific child with a particular need to arrive and to then address that need.

Identifying SEN in schools

Early identification, assessment and provision for any child who may have a SEN are crucial to children's educational and life outcomes. Consequently, the Code seeks to promote a common approach to identifying, assessing and providing for all children's SEN. To reflect this, the Code advocates a continuum of provision. In many cases, this graduated approach will commence with schools meeting children's learning needs through a differentiation of the curriculum. This would involve teachers tailoring their approaches to suit individual pupils' differing learning needs and styles. Such approaches enable teachers to become more skilled in mixed ability teaching, which can benefit all children and not just those with SEN.

The graduated approach

The Code makes clear that education providers must have arrangements in place to support children with SEN. As part of these arrangements clear guidelines for identifying and responding to children's SEN must be in place. The Code recognises that early identification of SEN coupled with effective provision will improve the long-term educational outcomes of children. In situations where children do not respond to the differentiation of lessons mentioned above, and therefore do not make adequate progress, there will be a need for the school to do something additional or different. This school-based SEN provision is described in the Code as a graduated approach.

In terms of the Children and Families Act and the Code of Practice 2014, a pupil has SEN where his/her learning difficulty or disability calls for special educational provision, namely provision different from or additional to that normally available to pupils of the same age (DfE, 2014b: Section 6.15).

The first stage in identifying children with SEN lies with teachers who should, as a normal part of their role, regularly assess all children's progress. The purpose of these assessments should be to identify those children who are not making the expected progress in terms of their age and individual circumstances. If after implementing 'high quality and targeted' teaching the progress of the children continues to remain problematic, a SENCo should assess whether or not a child has SEN in terms of the four broad categories of SEN. If, after this initial assessment it is determined that the child might have a SEN, the school must take action to remove barriers to learning and put effective special educational provision in place. This form of support should follow a staged process in which early decisions are 'revisited, refined and revised' so that schools may correctly identify, address and evaluate the SEN provision that will best suit the individual child (DfE, 2014b).

According to the Code, this school-based support should follow a four-stage process (see Nasen, 2014), where schools:

Assess – identify pupils who are making less progress.

Plan – plan for teaching that increases progress and raises attainment.

Do – schools will actively seek to improve educational provision to meet a wide range of needs through well-differentiated provision.

Review – schools will accurately review the progress of children and the arrangements for increasing progress and attainment, and make changes to teaching and learning where necessary.

READER REFLECTION

The Code of Practice advocates a continuum of provision that is often referred to as a 'graduated approach' in which the early identification of SEN is essential to meeting the educational needs of the child concerned. Reflect upon this statement in relation to the strategies that teachers and schools can put in place to ensure early identification and intervention are achieved.

When the school has been unable to help a child make adequate progress after implementing special educational provision, the school will seek outside advice from the local authorities' support services or from health or social work professionals. This might, for example, involve speaking to a speech and language therapist about a specific language programme or an occupational therapist on how teachers might work differently with the child in class. It might also include gaining information about the child's home circumstances that might help explain changes in a child's behaviour and attitudes to learning. The school can then use this to work with others to resolve a child's current difficulties. Central to this process should be the active consultation with the child and his/her parents in order to ensure his/her needs are addressed and that they play as full a part as possible in understanding any necessary modifications that may be considered. The Code also stresses the importance of working in partnership with parents in all aspects of a pupil's education and of that pupil's participation in making decisions and exercising choices in relation to their own education.

Education Health and Care Plans

The key test for considering whether a statutory assessment of SEN is necessary is whether the child concerned is making adequate progress. What 'adequate progress' is depends on the starting point and the expectations for a particular child. Essentially, however, what is considered to be adequate progress for a particular child is a matter for his/her teacher's professional judgement.

Most children will have their SEN met by their school but this will not be possible all of the time. If a child's needs cannot be met by the school, the local authority may consider the need for a statutory assessment and, if appropriate, will then make a multi-disciplinary assessment of that child's needs. Following this, the local authority may decide to formulate and implement an EHCP which will specify those needs and the special educational provision that will be required to meet these needs.

Conclusion

In this chapter you have learnt that during the past two decades there has been an increased impetus towards inclusive education for children with SEN, which is a far cry from the provision in the late nineteenth century that saw increasing numbers of children with SEN either excluded or destined to endure segregated schooling. Indeed, in the early part of the twenty-first century the shift has been quite dramatic, and for parents who request it, this now incorporates mainstream schooling for their children as a matter of right and entitlement. The exception to this is in cases where it would affect the 'efficient education' of other children at the school. Moreover, when parents want a special school for their son or daughter, they still have the right to state that preference. This seemingly indicates the sense of autonomy and decision making that rests with parents and with children themselves.

In your reading of this chapter you will have realised that these new rights, however, do not mean that every child will be able to go to the school of their choice. Whilst all parents are able to state their choice of school they are not automatically entitled to have this choice fulfilled. Consequently, in times when schools and local authorities are at the mercy of budgetary constraints, achieving the flexibility and responsiveness necessary to accommodate every child's needs with a school of their choice is still highly problematic.

In summary, this chapter has detailed that the concept of inclusive education is beginning to become more of a reality for parents of (and for) children with SEN. However, progress towards this modern conception of inclusion has not come about easily and in reality there is still much work to be done if schools' cultures, ethos and philosophies are to become more like those envisaged within the Salamanca Statement. Although legislation has significantly moved forward in recent years, the ambiguity of inclusion still poses challenges for service providers.

As we move forward with the next phase of educational reform based upon the Children and Families Act 2014, the views of children with SEN are now being considered as an integral component of the decision-making process regarding their educational choices. The past ten years have seen a shift from inclusive educational policy to practical and statutory guidance and who knows what the outcomes will be as we move through the twenty-first century. Perhaps the next stages of inclusion will involve a basic acceptance and empathy on the part of society that all children have the same entitlement to be valued and to access high-quality educational experiences, regardless of their individual needs.

Through the activity and the readings detailed below you will develop a deeper understanding of the 'workings' of the legislation that govern how children with SEN and disabilities should be treated within our educational system. Developing a knowledge and understanding of such legislation and policies will be invaluable in your work with professionals, families and children with SEN.

STUDENT ACTIVITIES

Reflect upon what the concluding statement to this chapter means and how it can be achieved over the forthcoming years.

The Equality Act 2010 requires schools to be proactive in promoting disability in schools. Discuss with a partner how schools can meet this requirement in the future, both from a policy and practice perspective.

Further reading

Arnold, N. (2014) *Children and Families Act 2014*. London: The Law Society.
This book, while designed for family lawyers, contains the full text of the 2014 legislation, with expert legal comment. The author also outlines the major changes that people will need to be aware of and how these changes will affect day-to-day practice.

Connors, C. and Stalker, K. (2007) 'Children's experiences of disability: pointers to a social model of childhood disability', *Disability and Society*, 22(1): 19–33.
This article will offer you an opportunity to review aspects of consultation and the empowerment of children with SEN.

Cook, A. (2014) 'Five things schools need to know about the SEN reforms', *The Guardian*. Available at: www.theguardian.com/teacher-network/teacher-blog/2014/feb/10/special-educational-needs-sen-reforms-five-things.
This is a very readable piece that succinctly summarises for teachers the main changes in the 2014 legislation.

7

MULTI-AGENCY WORKING

CHAPTER OBJECTIVES

- To introduce the key definitions of multi-agency working.

- To explore the development of multi-agency working for children with SEN.

- To examine how some of the key agencies and services work together to support children with SEN.

Introduction

This chapter will introduce you to the key definitions and the language surrounding multi-agency working. The chapter also provides an outline of the background and context to the development of multi-agency working, as well as analysing current legislation that governs this important area of practice. Additionally, the chapter examines some of the agencies and professionals that are involved in the day-to-day practice of supporting children with SEN.

Section 25 of the Children and Families Act 2014 places a legal duty on local authorities to guarantee that education, training, health and social care provision are integrated around the child with SEN (DfE, 2014a). It states that the aim of this reform is to:

> Ensure that services consistently place children and young people at the centre of decision making and support, enabling them to make the best possible start in life and challenging any dogma, delay or professional interests which might hold them back. (DfE, 2014a: 4)

READER REFLECTION

Read the quote below and consider how many 'professionals' might be involved with the child with SEN and his/her family over the course of one year.

There are times that having all different people in my life is too much. I spend a lot of my time in hospitals. I wish there were less appointments and less doctors to see. (Child cited in Stone and Foley, 2014: 49)

Multi-agency working: key definitions

In developing an understanding of multi-agency working, confusion can arise because of the plethora of language that is employed to describe how various agencies and services work together to support children with SEN (Hussain and Brownhill, 2014). It is important, therefore, that you develop an understanding of some of the more commonly employed language that dominates this area.

Examples of the words used to describe multi-agency working (Kaehne, 2014; Payler and Georgeson, 2013; Stone and Foley, 2014) include:

- integrated working
- multi-agency/cross-agency/interagency/trans-agency
- coordination
- cooperation
- collaboration
- partnerships
- 'joined-up thinking' and 'joined-up working'
- cross cutting
- network
- working together
- interprofessional working.

The range of language detailed above and its inability to express with clarity its meaning demonstrates the complexity of this area. For example, what is the difference between 'cooperation' and 'collaboration', or how in practice might 'partnerships' differ from 'networks' (Stone and Foley, 2014)?

WHAT ARE PARTNERSHIPS?

According to Doyle (1997) and Farrell (2004), partnerships can be described as arrangements between two or more parties who have agreed to work cooperatively towards collective and/or compatible objectives in which there is: shared authority and responsibility; a joint investment of resources; a joint liability or risk taking; and ideally, mutual benefits. Taken together, the following factors identify the nature of partnerships:

- shared common objectives and goals
- shared risks and mutual benefits
- contributions from both partners
- collective authority, responsibility and accountability.

partnership

Underlying this definition is the notion that partnerships represent a better strategy to address specific projects or goals in contrast to partners operating independently of each other. Indeed, this is certainly the case when working with children with SEN who may have a range of needs that have to be addressed. Consequently, a central feature of successful inclusion according to Rose and Howley (2007) is the commitment and desire for multi-agency and partnership working approaches.

READER REFLECTION

Adele is a child who has restricted ranges of physical movement and needs the services of a physiotherapist to support her physical activity and movement. Adele's physical development also needs to be supported within a school PE environment, so the PE teacher and physiotherapist need to work in partnership to support this child's physical development through the curriculum.

Reflect upon Adele's needs and then consider how partnerships between professionals might add value to the services that she is receiving. You should consider this from the perspectives of Adele, the teacher and the physiotherapist.

In trying to understand the language employed in this area, Frost (2005, cited in Stone and Foley, 2014: 13) believes that more transparency might be achieved if we think about these ideas in relation to a 'continuum of partnership' that ranges from 'co-operation to integration'. Frost details four levels of such partnership (Stone and Foley, 2014: 13), these being:

Uncoordinated – free standing service.

Level 1: cooperation – services work together towards consistent goals and complementary services, while maintaining their own independence.

Level 2: collaboration – services plan together to reach common outcomes and overcome issues of overlapping, duplication and gaps in their service provision.

Level 3: coordination – services work jointly in a planned and methodical way towards shared and agreed aims.

Level 4: merger/integration – here, services combine into one organisation in order to ensure effective and efficient service delivery.

According to Hussain and Brownhill (2014: 199), there are three major types of service provision available to children with SEN. These are:

Universal services – services that all children and young people can access without a special referral. For example, GPs, dentists, opticians, nurseries, schools, colleges and hospitals.

Targeted services – services that provide support for certain groups of children and young people and are often accessed, in the first instance, from within universal services. Such services might include children's centres, parental support and social services.

Specialist services – this form of service provision is usually required when universal services are unable to meet the individual needs of a child. These services might include family support workers, behaviour support workers, speech and language therapists, physiotherapists, youth offending teams, dieticians and child and adolescent mental health workers.

READER REFLECTION

Carefully read each of the case studies below and consider which services would be the most appropriate to meet the needs of that child. You might also specify which individual professionals would be the most suitable to provide support.

CASE STUDY 7.1

Amil

Amil has recently transferred to St. Mark's Secondary School. His teachers have noted that he is very quiet in class, but when he does speak, they find difficulty in understanding what he has to say. The Head of Year believes that Amil might have issues with his teeth, but is not sure what else might be affecting Amil's ability to speak.

CASE STUDY 7.2

Ben and Holly

Ben and Holly's daughter is just coming up to her third birthday. She is a delightful, happy and very active child. Ben and Holly want to find out what is the best school for their daughter to attend.

CASE STUDY 7.3

Peter and Bethany

Peter and Bethany are experiencing considerable issues in their family life. Bethany is having problems with heavy drinking and her husband, Peter, is undergoing long periods of depression. Both parents believe that the issues they are experiencing are exacerbated by their inability to cope with their five-year-old son who displays extreme behavioural issues.

Within the context of SEN, Watson et al. (2002) suggest multi-agency working necessitates the bringing together of a range of professionals across the boundaries of education, health, social welfare, voluntary organisations, parents and advocates – all those with the purpose of working towards holistic approaches to access and the entitlement of high-quality services for young people. Thus, if, as Bishop (2001) suggests, agencies and individual practitioners work together to support the educational development of children with SEN through holistic approaches, this has the potential to significantly enhance their quality of life and social, physical, emotional and intellectual development both inside and outside of school. However, it has been the case that over the past four decades many disabled children and their families have experienced barriers in trying to access opportunities and services. Research has strongly suggested that it is the complexities of service provision that have presented considerable obstacles for parents in developing and maintaining educational, home and social environments in which children can thrive (Cavet, n.d.).

The chapter now turns to consider how multi-agency working has developed over time and the challenge that parents, children and professionals experience in their attempts to provide coordinated packages of support.

READER REFLECTION

Reflect upon the statement that: agencies and individuals working together will significantly enhance the quality of life for children with SEN both in and outside of school.

Following your reflection, consider the case study below and list what you see as the advantages and challenges of the various health and educational professionals working together to provide a holistic approach to supporting Adam's needs, both in and outside of school.

CASE STUDY 7.4

Adam

Adam who is eight years old, attends a special school and has a profound physical and learning disability along with challenging behaviour. In addition to his day-to-day schooling, Adam receives weekly physiotherapy, speech therapy and behaviour therapy, and attends hospital on a monthly basis.

Multi-agency working: a brief history and overview of current practices

Multi-agency working is not a new phenomenon, indeed, its roots may be traced back to the mid-1800s when health and social workers came together to try to reduce poverty in England (Cheminais, 2009). More recently, multi-agency working has become a high priority for successive UK governments, who have accepted that well-planned and coordinated strategic service provision positively enhances the lives of young children and their families (Hussain and Brownhill, 2014). However, despite the rhetoric of the effectiveness of multi-agency partnerships, many serious case reviews have indicated that children have been badly let down by professionals not working together (Hussain and Brownhill, 2014).

In the modern era, the need for multi-agency working developed out of the death of Marie Colewell. The subsequent inquiry, in 1977, found that a lack of communication between agencies and service providers was a major contributory cause in Marie's death. It is from this beginning that Child Protection Committees were established to coordinate the provision of child protection services (Hussain and Brownhill, 2014). From this date forward a raft of measures and initiatives have been produced and introduced to develop joined-up thinking, and responses to the issue of social inclusion and child protection (Edwards et al., 2009). These included such things as the Children's Act 1989, Special Educational Needs Toolkit 2001; Every Child Matters and the subsequent Children Act of 2004; Children's Fund; Sure Start; Local Network funding; and extended schools initiatives (see Edwards et al., 2009). It seems that since the 1990s, multi-agency working has become a policy imperative for Labour, Conservative and Liberal Democratic politicians alike (Foley and Rixon, 2014).

Children Act 1989

This Act and the Every Child Matters agenda aimed to achieve a better balance in integrated service delivery between protecting children and enabling parents to challenge state intervention. It also encouraged service providers to work in 'greater partnership'. The legislation also strengthened the rights of families and children, and made it plain that health, education and social services should work together to support children (Hussain and Brownhill, 2014).

SEN Toolkit 2001

The SEN Toolkit was devised in 2001 by the Department for Education and Skills (DfES), following the introduction of the Code of Practice on the identification and assessment of children with SEN (DfES, 2001a). Although fairly dated, many schools still do employ this guidance to help them in their decision making in respect of children with SEN. The Toolkit's purpose was to support schools and local authorities by providing practical advice on how to implement the Code of Practice, with each section of the Toolkit designed to support schools and local authorities to work in partnership with a wide range of individuals and agencies in order to maximise entitlement and accessibility to high-quality inclusive education for children with SEN.

The Toolkit was constructed in collaboration with a multiplicity of professionals and people involved in meeting the needs of children and young people. These included children with SEN, pupils, parents, early education practitioners, teachers, headteachers, SENCos, local education authority officers, health and social workers and others within the voluntary sector. As a consequence of the wide range of consultation that took place, the Toolkit holds significant authority and standing (Atkinson, 2001), demonstrating the advantages of working through multi-agency partnerships to achieve the best services for children with SEN.

READER REFLECTION

Farrell (2005) suggests that successful inclusion of children with SEN occurs through ensuring there is a combination of:

- appropriate human resources
- adequate resources for an adapted curriculum.

Imagine that you are a headteacher who has to go to the school governing body to argue for more resources to support Robert, an eight-year-old child with cerebral palsy. Robert needs teaching assistant support in class and some additional resources to ensure the curriculum is modified to meet his needs. Consider how you would present your case to the governors, and justify why and how you would argue for both human and curriculum resources for Robert.

Children Act 2004

In 2004 the Children Act (DfES, 2004b) identified the need for a wide range of professionals, organisations, schools and agencies to work together to enhance children's services. Indeed, the Act stated that these different agencies had a legal duty to cooperate with each other (Tar, 2014). Through the encouragement of multi-agency partnerships, the government's Change for Children (DfES, 2005) agenda set out to provide a framework for more joined-up services in education, health, culture, social care and social justice for young people. The Children Act encouraged proactive collaboration across a wide range of stakeholders with the aim of promoting cooperation and shared working practices in order to improve the well-being of all children and young people.

Children and Families Act 2014

The Children and Families Act denotes that if children and young people with SEN are to achieve their ambitions then local education, health and social care services must work together to ensure that all children receive the correct support (Section 1.22). Indeed, the Act goes further in that Section 25 places a legal requirement on local authorities to ensure that integration between service providers takes place where this would promote well-being and improve the quality of service provision for children and young people with SEN.

Within the Code of Practice that supports this Act, a chapter is devoted to how services should work together. This chapter (DfE, 2014b: Section 25) details:

- the scope of joint commissioning arrangements
- how local partners should commission services to meet local needs and support better outcomes
- how partnership working should inform and support joint commissioning arrangements
- the role that children, young people, parents and representative groups such as parent carer forums have in informing commission arrangements
- responsibility for decision making in joint commissioning arrangements
- how partners should develop a joint understanding of the outcomes that their local population of children and young people with SEN and disabilities aspire to, and use it to produce a joint plan that they then deliver jointly and review jointly
- how joint commissioning draws together accountability arrangements for key partners
- the role of colleges as commissioners.

The Act makes clear that joint commissioning arrangements must provide services for all children and young people aged 0–25 and that such arrangements should provide for children with SEN, both those who have EHCPs as well as those children who do not. This pooling of resources not only requires agencies to ensure that everyone shares the same vision, but also to have the confidence to relinquish day-to-day control of decisions and resources while maintaining the high levels of accountability and commitment necessary to the development of child-centred, responsive services for children with SEN. In conclusion therefore the Act sets out the government's desire to reshape services for children with SEN by offering more intensive support for those who need it.

The Children and Families Act provides examples of the types of services that might be involved in joint commissioning arrangements. Such services might include: specialist support and therapies, such as clinical treatments and delivery of medications; speech and language therapy; assistive technology; personal care (or access to it); Child and Adolescent Mental Health Services (CAMHS) support; occupational therapy; rehabilitation training; physiotherapy; a range of nursing support; specialist equipment, such as wheelchairs and continence supplies; and emergency provision.

They could include highly specialist services needed by only a small number of children, for instance, children with severe learning disabilities or who require services that are commissioned centrally by NHS England. For example, some augmentative and alternative communication systems, or health provision for children and young people in the secure estate or secure colleges (DfE, 2014a: 40).

The Care Act 2014

The Care Act of 2014 also places a legal duty on local authorities to ensure that children and adult service providers cooperate and promote the integration of care, support and health services. The aim of such coordinated provision is that no young adult is left without the care and support they need to make the transition between childhood and adulthood.

The challenges of multi-agency working

Research by the Care Co-ordination Network UK (2001) has shown that, on average, families of children with SEN have contact with at least ten different professionals, and over the course of a year, can attend up to 20 appointments at hospitals and clinics. Therefore, it is vital that professionals and agencies work together through a multi-agency coordinated approach to support children with SEN and their families (Atkinson et al., 2002). Indeed, this partnership working is hugely important as regards the provision of holistic services that provide the best chance of a child with SEN succeeding and achieving physically, socially, emotionally and educationally. However, despite the evidence of the effectiveness of multi-agency working Townsley and Robinson (2000) and Kirk and Glendinning (1999) suggest that the range, diversity and different levels of support that families of children with SEN receive are in themselves problematic and therefore multi-agency working is essential if streamlined services are to be offered.

The literature base also identifies a number of challenges that can serve to undermine the effectiveness of multi-agency partnerships (see Atkinson et al., 2002). These challenges normally centre around four broad areas. These being:

- **Funding and resources** – one of the major challenges involved with the development of multi-agency partnerships is the simple question, 'Who is going to pay for these initiatives?'. This form of working, whilst being highly effective, is particularly demanding of staff time compared to that of single agency working.
- **Roles and responsibilities** – within any partnership arrangement, a fundamental question is, 'Who should lead the multi-agency team?'. Whose procedures and practices should dominate the approach taken with an individual child and their family?
- **Competing priorities** – each service provider in a multi-agency team may be held responsible by different government departments or indeed have different inspection regimes that they are accountable to. The question that can dominate multi-agency teams is, 'Who is accountable when something goes wrong?'.
- **Communication** – one of the major reasons for developing multi-agency partnerships was in response to the death of Marie Colewell. As stated above, the inquiry into Marie's death indicated that a lack of communication between professionals had been a contributory factor in this case. In 2002, a study by the National Foundation for Educational Research (NfER) (Atkinson et al. 2002) found that communication was still an issue in all forms of multi-agency working. This lack of communication was evident not only 'on the ground' between professionals but also at a strategic and operational level.

READER REFLECTION

Reflect upon how multi-agency approaches to supporting children with SEN and their families can offer improved access to services. Do you see any limitations in multi-agency approaches other than those offered above?

The key success factors involved in multi-agency working

According to research by NfER (Atkinson et al., 2002), successful multi-agency working is based upon effective systems and practices that ensure good communication, adequate resources in terms of staffing and time, but more importantly, that the professionals involved have the commitment and drive to ensure that this form of provision actually works in practice. It appears that successful multi-agency teams have a commitment and willingness, from all concerned, to engage in meaningful collaboration and cooperation. In addition, another key success factor is that all agencies understand their own roles and responsibilities as well as those of other agencies, and that multi-agency teams are led by people with vision and tenacity.

Lacey and Ouvry (2000) as well as Doyle (1997) have examined the impact of multi-agency partnership working from both the professional and parent–child perspectives. In relation to the professional context, Lacey and Ouvry have identified the terms 'role release' and 'role expansion' to articulate what is required by individuals and agencies to address the government's changing children's agenda, and as part of the requirement to foster more joined-up approaches to the support of children with SEN. 'Role release' implies that professionals will be required to transfer their skills and share expertise (Graham and Wright, 1999) with other professionals, whilst in contrast, 'role expansion' involves training professionals in the concepts and language of interdisciplinary working. Thus what is crucial to effective multi-agency partnership working will be the ability of various professional disciplinary areas to be able to share ideas and resources and to work much more cooperatively across professional boundaries.

In moving towards these partnerships, Atkinson et al. (2002) identified some of the potential positive outcomes of multi-agency work with children with SEN. These include:

- access to a wider range of services for children with SEN and their families
- easier, more responsive and holistic approaches to services or expertise that work across professional boundaries, and are more focused upon the individual needs of the child rather than getting caught up in any disputes or maintaining strict professional boundaries
- improved educational attainment and a better engagement in schooling for children with SEN
- improved support for parents
- children's needs being addressed more appropriately and within a holistic, rather than single, disciplinary context.

In addressing these areas, the Coalition government in 2014 set out to establish much more responsive services with timely support for children with SEN and their families. This should result in services that are easily accessible at key transition points in young people's lives and designed around the child and his/her family.

Within education, then, we are increasingly likely to see the continuation of multi-agency team approaches towards ensuring children with SEN gain their full entitlement and accessibility to the curriculum. Consequently, it is worth reiterating that teachers and schools must have a thorough understanding of the range of services that are on offer to support both children and teachers alike.

The second part of the chapter turns to examine some of the key services and people that are involved in the multi-agency partnerships.

Parents

Carpenter et al. (2001b) details that parents and teachers have one common interest that is the child. They relate that the government accepts this as an important principle in the partnerships between home and school. Indeed, in 1994 the government stated that:

> Professional help can seldom be wholly effective unless it builds upon parents' capacity to be involved, and unless parents consider the professionals have taken account of what they say and treat their views and anxieties as intrinsically important. (DoE, 1994, Section 2: 28, 12–13)

READER REFLECTION

Consider the statements made above in relation to parents and teachers. With a partner, mind map the areas in which a parent and teacher should work together to enable children with SEN to be fully supported. You may also wish to consider what skills the teacher and the parent would need to bring to this form of collaboration.

Parents play a crucial role in the education of their child, and research over two decades has indicated that their active involvement can lead to better outcomes for their child (Lendrum et al., 2015). Indeed, the original 1994 Code of Practice stated that:

> Children's progress will be diminished if their parents are not seen as partners in the education process with unique knowledge and information to impart. (DoE, 1994, Section 2: 28, 12–13)

The original Code therefore was the first in a plethora of initiatives that were designed to include parents in the education of children with SEN. For example, the Special Educational Needs and Disability Act 2001 amended the 1996 Education Act by introducing the Parent Partnership Services, which were to work independently of local authorities. Such services provided parents with information, training, advice and support as well as supporting networking and collaboration that informed parents what local SEN policy and practice was (NPP, 2014).

According to one local authority, Parent Partnerships Services should offer (see www.lancsngfl.ac.uk/projects/sen/index.php?category_id=186_):

- access to a confidential telephone helpline
- impartial information and advice around SEN issues
- support in preparing for and attending meetings
- help in filling in forms and writing letters/reports
- initial support in resolving disagreements with the child's school and the local authority
- contact details for other statutory and voluntary services
- links to local parent support groups and forums
- the chance to submit parents' views, which will help inform and influence local policy and practice training opportunities.

In August 2014 the Parliamentary Under-Secretary of State for Children and Families, Edward Timpson, wrote an open letter to parents. In this he detailed the government's commitment to high-quality partnerships with parents.

Timpson's letter stated:

Like any parent, I want the best for my child. Every parent should expect people who provide support for their children to make sure that support is the best it can possibly be. And every child and young person has the right to expect a good education, and the support they need to become independent adults and succeed in life.

The most important people in any child or young person's life are their parents. You know your children best of all. What you as parents think, feel and say is important. You should be listened to and you need to be fully involved in decisions that affect your children. That's what the new system is all about.

(Available at: www.gov.uk/government/uploads/system/uploads/attachment_data/file/348842/Parents_letter_Aug_2014_final.pdf)

Like previous Codes of Practice, the 2014 Code details the importance of parents and professionals working together to provide support to children with SEN. As with SENDA 2001, the Children and Families Act (DfE, 2014a) ensures that all local authorities provide children with SEN and their parents advice and information on the services and provision that are available in their local areas. This information is provided within a document known as *The Local Offer*. The government believes that effective participation of parents can lead to a closer fit between what families want and local authority services can reasonably provide.

⁕It would seem clear then that the role of parents in their children's education is crucial. Lendrum et al. (2015) summarises some of the benefits of parents and professionals working in partnership:

- engaged parents typically have higher aspirations for their children

- engaged parents facilitate and support extended learning opportunities

- parental involvement can increase a child's attendance at school

- parental involvement can lead to the improved behaviour and social skills of a child

- parental involvement can lead to greater academic achievement.

It seems evident then that professionals working in partnership with parents can have a positive impact on the quality of life for a child with SEN. However, in part, the level of impact is dependent upon 'the level and nature of engagement' of those involved in parental partnerships (Whittaker, et al., 2014: 479). Whilst many parents of children with SEN understand why they are involved with a range of professionals and the contribution that these integrated services can make, they nevertheless comment that they experience fragmented provision, a lack of 'child-centredness' in such arrangements, and that they fail to observe clear examples of practitioners who can work efficiently and effectively together (Stone and Foley, 2014). As Townsley et al. (2004, cited in Stone and Foley, 2014: 51) state:

> The sheer number of professionals who may be involved in supporting a disabled child in the community can often lead to a lack of continuity and coordination and may leave families uncertain about who to contact regarding a specific situation.

Todd's (2003, cited in Strogilos and Tragoulia, 2013) research documented many parents' experience of dissatisfaction with service providers because they held different priorities and made different assumptions about the children's and families' needs. The Lamb Inquiry (2009) reported that parents of children with SEN were infrequently consulted about their child's needs and aspirations, and what services the family believed would make a real difference to their child's education. This inquiry also reported that parents of children with SENs had lower levels of engagement and confidence in working with schools than those typically observed from parents whose children did not have SEN (see Lendrum et al., 2015). Strogilos and Tragoulia (2013) believe that there are serious gaps in the knowledge and understanding in relation to how parents and professionals should collaborate within applied educational settings.

Read the blogs below from parents of children with SEN. Write a list of the factors that have influenced these parental partnerships positively or negatively.

The relationship that you develop with your child's teacher when your child has multiple learning difficulties is an extremely complex one that sometimes requires a lot of time and patience. You not only have to support your child but you have to support the teacher too by listening to them and politely giving them suggestions as to how they might teach your child more effectively and respond to his or her needs. There are those teachers who simply do not understand my son's autism and others who do not want to understand. Look, I am not an expert, I have had good relationships with teachers and some really bad ones. I would recommend that developing a good working relationship is everything and you need to try to seek the teacher's point of view and you need to work hard to get them to see your point of view too.

My daughter Beth has ADHD and a hearing impairment. She was not diagnosed with ADHD until she was 12. By the time she was 14 education had become a real battle. We had to fight to get her a Statement of SEN. We had to fight to ensure that Beth got the specialised teaching that was set out in her statement. The school do not really talk to us anymore and we often find that they have passed on information to the paediatrician without even having the courtesy to inform us that they have done so. School is just one big stress factor for Beth now and I am sick of dealing with teachers who cannot be bothered to find out how me and our Beth actually feel about how we are being treated by the system.

Governments over the past three decades have attempted to address uncoordinated and fragmented services that children with SEN and their families experience (Foley and Rixon, 2014). One such example is the Scottish government's website, *Getting it Right for Every Child* (see www.gov.scot/Topics/People/Young-People/gettingitright). The Scottish government believes that 'getting it right for every child' should be the bedrock for multi-agency working.

Core components

Getting it Right for Every Child is founded on ten core components that can be applied in any setting and in any circumstance.

1. A focus on improving outcomes for children, young people and their families based on a shared understanding of well-being.
2. A common approach to the proportionate sharing of information where appropriate.
3. An integral role for children, young people and families in assessment, planning and intervention.
4. A coordinated and unified approach to identifying concerns, assessing needs, and agreeing actions and outcomes, based on the 'well-being indicators'.

5. Streamlined planning, assessment and decision-making processes that lead to the right help at the right time.
6. Consistently high standards of cooperation, joint working and communication, where more than one agency needs to be involved, locally and across Scotland.
7. A 'named person' for every child and young person, and a 'lead professional' (where necessary) to coordinate and monitor multi-agency activity.
8. Maximising the skilled workforce within universal services to address needs and risks as early as possible.
9. A confident and competent workforce across all services for children, young people and their families.
10. The capacity to share demographic, assessment and planning information, including electronically, within and across agency boundaries.

READER REFLECTION

Visit the Scottish government's website *Getting it Right for Every Child*. Carefully read the 'values and principles' that underpin this government initiative. Do you feel that these are a good basis for multi-agency working? Given your developing knowledge and understanding of this area, are there any values and principles that you feel are missing from this list?

Holistic approaches to including children with SEN within educational settings

One of the central components of successful inclusion is the ability of a wide range of professionals to work together to provide a coordinated support service to specific children with SEN. In relation to effective inclusion, Vickerman (2007) argues that taking a holistic approach to children with SEN is vital if teachers are to be aware of all the needs and issues they may face. In addition, it is highly important that teachers, SENCos and schools have access to the necessary resources, information and guidance to be in a position to take appropriate action to effectively include children with SEN. As a result, Kirk and Glendinning (1999) would argue the types of support teachers are likely to need when assisting children with SEN are those from specialists such as physiotherapists, occupational therapists, educational psychologists, nurses, and speech and language therapists, and sometimes specialist agencies will be required to support particular disabilities. In drawing together this multi-disciplinary team of professionals, the knowledge and understanding that can be gained by teachers in order to give a comprehensive understanding of a child with SEN are critical. Furthermore, teachers listening and reflecting upon the advice and guidance given by each professional will help to ensure that they provide a coordinated and person-centred approach to the specific needs of children (Jahoda et al., 2006).

Occupational therapists

In order for occupational therapists to qualify and practice, they are required to have a thorough appreciation of aspects of anatomy, physiology, neurology and psychology in order to assist with the assessment and support of children who often have functional difficulties. These therapists are primarily of use to teachers and children in that they have specific skills in observation and activity analysis and the implementation of carefully graded activities to develop, learn or re-learn skills in order for children to live independently. Furthermore, and in specific relevance to supporting children with SEN, paediatric occupational therapists' appreciation of neurology, child development and cognitive psychology offers teachers an insight into the functioning of gross and fine motor skills and movement in order to help them plan effective educational programmes (Lacey and Ouvry, 2000).

Physiotherapists

In contrast, physiotherapists have a knowledge and appreciation of anatomy and physiology, and are experts in analysing movement. They are particularly focused on aspects of children's movement based on the structure and function of the body and physical approaches to promoting health, preventing injury, treatment, and the rehabilitation and management of particular disability conditions. Consequently, in relation to supporting children with SEN, physiotherapists can help teachers to improve the quality and range of movements that are central to successful learning and participation.

Speech and language therapists

Speech and language therapists can offer essential information in helping children who have speech errors and communication and language development needs. They are of particular importance to teachers in helping them to ensure such children are able to communicate and interact in effective ways with their peers and tutors. In addition, teachers can reinforce any particular language programmes that are being worked on with a child with SEN.

Educational psychologists

Educational psychologists, on the other hand, will focus on learning outcomes, student attributes, and instructional processes that directly relate both to the classroom and the school. In addition, they can support pupils and teachers in ensuring individual needs are clearly understood, so they can plan for effective and supportive educational programmes. As part of the statutory assessment of SEN under the Code of Practice (DfE, 2014b), an educational psychologist can also help gather information for teachers, parents and professional support agencies. Furthermore, they are able to assist in evaluating children's thinking abilities and assessing individual strengths and difficulties. Together, the parents, teachers, SENCos and educational psychologist can formulate plans to help children learn more effectively, which is critical to the coordinated and multi-disciplinary partnership approaches (Keers et al., 2004) of supporting children with SEN.

Educational psychologists are professionals who work with children and young people in early years and educational settings. These professionals are 'experts' in learning difficulties, social and emotional problems, issues around disabilities as well as more complex developmental disorders. They offer a specialised service to support teachers, parents and the wider community as well as children and young people (see the British Psychology Society (BPS) website: http://careers.bps.org.uk/area/educational).

In 2013 there were 1799 educational psychologists working across 115 local authorities. The vast majority of educational psychologists work in stand-alone educational psychology services, but a significant number do work as part of multi-agency teams (Troung and Ellam, 2013). In research conducted in 2013 (Troung and Ellam, 2013), 81 per cent of the educational psychologists surveyed reported that they could not meet all the requests for their help and some reported that they could not meet the basic statutory aspects of their role.

READER REFLECTION

Watch the short video available on the BPS website (address above). Make a list of the services offered by educational psychologists. Do you think that based upon the information given, educational psychologists are simply expected to do too much?

The SENCo

The key link in the coordination of service provision for a child with SEN, their families and service providers within the school context is the SENCo. According to Section 6.85 of the Code, a SENCo has to be a qualified teacher who normally holds a National Award in Special Educational Needs Coordination. A SENCo has a very important role to play in determining, with the headteacher and governors, the strategic development of SEN policy and provision in their school. The SENCo also has day-to-day responsibility for the operation of SEN policy and coordination of the educational provision made to support children with SEN. Another major part of the role of a SENCo is to provide other teachers and colleagues with professional guidance, and work to support families so that all children with SEN in their school receive appropriate support and high-quality teaching (DfE, 2014b: Sections 6.87–6.89).

According to the Code (DfE, 2014b), the key responsibilities of a SENCo are:

• overseeing the day-to-day operation of the school's SEN policy
• coordinating provision for children with SEN
• liaising with the relevant designated teacher where a looked-after pupil has SEN
• advising on the graduated approach to providing SEN support

- advising on the deployment of the school's delegated budget and other resources to meet pupils' needs effectively
- liaising with parents of pupils with SEN
- liaising with early years providers, other schools, educational psychologists, health and social care professionals, and independent or voluntary bodies
- being a key point of contact with external agencies, especially the local authority and its support services
- liaising with potential future providers of education to ensure a pupil and their parents are informed about options and a smooth transition is planned
- working with the headteacher and school governors to ensure that the school meets its responsibilities under the Equality Act 2010 with regard to reasonable adjustments and access arrangements
- ensuring that the school keeps the records of all pupils with SEN up to date.

READER REFLECTION

Using Table 7.1 outline, in your own words, what you see as the different roles that the professionals listed above play in supporting children with SEN. You should then relate this specifically to how these professionals can support teachers, parents and children in order to ensure you have a full grasp of the varying roles that professionals take in supporting children with SEN.

Table 7.1 Supporting children with SEN

Professional	Your understanding of their role	How can these professionals support teachers, parents and children?
Occupational therapist		
Physiotherapist		
Speech and language therapist		
Educational psychologist		
SENCo		

According to Sloper (2004), health authorities should ideally have arrangements for ensuring local primary care trusts and GPs have the necessary information to support children with SEN from both a health and wider educational context. Health authorities should, as part of their expectations and requirements, be able to identify arrangements for the early identification of children with particular difficulties whilst providing advice, support and assessments as to whether they think a child has a SEN or not. Norwich (2007) believes that specific information from health authorities can be of help in identifying young children with physical, sensory or developmental difficulties, or particular medical conditions and, as a result, could provide schools with the necessary interventions and support to ensure effective access and inclusion within the educational system. Because of this, health authorities, as part of their partnership working with local authorities, should seek to:

- ensure all schools have a contact (usually the school health service) for seeking medical advice on children who may have a SEN
- coordinate advice from health services for a statutory assessment, and proactively participate in multi-agency meetings on assessments and making statements of SEN
- coordinate the provision to be made by the health services for a child with SEN
- make sure that there are appropriate mechanisms so that health advice is provided for annual review meetings and transition planning when appropriate.

Section 3.59 of the Code (DfE, 2014b) states that health services must be involved with children and young people with SEN. It states:

Health services for children and young people with SEN or disabilities provide early identification, assessment and diagnosis, intervention and review for children and young people with long-term conditions and disabilities, for example chronic fatigue syndrome, anxiety disorders or life-threatening conditions such as inoperable heart disease. Services are delivered by health professionals including paediatricians, psychiatrists, nurses and allied health professionals such as occupational therapists, speech and language therapists, rehabilitation trainers, physiotherapists and psychologists. In addition, public health services for children ensure a whole population approach to health and wellbeing including preventative services such as immunisation for the whole population and targeted immunisation for the most vulnerable.

Section 3.61 of the Code (DfE, 2014b) states:

The multi-disciplinary child health team, including paediatricians, therapists, clinical psychologists, dieticians and specialist nurses such as health visitors, school nurses and community children's nursing teams, provide intervention and review for children and young people with SEN and disabilities and should contribute to supporting key transition points, including to adulthood. They aim to provide optimum health care for the children, addressing the impact of their conditions, managing consequences for the families and preventing further complications.

READER REFLECTION

Using Table 7.2 review your understanding of the roles of health, education and social services in terms of the services, advice and guidance they can offer to each other, and what the benefits to you as the teacher and the child with SEN are likely to be.

Table 7.2 Benefits of health, education and social services agencies

Authority	What is your understanding of the role of this agency?	What are the benefits of collaborative working for the teacher of children with SEN?
Social services		
Health authorities		
Education authorities		

Conclusion

In this chapter you have learnt that parents, teachers, SENCos, health and social services, schools and youth services all play a pivotal role in supporting children with SEN. In addition, you have developed an understanding that the government aims to ensure services are responsive to the needs of families and that they offer further support at earlier stages with packages that are tailored to individual needs. Furthermore, this chapter has evidenced that despite such government commitments over a number of decades, it is still the case that children are being failed because of the lack of effective multi-agency working. The chapter concluded by arguing that a commitment on the part of all those involved in supporting children with SEN and their families to holistic and multi-disciplinary partnership approaches is essential if such children are to learn and progress in their schooling in the future.

The activities and further readings detailed below are included to develop further your knowledge and understanding of the workings of the multi-agency services that aim to support children with SEN and disabilities.

STUDENT ACTIVITIES

The Children Act 2004 identified the need for a wide range of professionals, organisations, schools and agencies to work together to enhance children's services. Discuss what the advantages of educational services working in partnership to support children with SEN can bring to the development of a quality education system.

The Scottish government's *Getting it Right for Every Child* is an important initiative in ensuring that multi-agency partnerships work in practice. With a peer, review the SEN websites for England and Wales and assess what, if any, initiatives are available to support multi-agency partnerships in these countries.

- The website for England is available at: www.gov.uk/childrens-services/special-educational-needs.

- The website for Wales is available at: http://wales.gov.uk/topics/educationandskills/?lang=en.

This chapter has covered some of the major service providers and professionals who work within multi-agency teams. Working with peers, review your understanding of the role that the professionals below have in supporting children with SEN:

- school nurses

- family support workers

- community mental health workers.

Further reading

Atkinson, M., Wilkin, A., Stott, A., Doherty, P. and Kinder, K. (2002) *Multi-agency Working: A Detailed Study*. London: National Foundation for Educational Research.
This report will help you appreciate, through a case study approach, the relative merits of multi-agency working.

Foley, P. and Rixon, A. (eds) (2014) *Changing Children's Services: Working and Learning Together* (Working Together for Children series). London: Policy Press.
This text concentrates on the ongoing and fundamental changes that have been happening to children's service across the UK. This text reviews and critically examines the realities of multi-agency working and questions the effectiveness of closer working relations between the professionals that support children with SEN.

Gasper, G. (2010) *Multi-agency Working in the Early Years*. London: Sage.
This book reviews multi-agency working in a time of immense change in the delivery of children and family services in England. It challenges the 'taken-for-granted ways' in which such partnership services are provided.

8

INTERNATIONAL PERSPECTIVES ON SEN AND INCLUSIVE EDUCATION

CHAPTER OBJECTIVES

- To introduce a range of international legislation and policies that govern the delivery of inclusive education on the 'world stage'.

- To develop a knowledge and understanding of how children with SEN are educated in Poland, India and USA.

Introduction

This chapter seeks to provide an international comparative analysis of the world of SEN, whilst identifying key trends and themes that have emerged and how they impact upon the quality of educational experience that children with SEN receive. In the first part of this chapter you will be introduced to a range of international policies related to SEN. In contrast, the second part of the chapter examines the policies and practices of specific countries. It commences by examining a European country (Poland) before moving on to examine how SEN and inclusion are conceptualised and organised in the USA and India. The second part of the chapter therefore provides case studies of the development, organisation and philosophical underpinnings of SEN and inclusion across a number of countries, and outlines the current educational practices, legislation and key trends that govern these provisions. Consequently, it is envisaged that after reading this chapter you will have a grasp of international policy related to SEN, alongside an appreciation of how different countries interpret this in practice.

If we accept the ideology of inclusive education, then we have to believe that all children and young people, no matter where they are located in the world, should have access to high-quality education. At the beginning of the twenty-first century inclusive education was high on the international agenda. Indeed, in 2010, The World Education Forum, convened in Dakar Senegal, stated that achieving Education for All would happen by 2015 (Meenakshi et al., 2015). The 'human ideology' of inclusive education then has 'appealed globally' and often has been described as a global movement with a global agenda (Johansson, 2014). However, despite such 'humane' ideology, inclusion has experienced difficulties in converting its initial idea into a practical reality on the world stage. For example, despite the United Nations Educational, Scientific and Cultural Organization (UNESCO) Convention against Discrimination in Education being formulated in 1960 and other international human rights treaties having existed since 1948, it is still the case that in 2015, millions of children, youths and adults experience exclusion from education around the world. Inclusion, then, whilst being high on the policy agenda of many countries since the Salamanca Statement of 1994, still witnesses that 72 million children throughout the world are not in school. UNESCO estimates that more than half of this number are girls, seven out of ten of these children live in sub-Saharan Africa or south or west Asia, and the group that experiences the most blatant educational exclusion are those who are disabled. Indeed, UNESCO suggests that one-third of all out-of-school children are those who we might consider as disabled.

READER REFLECTION

Read the following extract from UNESCO's education page, which is available at: www.unesco.org/new/en/education/themes/strengthening-education-systems/inclusive-education.

Education is not simply about making schools available for those who are already able to access them. It is about being proactive in identifying the barriers and obstacles learners encounter in attempting to access opportunities for quality education, as well as in removing those barriers and obstacles that lead to exclusion.

Throughout the chapter, make a note of the barriers and obstacles that learners face in their struggles to access high-quality learning placements.

Internationally, then, many educational authorities have seemingly embraced a philosophy of inclusion in order to address their social and moral obligations to educate all children. However, the competing needs of different types of disabilities and SEN expressed through various lobby groups have led to a wide range of different philosophies and practices for promoting inclusion across the world.

READER REFLECTION

Reflect upon why you think some international countries get on the inclusion bandwagon. As part of your consideration, try to identify what you see as the main reasons for some countries then taking this a step further and actioning inclusion, whilst others do not move beyond rhetoric and philosophical statements.

Problematising inclusion within international policy

Many of the issues with the internationalisation of the theoretic of inclusive education may be located in the fact that this concept has remained largely unproblematised and therefore it has been operated at a rather superficial level (Byrne, 2013). For example, the United Nations (UN) (2006: 66) defines inclusion as ranging from 'full-time placement of all students with disabilities into one regular classroom or placement into the regular classroom with varying degree of inclusion, including a certain portion of special education'. This definition would seem to be at odds with those 'full inclusionists' located within the English context (see Chapter 5). Furthermore, within the Salamanca Statement 'integration and inclusion' are used interchangeably and other issues of terminological ambiguity are detailed. Notably, the Statement indicates that the 'special needs' of children with disabilities should be considered (Byrne, 2013). This form of terminological ambiguity leads some to believe that inclusion as a concept within the international agenda is one which is heavily diluted and that its original 'reformist intent' has been undermined (Byrne, 2013). For other researchers, such as Armstrong et al. (2011), the concept of inclusive education is simply a Western construct that has difficulty translating into the many and varied international contexts.

Within the practice of inclusive education Smith and Thomas (2006) suggest the international inclusion debate has, for too long, focused on whether children with SEN should be educated in special or mainstream schools, rather than focusing upon the quality of education and support that they receive. Given that there is a developing trend towards including children with SEN in mainstream settings in the UK and internationally, its delivery in practice is, according to Farrell (2000), rather fraught with the complex issues and challenges of policy and practice.

READER REFLECTION

Consider the statement below.

Inclusive education is not an 'indigenous concept to India' but rather has developed as a result of Western influences in special education. Indeed, it may be observed that within the national language of Hindi no direct translation of this terminology exists. (Hodkinson and Devarakonda, 2011)

> With another student, detail what other barriers might stop the development of inclusion, bearing in mind that such countries have widely different cultures, traditions, languages and histories.

International action to date and future policy directions

> The major legislation that has governed the international formulation of special education and inclusive education is outlined below.
>
> 1948 – Article 26 of the Universal Declaration of Human Rights
>
> 1959 – United Nations Declaration on the Rights of the Child
>
> 1960 – UNESCO Convention against Discrimination in Education
>
> 1966 – Article 13(1) of the International Covenant on Economic, Social and Cultural Rights
>
> 1989 – UN Convention on the Rights of the Child
>
> 1993 – Standard Rules on the Equalisation of Opportunities for Persons with Disabilities
>
> 1994 – Salamanca Statement and Framework for Action
>
> 2006 – UN Convention on the Rights of Persons with Disabilities.
>
> (See Byrne (2013) for an insightful examination of the deficits in such international legislation.)

During the past 30 years there has been an increasing pattern of UN conventions setting out the expectations of international member states as related to disability and SEN. In 1993, for example, the UN Standard Rules on the Equalization of Opportunities for Persons with Disabilities noted that the rights of disabled people had been the subject of significant attention within the UN over the previous three decades. For example, it highlighted that the most important outcome of the International Year of Disabled People (1981) was the introduction of the World Programme of Action for Disabled People. This programme emphasised the right of disabled people to the same opportunities as other citizens (Davis, 2000). A further significant development was that disability was to be considered a function of the relationship between disabled people and their environment. This programme then highlighted the importance of countries' interaction with disabled people and the agencies that supported them. It stated that societal and cultural responses to accommodate and include, or contrastingly to observe, that disability was located solely within the person were of crucial importance to the establishment and development of disability policies and practices (see Chapters 3 and 4).

As part of the developing shift towards social models of disability (Barnes, 1992) a global meeting of experts to review the implementation of the World Programme of Action was held in Stockholm in 1987. It suggested that guiding philosophies should be developed to highlight the priorities for action in the years ahead, and that the basis of these should be a recognition of the rights of disabled people. Consequently, the meeting recommended that the UN General Assembly convene a special conference to draft an international convention on the elimination of all forms of discrimination against persons with disabilities to be ratified subsequently by member states by the end of the decade.

READER REFLECTION

The World Programme of Action meeting held in Stockholm put forward the idea that a 'guiding philosophy' should be established to highlight the priorities for inclusive education for children with SEN. Furthermore, this should embrace the social model of disability and the fundamental rights of disabled people to have equal access to society.

Review the models of disability that you encountered at the start of this book. Employing these models, what would be your guiding principles in the development of a system of inclusive education?

The UN Convention on the Rights of the Child 1989

In 1989 a Convention on the Rights of the Child instigated the first legally binding international agreement to address the full range of human rights, including civil, cultural, economic, political and social rights for young people. The reason for implementing this convention was that world leaders had decided that children needed a special convention just for themselves because people under 18 years of age are often in need of special care and protection that adults do not require. The convention set out these rights in 54 articles and identified the basic human rights that children everywhere should have, which included:

- the right to survival
- an opportunity to develop to the fullest
- protection from harmful influences, abuse and exploitation
- full participation in family, cultural and social life.

Alongside these were four core principles:

- non-discrimination
- a devotion to the best interests of the child
- the right to life, survival and development
- respect for the views of the child.

READER REFLECTION

Consider the barriers to successful inclusive education that were detailed at the start of this chapter. How might these undermine the four core principles of the United Nations Convention of the Rights of the Child?

The core principles identified above support the notion of equality of opportunity discussed in more detail in Chapter 1 (see Finkelstein, 1980; Johnstone, 2001) and suggest what countries should be doing to tackle those barriers to the participation of children (including those with SEN) within society. The articles noted below specifically relate to this development of international inclusive SEN policies and practices.

Article 2: All human rights applying to children without discrimination on any ground particularly.

Article 12: The right of the child to express an opinion and to have that opinion taken into account, in any matter or procedure affecting the child. This emphasises the notion of empowerment and the self-advocacy of children to have a voice in decisions which impact upon them.

Article 23: The right of disabled children to enjoy a full and decent life, in conditions which ensure dignity, promote self-reliance and facilitate the child's active participation in the community. It also advocates the right of the disabled child to special care, education, health care, training, rehabilitation, employment and recreation opportunities. Moreover, all of these are to be designed with the intention of fostering the child to achieve the fullest possible levels of social integration and individual development.

Article 28: This states the child's right to an education and that it shall be provided on the basis of equal opportunity.

Article 29: This states that a child's education should be directed at developing that child's personality and talents, and mental and physical abilities, to their 'fullest potential'.

Historically, the UN Convention on the Rights of the Child 1989 was not the first to address children, as its instigation marked the 30th anniversary of an earlier declaration of the rights of the child in 1959 and the tenth anniversary of the International Year of the Child in 1979. But since its adoption in 1989, and after more than 60 years of advocacy on children's rights, what was significant about the 1989 UN convention was that it was ratified more quickly and by more governments (except Somalia and the USA) than any other previous human rights instrument, while additionally and specifically addressing those children with SEN. Indeed Nind et al. (2003) suggest that pivotal to the successful implementation of the 1989 convention was that it was at the time the only international human rights treaty that expressly gave non-governmental organisations (NGOs) a role in monitoring its implementation under Article 45a. The uniqueness of enabling NGOs to have a role in supporting the UN convention lay in the fact that for the first time this gave organisations (excluding government representatives) a central opportunity to influence and shape the policies and practices of international child development, including those with SEN.

In summary, the 1989 Convention brought about a paradigm shift in UN policy direction through which children with SEN were considered as being integral to any successful young people's international strategy development (Thomas and Loxley, 2001). Therefore, as disability movement perspectives sought to assert their human rights to be included within society (Slee, 1998), this convention supported a developing trend of including children with SEN as an integral component of children's development activities.

READER REFLECTION

Article 12 of the UN Convention on the Rights of the Child gave the right to any child of expressing an opinion and to have that opinion taken into account in any matter or procedure affecting them. Furthermore, the convention gave NGOs a pivotal role in implementing its implementation.

Reflect upon the statement from this article and consider how the voices of children with SEN can be heard, and how this can have the potential to shape inclusive education policies and practices in the future.

UN Standard Rules 1993

Following substantial debate and discussion by international member states of the UN, a total of 22 standard rules were eventually established in order to provide a benchmark for policy making and action covering the entitlement and accessibility of disabled people to society. In relation to education and disability, Rule 6 is of most significance in that it states that countries should recognise the principle of equal educational opportunities for children with disabilities within integrated settings and that they should ensure these are an integral part of the educational system. This reinforces the encouragement of the social model of disability and the new orthodoxy of the drive towards inclusive education.

Indeed, in order to implement inclusive education, the UN suggested member states should have a clear policy that is understood at school as well as at the wider community level that allows for a flexible curriculum plus any additions and adaptations to the school curriculum alongside ongoing teacher training and support (Rose, 2001). Moreover, the UN argued that where 'ordinary schools' cannot as yet adequately make inclusive provision, special school education could be considered. However, this should be aimed at preparing the student for inclusion within the mainstream eventually. Thus, these UN rules constituted the first articulated drive towards inclusive schooling for children with SEN, by recognising the need for schools and teachers to adapt and modify their curriculum, teaching styles and practices to accommodate individual needs.

Central to the international drive for schools to become more inclusive was the responsibility of schools, teachers and policy makers to change their existing structures to accommodate the diversity of all children with SEN (Avissar, 2003; Vickerman, 2007). This supports the challenges of the 1960s and 1970s on the orthodoxy of segregation within the UK (Wearmouth, 2001), and the development and emergence of inclusive environments in the 1990s and into the twenty-first century (Gibson and Blandford, 2005). As such, individuals and agencies supporting children with SEN have had to respond to what has become a significant policy and practice shift from isolated and segregated schooling through to an acknowledgement of equal rights and the entitlement to mainstream education.

READER REFLECTION

A significant development of the 1993 UN Standard Rules on the Equalization of Opportunities for Persons with Disabilities was a recognition that disability was to be considered to be a function of the relationship between disabled people and their environment, which is commonly referred to as the 'social model of disability'. Furthermore, the rules acknowledged the drive towards the provision of integrated settings for the education of children with SEN as opposed to previously segregated approaches.

In reviewing the statement above, reflect upon what issues you think schools and teachers would have to adopt in implementing the 'social model of disability', which involves organisations being proactive in meeting and accommodating the needs of children with SEN, rather than children having to fit into existing and sometimes 'restrictive' structures.

The UNESCO Salamanca Statement 1994

The Salamanca Statement (see Chapter 5) was a significant international directive in that it called upon the international community to endorse the approach of working towards inclusive schools by implementing practical and strategic changes across the world. In June 1994, representatives from 92 governments and 25 international organisations attended the World Conference on Special Needs Education in Salamanca, Spain, and agreed upon a dynamic statement on the education of all disabled children and called for inclusion to be internationally considered as the norm rather than the exception (O'Hanlon, 1995).

The conference also adopted a new framework for action of which the guiding principle advocated that 'ordinary schools' should accommodate all children, regardless of their physical, intellectual, social, emotional, linguistic or other needs.

The framework for action stipulated that disabled children should attend their neighbourhood school, which should make appropriate provision to accommodate their individual needs. The statement argued that 'regular schools' with this inclusive orientation were the most effective means of: overcoming discriminatory attitudes; creating welcoming communities; building inclusive societies; and achieving education for all (Mittler and Daunt, 1995).

The World Conference on Special Needs Education in Salamanca called upon all international governments to:

- give the highest policy and budgetary priority to improve education services so that all children can be included, regardless of their differences or difficulties
- adopt as a matter of law or policy the principle of inclusive education and seek to enrol all children in 'ordinary schools' unless there are compelling reasons for doing otherwise
- develop demonstration projects and encourage international exchanges with countries with more progressive inclusive policies and practices
- ensure that organisations of disabled people, along with parents and community bodies, are involved in the planning and decision-making of policies and practices for children with SEN
- place greater effort into pre-school strategies to promote inclusive practices
- ensure that both initial and in-service teacher training addresses the provision of inclusive education.

The Salamanca Statement (UNESCO, 1994) called upon international communities to endorse an inclusive approach to schooling and to support the development of SEN as an integral aspect of all education programmes. In working towards these ideals the World Conference called upon agencies such as UNESCO, the UN Children's Fund, the UN Development Fund and the World Bank for their endorsement and support in meeting these inclusive education ideals. This also reinforces the importance of multi-disciplinary and multi-agency approaches (Watson et al., 2002) to the successful adoption of inclusive educational practices (see Chapter 7). Additionally, the World Conference asked the UN and its associated agencies to strengthen their inputs whilst improving their networking to foster the more efficient support of integrated SEN provision. As such, non-governmental organisations were asked to strengthen their collaboration with official national bodies and to become more involved in all aspects of inclusive education. UNESCO was asked to:

- ensure that SEN formed part of every discussion dealing with 'Education for All'
- enhance teacher education related to SEN and inclusion and gain support from teaching unions and related professional associations
- stimulate the academic community to do more research into inclusive education and disseminate the findings and reports across international boundaries in order to share practice and work towards advancing educational attainment and accessibility for children with SEN

- use its funds over the five-year period from 1996 to 2001 to create an expanded programme for inclusive schools and community support projects, which would enable the launch of international pilot projects in which those countries with less advanced education systems could work towards more inclusive ideals.

The framework for action within the Salamanca Statement (UNESCO, 1994: 11) states, 'inclusion and participation are essential to human dignity and to the enjoyment and exercise of human rights. Within the field of education this is reflected in bringing about a genuine equalisation of opportunity.' Thus SEN provision must embody proven methods of teaching and learning in which all children can benefit, but at the same time must recognise that human differences are normal and that learning must be modified to meet the needs of the individual child, rather than the child fitting into existing processes. As such, the fundamental principle of the inclusive school is premised upon the notion that all children should learn together, where possible, and that 'ordinary schools' must recognise and respond to the diverse needs of their students, whilst also having a continuum of support and services to match these needs.

READER REFLECTION

Reflect upon your views and perspectives in relation to the Salamanca Statement, which argues that:

'regular schools' with an inclusive orientation are the most effective means of combating discriminatory attitudes; creating welcoming communities; building inclusive societies; and achieving education for all.

As part of your reflection and agreement or opposition to the statement above you should identify some key points based on the chapter so far to justify your comments.

The UN Convention on the Rights of Persons with Disabilities 2006

In December 2006 the UN Convention on the Rights of Persons with Disabilities launched a citation, which noted only 45 of its 192 member states had specific legislation protecting the rights of disabled people. This first convention of the new millennium had set out to encourage the enactment of laws and policies upon all its member states in favour of disabled people with the aim of including them in everyday life, and at the same time providing equal access to educational services for everyone. Indeed, the treaty was created to have a concrete effect on the lives of disabled people by ensuring the enacted laws were not only put into policy but more importantly were implemented in practice, thus reiterating the trend towards inclusivity within the international community (Fisher and Goodley, 2007).

It has been estimated that the worldwide number of children under the age of 18 with a disability varies between 120 and 150 million (UNESCO, 2004). Moreover, two-thirds of people worldwide with disabilities live in developing countries and these poor countries in particular suffer from the resultant waste of potential that goes hand in hand with the exclusion of people solely due to their disability (Timmons, 2002). A key feature of the UN convention emphasises the need for international cooperation and that all phases of the new international development programmes should include a disability dimension. As such, developing countries will receive support from a range of international agencies to implement the 2006 UN Convention on the Rights of Persons with Disabilities, with the aim here being to raise the aspirations and achievements of those children with SEN.

In summary, this convention is centred upon the instigation of a significant 'paradigm shift' from medical models (seeing the causation and location of disability with the person) to a social model approach (seeing the problem with society and the barriers it creates for disabled people) (see Chapter 2). Thus, the UN is seeking to promote the notion of educational inclusion, alongside a recognition that countries worldwide need to be proactive in identifying what they can and should do to adapt their services to accommodate the needs of children with SEN. Central to future international developments in SEN is the need for a commitment that no child is discriminated against on the basis of their disability and that all should have access to a high-quality educational experience. However, whether this is located within mainstream or segregated school settings is subject to much international debate as countries' differing cultures and financial situations determine the quality and nature of education provided for children with SEN (Farrell, 2000; Smith 2006; Warnock, 2005).

A review of contrasting international perspectives

The first part of this chapter offered an international context to the various UN declarations and ideologies being promoted to support children with SEN. However, as discussed earlier, the countries involved adopted different approaches to and interpretations of these directives. The second half of this chapter seeks to provide an overview of various countries' approaches to the inclusion of children with SEN.

Poland

CASE STUDY 8.1

SEN and inclusion in Poland

Poland is a European country whose territory was defined at the end of the Second World War. It is a country that is relatively homogeneous, and compared to many other European countries, it has a relatively low number of migrants in its education system (Wazna-Pajak, 2013). After a period of communist control, it is now a country with a parliamentary and cabinet system of government. In Poland, formal education begins at the age of six in reception classes and from ages seven to 12, children move into the primary phase of education (grades 1 to 6). Similar to the UK, secondary education begins at age 12 and lasts until the age of 16 (Starczewska et al., 2014).

From the eighteenth century people with disabilities' right to life has been protected by the state. Statistics, cited by Starczewska et al. (2014), suggest that some five million people in Poland have a disability and that a significant proportion of these are children. Recent education acts have created the possibility for children with disabilities to be educated within the public education system. Whether a child is, or is not admitted to mainstream schooling though is based upon the decision of professionals located in the Guidance and Counselling Centre (Sheligevich-Urban, 2011). Within education in Poland, children with disabilities continue to be largely segregated from mainstream educational settings (Starczewska et al., 2014).

READER REFLECTION

It would seem then that whether a child is or is not educated in the mainstream in Poland rests with the decisions made by educational professionals. Who else do you think should be involved in making the decision to educate a disabled child in a mainstream educational setting?

Defining inclusion in Poland

In a research project I was involved with, we found that the majority of the teachers defined integration as including children with disabilities into mainstream schools. Indeed, one of the teachers believed that inclusion was an alternative to integration and that both of those words meant the participation of children with SEN in mainstream schooling. Another participant denoted that integration was a 'willingness to bring children with disabilities and without disabilities closer together, willingness to cooperate and interact, mutual understanding' (Starczewska et al., 2012). For one teacher, integration was conceptualised around the need for specialised support, they commented that 'pupils with disabilities are in mainstream class, supported by a special educational needs teacher'. For these teachers then, integration was inclusion – the concept was interchangeable (Starczewska et al., 2012).

In 1994 Poland signed the Salamanca Declaration. This committed it to a paradigm shift in terms of its educational provision, which had to move from a system of segregated special schools to a policy of inclusive education. However, a review of the literature available for education in Poland still denotes that integration and inclusion are employed interchangeably by educational professionals (see Starczewska et al., 2012) and little real progress had been made to convert the idea of inclusion into practice within Polish classrooms.

The barriers to the development of inclusive education in Poland

According to research by Firkowska-Mankiewicz (2000) only around 2 per cent of children with disabilities in Poland are actually educated in mainstream schools. Interestingly, the highest number of pupils integrated into the mainstream are those with moderate learning disabilities, followed by those with physical disabilities and then those with social and emotional difficulties or children who have sensory impairments (Starczewska et al., 2014). Research from Poland suggests that 'integrative' education is being stalled by the fact that:

- teachers are having difficulty including older children (Starczewska et al., 2012)
- schools cannot satisfy the individual needs of their pupils (Wapiennik, 2005)
- 'integration' is not leading to the closures of special schools (Gajda, 2008)
- the training of teachers in SEN is problematic (Starczewska et al., 2012).

READER REFLECTION

Read the information below from the research of Starczewska et al. (2012). What are the major issues, in terms of teacher training, that are stalling the implementation of inclusive education in Poland?

Through this research project it was found that the qualifications required of teachers in Poland were specified in the Act on the Charter of Teachers (1982, amended in 2004). This Act states that teachers must have at least an undergraduate degree and a teaching certificate to be able to teach children. According to Wapiennik (2005), the quality of education for teachers at the university level was usually outdated and lacked pedagogical knowledge in the field of intellectual disabilities. More recent legislation though has specified new standards for training within the area of special needs. However, this still requires only a minimal knowledge of special education. Furthermore, we discovered that teachers in mainstream schools receive no mandatory in-service training in disability issues.

Starczewska et al's (2014) summary of the Polish inclusive education is somewhat pessimistic in that it states:

An analysis of the literature intimates that inclusion is a concept that has little meaning in the Polish educational system. Furthermore, the review highlights the difficulties that pupils with disabilities have in gaining access to mainstream integrative provision and the lack of appropriately trained school personnel to facilitate high quality teaching and learning. It would seem that in relation to the inclusive segregation continuum, Poland's education system is far closer to the segregation end, particularly for children with profound disabilities living in its rural hinterlands.

The USA

CASE STUDY 8.2

SEN and inclusion in the USA

America, or as it is more usually known the USA, is a country made up of 50 states. The country covers some 3.8 million square miles and is populated by around 318 million people. The USA is the fourth largest country by land mass and third largest by population (US Census Bureau, 2014).

Education in the USA is provided by both the public and private sectors. In the autumn term of 2014 some 49.8 million students attended public school in America and 5.0 million pupils attended private schools (NCES, 2014). Education is compulsory for children who have reached their fifth birthday and state education ends at 16 or 18 depending upon individual states. Education in the USA is divided into grades ranging from kindergarten and first grade through to the twelfth grade, which is the final year of high school.

Inclusive education in the USA

While some developing international countries may be working towards ensuring all children have a basic right to education, in the USA around 96 per cent of children with disabilities are presently educated within mainstream schools and almost half spend the majority of their school day in 'general inclusive' classrooms, as opposed to being withdrawn for segregated lessons. This picture demonstrates a progressive increase in the number of children with SEN being included in mainstream settings since 1976 (NCES, 2014). Furthermore, the Public Law 108–446: Individuals with Disabilities Education Improvement Act (IDEA) of 2004 continues to advocate the inclusion of children with SEN within mainstream education settings. This law not only advocates accessibility to a high-quality education for children with SEN, it also promotes accountability for results; enhanced parental involvement; the use of proven practices and resources; greater flexibility; and reduced paperwork burdens for teachers, states and local school districts (Block and Obrusnikova, 2007).

The IDEA is the main federal programme within the USA that authorises state and local aid for special education and related services for children with disabilities, including those students with learning disabilities. On 3rd December 2004, President Bush signed the Individuals with Disabilities Education Improvement

Act (Public Law 108–446), which made significant changes, including new provisions regarding how schools could determine whether a child had a specific learning disability and how they could receive special education services (see http:// idea.ed.gov).

As a result, the USA can be considered as one of the more progressive international countries that has actively promoted the full inclusion of children with SEN. Indeed, the country has had a long history of policy and practice developments in inclusive education, dating back to 1975 when President Gerald Ford advocated that every public school district in the country must provide all its students with disabilities, aged from three to 21 years of age, with an individualised, free and appropriate public education that was to take place within the 'least restrictive environment'. President Ford's desire to foster educational environments that were 'least restrictive' were initially introduced in 1975 through the Public Law 94–142: Education of All Handicapped Children Act, and this has since been regularly updated in 1983, 1990, 1997 and 2004.

The notion of 'least restrictive environments' is worth taking note of. According to Winnick (2005), the least restrictive environments for children with SEN are within mainstream education and so this should be used whenever and wherever possible. However, Warnock (2005) has argued that for many children with SEN segregated schooling may be the most appropriate environment for some to have the best access to education. This highlights the complexity of developing SEN provision within countries' national laws as well as with regard to UN directives that promote full inclusion within the mainstream.

READER REFLECTION

The IDEA 2004 has three main phases:

- Stage 1: 'Get 'em in' – involving opening the doors of public schools to children with SEN.

- Stage 2: 'Get 'em through' – involving teacher educators, related support services, staff and parents working to keep children with SEN from dropping out.

- Stage 3: 'Get 'em ready' – involving preparing children with SEN for further education, employment and independent living.

Reflect upon the three stages from IDEA 2004 above and consider the strategies that need to be in place to ensure each of the stages are fulfilled for children with SEN.

According to Bender et al. (1995) and Block and Obrusnikova (2007), the US model of inclusion is rooted in the philosophy of educating children with SEN alongside their non-disabled peers, while at the same time supporting them fully from initial entry and access to school through modifications to schools and curricula, and then on into preparation for employment. This model exemplifies the notion of fostering the 'least restrictive' environments (Winnick, 2005), suggesting a child with SEN should have the opportunity to be educated with their non-disabled peers to the greatest extent possible, while also having an entitlement to the same activities and programmes that any other non-disabled person would be able to access.

READER REFLECTION

American law does not clarify the nature of the least restrictive environment, however in a landmark case (*Daniel v the State Board of Education* (1989), cited in Daniel, 1997) it was determined that children with SEN had a right to be included in both academic and extra-curricular programmes of 'general education'.

As part of this significant ruling, it was acknowledged that in determining what constituted a 'least restrictive environment' four fundamental factors should be considered, namely:

- the educational benefits of integrated versus segregated settings

- the non-academic benefits of inclusion (primarily social interaction with non-disabled peers)

- the effect of a student with a SEN on their teacher and peers

- the costs of all supplementary services required for a child with SEN to stay within an inclusive setting.

Read the four fundamental factors noted above and then devise your own definition of the term 'least restrictive environment'. Try to identify factors additional to those noted above that you would use to determine the most appropriate inclusive setting for children with SEN.

India

CASE STUDY 8.3

SEN and inclusion in India

India is a vast country that cannot be easily quantified or described. It is a unique country of historical traditions and modern developments and one where incredible poverty sits side by side with immense wealth. India is the world's largest democracy and it is estimated that it has 17 per cent of the world's population, some 1,027 million people. In India, there are 16 officially recognised

(Continued)

(Continued)

languages as well as over 314 spoken dialects, four major religions and some 200 million children who are eligible to attend schools. The Indian school system, then, is the second largest in the world (Hodkinson and Deverakonda, 2011).

From 2002, all children in India up to the age of 14 have had a right to access eight years of free education. However, whilst India is a country that is working hard to ensure that all children attend school, it is noticeable that the Indian government is faced with a very difficult task to fulfil its aim of free universal primary education for all. Indeed, despite the Indian government's attempts to include all children in school, it is still the case that between 35 million and 80 million children do not attend school (Singal and Rouse, 2003). Furthermore, it is also reported that 53 per cent of children drop out of school before they reach Grade 7. UNESCO believes that despite intensive efforts and a very real commitment to providing universal education by 2015, the Indian government will fail on this educational promise (Hodkinson and Deverakonda, 2011).

The state education system in India

The Indian education system provides a mainly uniform structure of provision across the 28 regional states (Singal, 2006a). Nursery and pre-primary education is not compulsory and there is also a great discrepancy in educational provision between rural and urban areas (Singal, 2006b). State education in India, then, commences when a child is six years of age and the first five years of education is within primary education (Grades 1–5). Grades 6–7 begin at the age of 11 where pupils are educated in what are known as 'upper primary classes' (Singal, 2006a). The main focus of the state educational system in India is upon the provision of basic reading, writing and numeracy skills (Singal, 2006a).

Since the 1990s the Indian educational system has changed substantially, as many private and charitable bodies have moved in to deliver educational programmes on the state's behalf. Singal (2006a) estimates that nearly one-quarter of education is now provided by private or non-governmental organisations.

READER REFLECTION

Read the following information, which relates to the Indian education system and consider what barriers the Indian government faces in its aim to provide universal free primary education to all of its children. Do you think, as Sharma does, that it is only through legislation that these barriers can be overcome?

The Hindu Business Line (2007) believes that education in India is mainly delivered in poorly-lit classrooms where large classes are often taught by a person who may not have completed state education themselves.

> Sharma (Baquer and Sharma, 1997) states that as India is such a large country, where resources are so scarce and one in which societal attitudes are sometimes so damaging, it is only through well-directed legislation that all children might be included in schools

The development of inclusive education in India

The education of children with SEN within the Indian context was mainly conceptualised within a segregated special schooling system. Up until the 1970s many educational and medical professionals believed that pupils with SEN were simply not capable of being educated in mainstream settings. However, the past two decades or so have observed significant and major educational reforms in India that have been influenced by international developments (Raghavan, 2014). In 1994 India endorsed the objectives of the Salamanca Statement and began to promote a policy of inclusive education (Raghavan, 2014). In 1995, the Indian government passed the landmark Person with Disabilities (PWD) Act, which ushered in a new era for children with disabilities in India (Das et al., 2013).

The PWD Act was observed to be a landmark step in Indian education because it required all central and state governmental institutions to provide free and appropriate access to children with disabilities. As part of this legislation, state schools were required to keep 3 per cent of all its places for pupils with SEN. India, then, is one of the few countries that employ positive discrimination to ensure that all of its pupils has the right to be educated.

In 2000, it was recommended (NCERT, 2000) that the Indian education system would be improved if it was based upon an inclusive educational model. From this time forward, the Indian government has launched a multitude of initiatives, such as the Integrated Education for Disabled Children and the District Primary Education Programme, to speed the development of inclusive education.

The barriers to the development of inclusive education in India

From the very beginning, the development of inclusive education was stalled because politicians, teachers, pupils and parents had no clear understanding of what inclusion meant. Indeed, many educators referred to inclusion as a Western construct and as such inclusive education has often been dismissed or misunderstood (Madan and Sharma, 2013). This issue has meant that inclusion and integration have been employed interchangeably within policy and legislative acts and by education professionals alike. This 'terminological ambiguity' (Hodkinson and Deverakonda, 2011) has led to a lack of clarity and indeed even an elusiveness in professionals' understanding of the practice of inclusive education (Madan and Sharma, 2013).

A further barrier to the ideal of inclusion is the location of children with SEN in mainstream schools being controlled by educational professionals such as psychologists and special educators. These professionals are required to judge whether individual children have the necessary capabilities in terms of communication, mobility, dressing and toileting skills that would enable them to be able to access education in mainstream schools (Hodkinson and Deverakonda, 2011). It is apparent that this power to exclude children has been widely employed, as it is reported that during the first decade of inclusive education there was a twofold increase in the number of children attending special and segregated schools (Singal, 2005).

A major barrier to the Indian government's commitment to inclusion is the teachers, who are required to operate inclusive education within the schools themselves. Sharma and Deppler (2005: 4) believe that Indian universities 'fail to train teachers adequately' about educating children in inclusive settings. It is somewhat disturbing to note that the vast majority of Indian school personnel in post today do not have the requisite training to enable them to provide successful inclusive education (Hodkinson and Deverakonda, 2011). A further significant issue is that of educational professionals' attitudes towards children with SEN. Practitioners in India it seems view inclusive education not as a fundamental human right but as 'an act of kindness' (Singal, 2006a). Other research also notes that many teachers do not believe that all children should be educated in the mainstream, and more worryingly, that some teachers hold negative attitudes towards children with SEN (Shama, 2002; Singal and Rouse, 2003; Singal, 2006b). What is apparent is that whilst significant numbers of children with SEN are included into the mainstream system, many simply drop out because of a lack of sensitivity displayed towards their educational needs (Panda, 2005).

In summary, it would seem that despite the good intentions shown by the government towards the development of inclusive education, the latter part of the twentieth century witnessed the Indian education system struggling to cope with the vast number of children with SEN who wanted to access the system (Mani, 2000).

READER REFLECTION

Imagine that you are a government education minister who has been tasked with the responsibility for meeting UN international directives on promoting the inclusion of children with SEN within mainstream settings in one of the countries detailed above. Make a list of the ways in which you would tackle this complex challenge and what policy and practice directives you would advocate. In addition, consider which key agencies you would need to engage with in order to ensure that you have fully consulted and represented all stakeholders' views.

This review of differing and different education systems shows how the USA contrasts with Poland and India in its development of inclusive education for children with SEN. The review of these countries' education systems also demonstrates the complexities of and variations in how they are working towards establishing acceptable levels of schooling for all (Baker and Zigmond, 1995). Indeed, it demonstrates the unique role of the UN and the significant challenges it faces in working with its 192 member states to encourage international commitments towards not only inclusion but, for some countries, the commitment to a basic right to education. However, in noting these varying perspectives, this chapter will now move towards an examination of internationally significant initiatives established in the late 1980s and early 1990s (Kavale, 2000; Snyder et al., 2001), which have been instrumental in encouraging access and the entitlement of children with SEN to be educated within ordinary schools. A key factor will be the ability of international governments, policy makers, teachers and parents to work together to share and disseminate practices with the ultimate goal of raising aspirations and the entitlement to high-quality, appropriate education for all who are marginalised and under-represented within society.

READER REFLECTION

Make notes on what you see as the key issues, similarities and differences between the international perspectives of SEN and inclusive schooling noted above. As part of your reflection, consider what you think different countries can learn from each other in relation to inclusive policy and practice, and how this could be disseminated to improve access and the entitlement to high-quality education for children with SEN.

International directions in inclusive policy and practice

As noted earlier in this chapter, the first UN convention of the new millennium, the Convention on the Rights of Persons with Disabilities (UN, 2006), was adopted by the UN General Assembly on 13th December 2006 and has been signed by a total of 101 governments to date. Due to the diverse international views and stages of development that are encompassed by inclusive policies and practices, this was a challenging convention to agree. However, the negotiators succeeded in shifting the position on education from one of a choice between segregated or mainstream education, to the right to attend inclusive primary and secondary schools.

The Convention is based upon a 'paradigm shift' (Norwich, 2007; Pijl et al., 1997) from a medical model to a social model approach. This movement in philosophy has been fundamental in moving international SEN developments forward to a position of society changing and responding to the needs of children with SEN, whilst at the same time recognising their fundamental right to an education that is inclusive. In addition, the convention also recognises the complexity of interpreting inclusive education (which is more than merely about location and more importantly includes the context within which the schooling takes place).

The Chair of the ad hoc committee that negotiated the convention applauded the role that disabled people and their organisations had played in the development process, with over 800 agencies taking part in the negotiations. This acknowledges the significant shift towards self-representation and the empowerment of both disabled people and the organisations that represent them to determine their futures. Article 24 of the Convention requires signatories to ensure that all disabled children and young people, 'can access an inclusive, quality, free primary and secondary education on an equal basis with others in the communities in which they live' (UN, 2006: Article 24, 2b). It continues by stating, 'reasonable accommodation of the individual's requirements' (UN, 2006: Article 24, 2c) should be made along with the support that is provided, 'within the general education system, to facilitate their effective education' (UN, 2006: Article 24, 2d). What is particularly significant within the convention is that Article 24 allows for the possibility of segregated education for children with sensory impairments, thus 'ensuring that the education of persons, and in particular children, who are blind, deaf and deafblind, is delivered in the most appropriate languages and modes and means of communication for the individual, and in environments which maximise academic and social development' (UN, 2006: Article 24, 3c).

In summary, Article 24 of the Convention marks a significant step forward in the development of inclusive education for children with SEN, with its main features recognising that:

- all disabled children are entitled to an education in an 'inclusive system'
- disabled people should not be excluded from the general education system on the grounds of their disability
- a focus upon removing barriers to the development (to their fullest potential) of disabled people's personality, talents and creativity, as well as their mental and physical abilities, is paramount
- all disabled people should receive the support they need within general education systems
- large classes make inclusive education more difficult and this should be challenged when implementing the convention
- every state will need to engage with disabled people's organisations in implementing the articles and convention
- disabled people's organisations need to develop their capacity to advocate for inclusive education
- all disabled children and learners need to be consulted.

READER REFLECTION

Read the key points noted above from Article 24 of the UN Convention on the Rights of Persons with Disabilities 2006 and compare how these have developed since the directives of the late 1980s and early 1990s. In doing so, try to summarise what you see as the central components of inclusive education for children with SEN in the twenty-first century.

There is growing recognition among organisations engaged in development activities of the need to include children with SEN in educational activities. However, there remains much room for the expansion of such programmes, as well as for more documentation of good practices. Indeed, the World Bank found that during the fiscal years 2002–2006 only 5 per cent of new international lending commitments had a disability component. Therefore, in March 2007, the World Bank issued a guidance note to assist its projects in better incorporating the needs of disabled people, integrating a disability perspective into ongoing sector and thematic work programmes, and adopting an integrated and inclusive approach to disability. These developments represented a significant paradigm shift as they identified disability as an issue to be considered in all programming, rather than as a stand-alone thematic issue. Within this framework, there is still space for disability-specific actions and programming based on the needs of the particular international contexts of individual countries.

The UN Convention obligates states to be proactive in taking appropriate measures to ensure that disabled people participate in all facets of society on an equal basis with others. However, all such efforts should be guided by the overall goal to integrate and include disabled people in every aspect of programme development, although finding the appropriate methods of doing so will not be possible without the participation of disabled people at every stage of this process. Thus, empowerment and the self-representation of disabled people, combined with an international commitment to acknowledge the rights of children with SEN to a high-quality education, will be paramount if this new millennium is to see a major change in the policies and practices of inclusive education.

In 2014, UNESCO worked with governments and international partners to address exclusion from education in all its forms. As a result of this international cooperation UNESCO formulated *Ten Questions on Inclusive Education*. This document, they believe, is useful in assessing the success, or otherwise, of a country's attempts to deliver 'Education for All'.

Ten questions on inclusive education:

1   Beyond the figures, what do we know about the excluded?

   UNESCO details that exclusion has many faces such as poverty and marginalisation. What is it that countries are doing to ensure that children avoid the 'enormous risk' of missing out on an education?

2   Why, when schools are promoting access to schools, do they not ensure that access is to quality education?

   UNESCO suggests that it is not enough to simply include children. Governments must also implement strategies to keep children at school and examine what they are actually learning, and importantly, in what conditions they are studying.

   (Continued)

(Continued)

3   How does inclusive education promote successful learning?

UNESCO believes that inclusion must be accompanied by policies to enhance educational quality and that such policies should work on a principle of 'access to success'. This, it believes, has implications not only for children but also for teachers, curriculum and ways of interacting across the schools and their communities.

4   What are the principles of inclusion?

How we define and operationalise inclusion is for UNESCO very important, as this affects how curriculum and pedagogy are organised and how school systems are managed.

5   The notion of inclusion is still often associated with children who have special needs. Why?

Too often, UNESCO states, inclusion programmes are targeted at one marginalised or excluded group at the expense of another. It believes this results in second-rate opportunities for all children.

6   How does education need to change to accommodate everyone?

Inclusion involves a change in how teachers, children and parents view schools and education in general. Inclusive education according to UNESCO is an approach that must transform education systems in order for them to respond to the diversity of all learners.

7   How do curricula need to change to improve learning and encourage the inclusion of all pupils?

UNESCO states that the curriculum has an instrumental role to play in fostering tolerance and promoting human rights. It believes that it is a powerful tool for breaking down barriers, transcending cultural, religious and other differences. An inclusive curriculum, UNESCO argues, must take gender, cultural identity and the language background of a child into consideration.

8   Teachers have a foremost influence on learning, yet their status and working conditions in many countries make it difficult to promote inclusion. What can be done to improve their lot?

Teachers are the linchpins in any educational system and as such are of critical importance to attempts to introduce inclusive education. UNESCO believes that teachers' attitudes and practices towards learners from different backgrounds are crucial to the success of the policies of Education for All.

9   Is inclusive, quality education affordable?

An argument sometimes levelled at inclusion policies is that it is an expensive form of educational system. UNESCO believes that educating all children for success is more cost effective than students continually failing in education systems and having to repeat schooling.

---

10   Does inclusive, quality education lead to more inclusive societies?

UNESCO states that exclusion starts very early in life. A holistic vision of education is imperative. Comprehensive early childhood care and education programmes improve children's well-being, prepare them for primary schools and give them a better chance of succeeding once they are in school. All evidence shows that the most disadvantaged and vulnerable children benefit most from such programmes.

(See www.unesco.org/new/en/education/themes/strengthening-education-systems/inclusive-education.)

Conclusion

This chapter has detailed that governments, international agencies and organisations are all working with renewed vigour in this millennium towards the goal of equality for children with SEN following the adoption of the UN Convention on the Rights of Persons with Disabilities at the end of December 2006. According to the UN, there are approximately 650 million people with disabilities in the world (of whom 120–150 million are estimated to be children) who represent 10 per cent of the global population. An estimated 80 per cent of these disabled people live in developing countries, with many in conditions of poverty and deprivation (Kristensen, 2002). In reading this chapter it is important to understand that in both developed and developing countries, the evidence suggests that disabled people are disproportionately represented.

In this chapter you have learnt that although international inclusive education has progressed significantly in some countries, there is still much to be achieved in offering a fundamental right to a basic education for some children. The UN set eight goals for development called the Millennium Development Goals. These established an ambitious agenda for improving the human condition by 2015 and included:

- eradicating extreme poverty and hunger
- achieving universal primary education
- promoting gender equality and empowering women
- reducing child mortality
- improving maternal health
- combating HIV/AIDS, malaria and other diseases
- ensuring environmental sustainability
- developing a global partnership for development.

This chapter has made plain that despite the rhetoric and the very real attempts to ensure that inclusive education and the Millennium Goals became a reality by 2015, it is the case that these goals have not yet been realised. In concluding your reading of this chapter it is important for you to understand that it is clear international legislation and initiatives, to date, have not ended the struggle for universal education for all. However, it is also important to realise that this should not preclude professionals and parents from having high aspirations for all of the world's children. Furthermore, it should not impede governments and professionals working tirelessly to ensure that children throughout the world have their individual educational needs met.

The activities and reading outlined below are included to deepen your knowledge of the international definitions and systems of inclusive education. In addition, they aim to challenge the notion that the system of inclusion in England is so good that it deserves to be operationalised throughout the world.

STUDENT ACTIVITIES

Using the ten questions on inclusive education above, critically examine inclusive education in England. Is the English educational system a good example of inclusive education for other countries in the world to copy?

The UN Convention of 2006 noted in this chapter advocates that disabled people are actively involved in the decision-making process about their services. Reflect upon what strategies you could implement to ensure that this goal is achieved when developing inclusive educational policies and practices.

Further reading

Armstrong, D., Armstrong, A.C. and Spandagou, I. (2011) 'Inclusion: by choice or by chance?', *International Journal of Inclusive Education*, 15(1), 29–39.
This journal article examines the international development of inclusive education and raises key questions in respect of inclusion's definition and implementation.

United Nations (2006) *Convention on the Rights of Persons with Disabilities*. Available at: www.un.org/disabilities/default.asp?id=259.
This document is one of the international publications related to disability and will help you to compare and contrast how issues have evolved over several years in different countries.

United Nations Educational, Scientific and Cultural Organisation (UNESCO) (1984) *The Salamanca Statement and Framework for Action on Special Needs Education*. Available at: www.unesco.org/education/pdf/SALAMA_E.PDF.
This document is worth reading as it had a significant influence on engaging an international commitment to inclusive education.

9
CONCLUSIONS

CHAPTER OBJECTIVES

- To review and critically examine the key themes examined in the book.
- To discuss the future direction of SEN and inclusion.

Introduction

This chapter draws together the key themes examined within the book. We will review these in order to draw the complexities of SEN and inclusive provision together. From this you will be prompted to construct your own assessment of the key issues involved in SEN and inclusion. The key themes will address: transformations in disability; proposed models of SEN; international dimensions; and future directions.

Transformations in disability

Previous chapters have navigated you through a series of complex and diverse issues related to SEN and inclusion. We have previously referred to the work of Farrell (2000) who has commented that the SEN world is dominated by professionals, families and administrators who try to work together to meet individual children's needs. Behind this world however are a range of government departments and educational policies that provide regulation and scrutiny of the provision on offer. If we are to fully understand the context of SEN and inclusion we must be able to recognise the complex interplay between these professional, political and statutory worlds (Norwich, 2002).

The discussion within previous chapters acknowledged that SEN operates on a continuum in which there is no clear distinction between pupils who have a SEN and those who do not (Postlethwaite and Hackney, 1989). Conceptualising differences such as disability and the SEN of children is therefore complex and often fraught with difficulties, as there are so many contrasting and opposing views as to what counts as a SEN or disability. These concepts are constantly changing as new ideologies, policies and practices emerge, but what is important to your understanding is that you have an appreciation of the history of SEN and how this contributes to current thinking.

In relation to reviewing the historical development of legislative frameworks the book has provided a comprehensive overview of the early education Acts from the late nineteenth century through to the transformational Warnock Report (DES, 1978) and on to the 1981 Education Act. We saw how the work of Warnock in 1978 stimulated the drive towards today's inclusive education stance. The Warnock Report (DES, 1978) estimated that as many as 20 per cent of children during their time at school may experience a SEN that would necessitate additional educational provision being made for them. The report suggested that around 2 per cent of all children and young people of school age might have an educational need that was so severe that they would require a Statement of SEN.

Thirty years later, government data continue to show approximately one in five children is identified as having a difficulty with learning that requires extra help to be given in class. The data also reveal Warnock's figure of 2 per cent under-estimated the number of children and young people who would need the highest level of special educational provision. Consequently, the complex and diverse nature of SEN continues today as does the debate on how, what and where to support these children.

READER REFLECTION

Review your own interpretation of the transformations of disability policy and practice and, as part of this, draw a picture/table that identifies the varying issues and complexities surrounding SEN provision.

Models of SEN

While special and inclusive education has been viewed by society and individuals from a diverse range of perspectives (Slee, 1998), I would like to briefly return to the three central ideological frameworks (Skidmore, 1996), which were focused upon previously and are now described below.

- **Psycho-medical model:** this locates children's disabilities and SEN unproblematically in their individual pathology. The model is also recognised as the individual tragedy, deficit or medical models in which the location and causation of disability rest solely with the child. Thus, the child has to change and/or adapt to be accommodated within society's pre-existing structures.
- **Social model:** this presents disability and SEN as being the result of society's actions, values and beliefs, which seek to enforce social marginalisation upon minority groups (Slee, 1998). The model recognises therefore that society has a responsibility to modify/adapt its structures to accommodate children with SEN rather than the other way round.

- **Disability movement perspective:** this provides a more emergent perspective where disabled people seek to assert their human rights through the employment of politics, legal systems and the disability movement. This recognises the emerging empowerment agenda, which is discussed further in this chapter as part of the emerging 'bio-psychosocial model'.

Models of SEN have emerged from a complex interplay of competing theories, policy and practical findings. They continue to develop all the time and the current prevailing ethos is one of inclusion. Previous chapters have suggested that 'there is no logical purity in education', but rather there is 'ideological impurity' in which there needs to be recognition of a range of 'multiple values' (Norwich, 2002: 483) and interpretations of what constitutes SEN.

Recently the rights-based model has come to the fore and at its very core it has the principle that all children should attend a mainstream school that is based within their local community (Kenworthy and Whittaker, 2000). This model of disability seeks to challenge the widely held belief regarding the legitimacy of segregated education based on the premise that it is impossible to include all children within mainstream education. This has been a point of much debate and consternation as professionals, parents, children, disability rights groups and government continue to debate what the most appropriate educational location is for a child with SEN. My view is that a mixed provision should be on offer in which children are at the centre of the decisions that are made about them regarding their educational location.

The bio-psychosocial model
In recent times we have seen the development of a new perspective on disability, which progresses the psycho-medical (medical) and social models to today's stance of the bio-psychosocial model. This model offers a more generalised approach, suggesting biological, psychological and social factors all play a significant role in human functioning and how disability is defined and interpreted. This is in stark contrast to the medical and social models, which take individualistic approaches from either the child or society to change/adapt. Thus the bio-psychosocial model embraces both of these models whilst recognising the complexity of SEN and the need for children with SEN (via the disability rights movement) to work with society to remove barriers and allow full accessibility to education.

READER REFLECTION

Review your understanding of the various models of disability that have emerged over the years. As part of your review, put into your own words/interpretation what you understand the bio-psychosocial model to represent for future policy and practice in SEN.

International dimensions

As part of the examination of British educational provision, we have examined some distinctive international perspectives on SEN. Two fundamental aspects of international policy related to SEN that are worth briefly returning to are the 1994 Salamanca Statement (UNESCO, 1994) and the UN Convention on the Rights of Persons with Disabilities 2006. These were instrumental in moving provision forward within a human rights (bio-psychosocial model) based context. We saw that many international communities and educational authorities adopted a philosophy of 'inclusion' to address their social and moral obligations to educate all children.

Consultation and empowerment

The UN Convention of 2006 obligates international member states to undertake proactively the appropriate measures to ensure disabled people participate in all facets of society on an equal basis with others. There is still difficulty in determining the appropriate balance between mainstreaming strategies and targeted, disability-specific approaches in what is often referred to as the 'twin-track approach'. Thus, whilst the goal should be to integrate and include disabled people in all aspects of development programming, finding the appropriate methods of doing so may be problematic.

Indeed, the empowerment and self-representation of disabled people combined with an international commitment to acknowledge the rights of children with SEN to a high-quality education will be paramount if the new millennium is to see a major shift in the policies and practices of inclusive education. This requires a transformational approach that recognises the need to employ varying models and practices in order to accommodate the multiplicity of children's needs.

READER REFLECTION

The consultation and empowerment agenda is moving with vigour and purpose within the disability/SEN field. Review your interpretation of the empowerment/human rights agenda and how you can respond to this when supporting children with SEN.

Future directions

It has been suggested that disability, as conceptualised within Western societies, is grounded upon superstitions, myths and beliefs about people with impairments that evolved in earlier and less enlightened times. Finkelstein (1980) outlined three periods.

- **The feudal period:** in which people with impairments were routinely integrated within their villages and local communities rather than excluded from society (Oliver, 1990b).

- **The industrial capitalism period:** when the new social and economic order with its rapidly expanding cities and towns forced the decline of local and family-based support systems, which led to some people with impairments becoming disadvantaged and excluded from employment and society.
- **The post-industrial period**: within which disability was reconceptualised and moved away from the notion that it is an 'individual tragedy' and replaced with the premise that disability is nothing more than a form of social oppression. From this, the disability and human rights-based movements were developed.

The return of the Labour government in 1997

In 1997 the Blair government was elected on a commitment to review the 1995 DDA and it was hoped by many that this new administration would take the opportunity to emphasise a 'more social construction in which disability is seen to be a product of external environmental factors' (Keil et al., 2006). However, its first piece of disability legislation, SENDA (DfES, 2001b), did nothing more than alter Part 4 of the 1995 DDA to bring educational provision in line with other discrimination legislation.

As such this legislation's definition of disability was based upon the medical rather than the social model of disability. New legislation was then enacted to attempt to address this issue. However, in reality this still did little to reconceptualise disability, although it did place a general duty on public institutions to promote disability equality. More than a decade after the enactment of the 1995 DDA it would appear that this government's conceptualisation and articulation of disability remained unchanged.

Consequently, it can be argued that, whilst some shift had been observed, disability was still considered officially as an individual medical tragedy that was based squarely upon personal impairment rather than social prejudice and discrimination. Indeed, whilst two decades of literature leave one in no doubt that inclusion in general and inclusive education in particular has become the new orthodoxy of educational thinking (Allan, 1999), there is still much work to be done.

Inclusion by 2010 then had become the new 'buzz word' (Evans and Lunt, 2005: 41) that gained high status and acquired international currency (Ainscow et al., 2010) within educational and social policy initiatives. However, it was apparent that this was a concept that might be defined in a variety of ways (Ainscow et al., 2010; Clough and Corbett, 2000).

New Labour then took a 'powerful inclusion stance' (Coles and Hancock, 2002: 10), but by adopting a top-down approach to policy implementation they appeared to be forcing their own version of inclusion upon schools and colleges. Therefore, whilst it might appear that New Labour was fully committed to the ideology of inclusive education defined by a previous minister of education as, 'ensuring that every child has the opportunity to achieve their full potential' (DfES, 2004a: 2), it also appeared that their particular view on inclusion was not without its critics.

We observed how New Labour's attempts to define inclusion along a continuum that places inclusive education in the realms of 'equality for all' actually led to more children attending special school than ever before. It was suggested in earlier chapters that whilst New Labour was well versed in 'inclusion speak', it was the case that its motivational drivers and its implementation of inclusion policy were like its definition of inclusion – highly suspect.

READER REFLECTION

Review what you see as the key developments and changes in SEN policy and practice under the Labour government up until 2010. Consider the strengths and weaknesses of these initiatives and the impact they had upon children with SEN.

The Coalition government: ending the bias towards inclusion

From 2010 we witnessed a fundamental change in the ideology that underpins the provision for children with SEN. It was clear from the earliest time that the government, headed by David Cameron, did not observe inclusive education to be the sole objective of educational provision for children with SEN. Indeed, as commented upon in Chapter 1, this government made clear through the tone of its rhetoric that the medical model of disability had been returned to the centre of educational policy and provision. Indeed, it became clear that any hope that 'full inclusionists' might have had that all special school would be closed had been cast aside in Cameron's conviction to end the ideologically bias towards inclusion. Whilst Cameron determined that policy and provision should, quite rightly, not be driven by ideology, it is of interest to note that the 2014 legislation is replete with references to employment and employability. This notion of employability placed at the centre of legislation would itself appear to be an example of Conservative ideology driving the governing principles of educational provision. The stories of 'special school survivors' that you have read strongly suggest that government interference and ideologically driven policies have been unsuccessful in the past because they have failed to take into consideration the views and wishes of those who are important – namely the children who experience education in this country. Whilst there is some hope that there will more consultation with children in the future because of the 2014 Children and Families Act, experience has shown that policies since the 1940s that have included the notion of pupil's voice have not been able to deliver on this commitment. Perhaps it is time for politicians from every political party to begin thinking about who education is really for. Is it for children and their families or is it so that we may produce economic units of production? This question is significant for all children but especially for those who have SEN.

Bearing this in mind, I leave you with a quote from Luke Jackson, a child with Asperger's syndrome, who wrote a book on his experiences of living with a SEN and his involvement with a range of services. The message he gives is an important one, as it embraces the human rights-based approach to inclusivity so well:

I used to have a teacher who helped me at school, but at the time I didn't have a clue what she helped me with ... whatever level of understanding the child you are working with has got, then I reckon you should still try to involve the child so they know what is going on. (Jackson, 2002)

Further reading

Forlin, C. (ed.) *Future Directions for Inclusive Teacher Education: An International Perspective*. London: Routledge.
This book details how inclusive education has impacted upon the world stage and how further inclusive education might progress. It has been written by international scholars, and, whilst targeted at teacher educators, is a useful text.

Oliver, M. (1988) 'The social and political context of educational policy: the case of special needs', in L. Barton (ed.), *The Politics of Special Educational Needs*. London: Falmer, pp. 13–31.
This book offers a useful insight into the social and political context of SEN and inclusion. It will help in assisting you to contextualise evolving provision and how this has changed over many years.

Tilstone, C. and Rose, R. (eds) (2003) *Strategies to Promote Inclusive Practice*. London: Routledge.
This book provides a recent overview of strategies to develop inclusive practice. It will offer you the opportunity to review and reflect upon issues related to inclusion and assist you in contextualising the issues of putting policies into practice.

REFERENCES

Abberley, P. (1987) 'The concept of oppression and the development of a social theory of disability', *Disability, Handicap and Society,* 2(1): 5–19.

Ainscow, M. (1995) 'Education for all: making it happen', *Support for Learning,* 10(4): 147–54.

Ainscow, M., Booth, T. and Dyson, A. (2006) 'Inclusion and the standards agenda: negotiating policy pressures in England', *International Journal of Inclusive Education,* 10(4–5): 295–308.

Ainscow, M., Farrell, P. and Tweddle, D. (2010) 'Developing policies for inclusive education: a study of the role of local education authorities', *International Journal of Inclusive Education,* 4(3): 211–29.

Allan, J. (1999) *Actively Seeking Inclusion: Pupils with Special Needs in Mainstream Schools.* London: Falmer.

Allan, J. (2003) 'Productive pedagogies and the challenge of inclusion', *British Journal of Special Education,* 30(4): 175–9.

Allen, N. (2005) *Making Sense of the Children Act 1989* (4th edition). London: Wiley-Blackwell.

Armstrong, A.C., Armstrong, D. and Spandagou, I. (2009) *Inclusive Education: International Policy and Practice.* London: Sage.

Armstrong, D., Armstrong, A.C. and Spandagou, I. (2011) 'Inclusion: by choice or by chance?', *International Journal of Inclusive Education,* 15(1): 29–39.

Armstrong, F. and Barton, L. (1999) *Disability, Human Rights and Education.* Buckingham: Open University Press.

Atkinson, M. (2001) *Multi-agency Working: A Detailed Study, Local Government Association for England.* London: National Foundation for Educational Research.

Atkinson, M., Wilkin, A., Stott, A., Doherty, P. and Kinder, K. (2002) *Multi-agency Working: A Detailed Study.* London: National Foundation for Educational Research.

Audit Commission (2002) *Special Educational Needs: A Mainstream Issue.* London: The Audit Commission.

Avissar, G. (2003) 'Teaching an inclusive classroom can be rather tedious: an international perspective, Israel, 1998–2000', *Journal of Research in Special Educational Needs,* 3(3): 154–61.

Bailey, J. (1998) 'Australia: inclusion through categorisation', in T. Booth and M. Ainscow (eds), *From Them to Us: An International Study of Inclusion in Education.* London: Routledge, pp. 186–92.

Baker, J. and Zigmond, N. (1995) 'The meaning and practice of inclusion for students with learning disabilities: themes and implications from five cases', *The Journal of Special Education,* 29(2): 163–80.

Baquer, A. and Sharma, A. (1997). *Disability: Challenges vs. Response.* New Delhi: Concerned Action Now.

Barnes, C. (1992) *Disabling Imagery and the Media*. Halifax: Ryburn/BCOCP.

Barnes, C. (1997) 'A legacy of oppression: a history of disability in Western culture', in L. Barton and M. Oliver (eds), *Disability Studies: Past, Present and Future*. Leeds: Disability Press.

Barnes, C. and Mercer, G. (2003) *Disability*. Cambridge: Polity Press.

Barnes, C. and Mercer, G. (2010) *Exploring Disability* (2nd edition). Cambridge: Polity Press.

Barnes, C., Oliver, M. and Barton, L. (eds) (2002) *Disability Studies Today*. Cambridge: Polity Press.

Bartlett, S. and Burton, D. (2012) *Introduction to Education Studies* (3rd edition). London: Sage.

Barton, L. (1997) 'Inclusive education: romantic, subversive or realistic?', *International Journal of Inclusive Education*, 1(30): 231–42.

Barton, L. (2003) 'Inclusive education and teacher education: a basis for hope or a discourse of delusion?', inaugural professorial lecture. London: Institute of Education.

Batty, D. (2005) 'Children's services: the issue explained', *The Guardian*, 18th May.

British Broadcasting Corporation (BBC) (n.d.) 'Forty years of Chronically Sick & Disabled Persons Act'. Available at: http://news.bbc.co.uk/local/lancashire/hi/people_and_places/newsid_8697000/8697441.stm.

Beacham, N. and Rouse, M. (2011) 'Student teachers' attitudes and beliefs about inclusion and inclusive practice', *Jorsen*, 21(1): 3–11.

Beckett, A.E. (2014) 'Non-disabled children's ideas about disability and disabled people', *British Journal of Sociology of Education*, 36(6): 856–75.

Bender, W., Vail, C. and Scott, K. (1995) 'Teachers' attitudes toward increased mainstreaming: implementing effective instruction for students with learning disabilities', *Journal of Learning Disabilities*, 28(2): 87–94.

Benjamin, S. (2002) *The Micropolitics of Inclusive Education – An Ethnography*. Buckingham: Open University Press.

Beveridge, S. (2004) *Children, Families and Schools: Developing Partnerships for Inclusive Education*. London: Routledge.

Bishop, R. (2001) *Designing for Special Educational Needs in Mainstream Schools*. London: Blackwell Synergy.

Block, M. and Obrusnikova, I. (2007) 'Inclusion in physical education: a review of the literature from 1995–2005', *Adapted Physical Activity Quarterly*, 24: 103–24.

Booth, T. (2000) 'Inclusion and exclusion policy in England: who controls the agenda?', in F. Armstrong and D. Armstrong (eds), *Inclusive Education*. London: David Fulton.

Borsay, A. (2005) *Disability and Social Policy in Britain Since 1750*. Basingstoke: Palgrave Macmillan.

Bowen, P. (n.d.) *Human Rights: Transforming Services*. Institute for Social Care Excellence. Available at: www.scie.org.uk/news/events/previousevents/humanrights06/socialcare-bowen.pdf.

Brainhe (2007) *Best Resources for Achievement and Intervention re Neurodiversity in Higher Education*. Available at: www.brainhe.com.

Brothers, M., Scullion, P. and Eathorne, V. (2002) 'Rights of access to services for disabled people', *International Journal of Therapy and Rehabilitation*, 9(6): 232–6.

Brown, J. (2014) 'Rights and legislation', in C. Cameron (ed.), *Disability – A Student's Guide*. London: Sage.

Burt, C. (1937) *The Backward Child*. London and Aylesbury: University of London Press Ltd.

Byrne, B. (2013) 'Hidden contradictions and conditionality: conceptualisations of inclusive education in international human rights law', *Disability and Society*, 28(2): 232–44.

Cabinet Office (2010) *The Coalition: Our Programme for Government*. London: Cabinet Office. Available at: http://programmeforgovernment.hmg.gov.uk/schools.

Cairns, B. and McClatchey, K. (2013) 'Children's attitudes towards disability', *British Journal of Special Education*, 40(3): 124–9.

Cameron, C. (2013) 'The affirmation model', in C. Cameron (ed.), *Disability Studies: A Student's Guide*. London: Sage.

Care Co-ordination Network UK (2001) Information sheet. Available at: www.york.ac.uk/Institute/spru/ccnuk.

Carpenter, B., Ashdown, R. and Bovair, K. (2001a) *Enabling Access: Effective Teaching and Learning for Pupils with Learning Difficulties*. London: David Fulton.

Carpenter, B., Stevens, C., Bovair, K. and Ashdown, A. (2001b) *Effective Teaching and Learning for Pupils with Learning Difficulties*. London: David Fulton.

Carrier, J.G. (1986) 'Sociology and special education: differentiation and allocation in mass education', *American Journal of Education*, 94(3): 282–312.

Cavet, J. (n.d.) *Working in Partnership Through Early Support: Distance Learning Text. Best Practice in Key Working: What Do Research and Policy Have to Say?*. London: Care Co-ordination Network UK. Available at: www.ncb.org.uk/media/513338/best_practice_in_key_working.pdf.

Charlton, J.I. (2000) *Nothing Without Us. Disability Oppression and Empowerment*. Berkeley, CA: University of California Press.

Cheminais, R. (2009) *Effective Multi-Agency Partnerships: Putting Every Child Matters into Practice*. London: Sage.

Clough, P. and Corbett, P. (2000) *Theories of Inclusive Education: A Students' Guide*. London: Paul Chapman.

Clough, P. and Garner, G. (2003) 'Special educational needs and inclusive education: origins and current issues', in S. Bartlett and D. Burton (eds), *Education Studies: Essential Issues*. London: Sage.

COI (2001) *Images of Disability*. London: COI Communications and Department for Work and Pensions.

Coles, C. and Hancock, R. (2002) *The Inclusion Quality Mark*. Croyden: Creative Education.

Contact (1991) *Contact*. No. 70, winter, pp. 45–48. Available at: www.um.es/discatif/PROYECTO_DISCATIF/Textos_discapacidad/Barnes_1.pdf.

Conservative Manifesto (2010) *Invitation to Join the Government of Britain*. London: Conservative Party.

Copeland, I.C. (2001) 'Integration versus segregation: the early struggle', *British Journal of Learning Disabilities*, 29(1): 5–11.

Corbett, J. (2001) *Supporting Inclusive Education: A Connective Pedagogy*. London: RoutledgeFalmer.

Corbett, J. and Norwich, B. (2005) 'Common or specialised pedagogy?', in M. Nind, J. Rix, K. Sleehy and K. Simmons (eds), *Curriculum and Pedagogy in Inclusive Education: Values into Practice*. Abingdon: RoutledgeFalmer.

Council for Disabled Children (n.d.) *Children's Services*. Available at: www.councilfordisabledchildren.org.uk/media/80188/CDC_LH_Chap_3c.pdf_.

Council for Disabled Children (2014) *Independent Supports: Questions and Answer*. Available at: www.ncb.org.uk/media/1102886/independent_support_q_and_a.pdf.

Council of the European Union (2010) *Council Conclusions on the Social Dimension of Education and Training*, 3013th Education, Youth and Culture meeting, Brussels, 11th May 2010. Available at: www.european-agency.org/news/news-files/Council-Conclusions-May-2010-Social-Dimension.pdf.

Coune, E. (2003) *The SENCO Handbook* (4th edition). London: Fulton.

Croll, P. and Moses, M. (2000) 'Ideologies and utopias: education professionals' views of inclusion', *European Journal of Special Needs Education*, 15(1): 1–12.

Croll, P. and Moses, D. (2003) 'Special educational needs across two decades: survey evidence from English primary schools', *British Educational Research Journal*, 29(5): 731–47.

Crowther, N. (2007) 'Nothing without us or nothing about us?', *Disability and Society*, 22(7): 791–94.

Centre for Studies on Inclusive Education (CSIE) (2005) *Evidence to the UK Parliament's Inquiry into Special Educational Needs*. Available at: http://inclusion.uwe.ac.uk/csie/campaigns.htm.

Centre for Studies on Inclusive Education (CSIE) (2008) *Ten Reasons for Inclusion*. Available at: www.csie.org.uk/resources/ten-reasons-02.pdf.

Cumberbatch, G. and Negrine, R. (1992) *Images of Disability on Television*. London: Routledge.

Daniel, P. (1997) 'Educating students with disabilities in the least restrictive environment: a slippery slope for educators', *Journal of Educational Administration*, 35(5): 397–410.

Das, A.K., Kuyini, A.B. and Desai, I. (2013) 'Inclusive education in India: are the teachers prepared?', *International Journal of Special Education*, 28(1): 27–36.

Davis, J.M. (2014) 'Disability and childhood journey towards inclusion', in S. Swain, C. French and C. Barnes (eds), *Disabling Barriers – Enabling Environments* (3rd edition). London: Sage.

Davis, J.M. and Watson, D. (2001) 'Where are the children's experiences? Cultural and social exclusion in "special" and "mainstream" schools', *Disability and Society*, 16: 671–87.

Davis, K. (1996) 'Disability and legislation: rights and equality', in G. Hales (ed.), *Beyond Disability: Towards an Enabling Society*. London: Sage.

Davis, T. (2000) *Moving from Residential Institutions to Community Based Services in Eastern Europe and the Former Soviet Union*. Available at: www.worldbank/sp.

Deal, M. (2003) 'Disabled people's attitudes toward other impairment groups: a hierarchy of impairments', *Disability and Society*, 18(7): 897–910.

de Boer, A., Pijl, S.J. and Minnaert, A. (2012) 'Students' attitudes towards peers with disabilities: a review of the literature', *International Journal of Disability, Development and Education*, 59(4): 379–92.

de Laat, S., Freriksen, E. and Vervloed, M.P.J. (2013) 'Attitudes of children and adolescents toward persons who are deaf, blind, paralyzed or intellectually disabled', *Research in Developmental Disabilities*, 34(2): 855–63.

Department of Education and Science (DES) (1978) *Special Educational Needs: Report of the Committee of Enquiry into the Education of Handicapped Children and Young People (The Warnock Report)*. London: HMSO.

Department of Education and Science (DES) (1981) *The 1981 Education Act*. London: HMSO.

Department for Education (DfE) (2011) *Support and Aspiration: A New Approach to Special Educational Needs and Disability*. London: DfE.

Department for Education (DfE) (2013a) *Special Educational Needs in England: January 2013*. Available at: www.gov.uk/government/publications/special-educational-needs-in-england-january-2013.

Department for Education (DfE) (2013b) *Children with Special Educational Needs: An analysis – 2013 (SFR42/2013)*. Available at: www.gov.uk/government/publications/children-with-special-educational-needs-an-analysis-2013.

Department for Education (DfE) (2013c) *Teachers' Standards Guidance for School Leaders, School Staff and Governing Bodies*. Available at: www.gov.uk/government/uploads/system/uploads/attachment_data/file/301107/Teachers__Standards.pdf.

Department for Education (DfE) (2014a) *Children and Families Act*. London: HMSO.

Department for Education (DfE) (2014b) *Special Needs Code of Practice*. London: HMSO.

Department for Education (DfE) (2014c) *SEN and the National Curriculum: The DfE's Advice*. Available at: http://community.tes.co.uk/national_curriculum_2014/b/sen_and_the_new_national_curriculum/archive/2014/01/06/sen-and-the-national-curriculum-the-dfe-39-s-advice.aspx.

Department for Education (DfE) (2014d) *The National Curriculum in England. Framework Document*. Available at: www.gov.uk/government/publications/national-curriculum-in-england-framework-for-key-stages-1-to-4/the-national-curriculum-in-england-framework-for-key-stages-1-to-4.

Department for Education and Employment (DfEE) (1997) *Excellence for All Children. Green Paper*, 22nd October. London: HMSO.

Department for Education and Employment (DfEE) (1998) *Meeting Special Educational Needs: A Programme of Action*. London: HMSO.

Department for Education and Skills (DfES) (1997) *Excellence for all Children*. London: Department for Education and Skills.

Department for Education and Skills (DfES) (2001a) *Special Educational Needs and Disability Act*. London: Department for Education and Skills.

Department for Education and Skills (DfES) (2001b) *Special Educational Needs Toolkit*. London: HMSO.

Department for Education and Skills (DfES) (2003) *The Report of the Special Schools Working Group*. Annesty: Department for Education and Skills.

Department for Education and Skills (DfES) (2004a) *Removing Barriers to Achievement. The Government's Strategy for SEN*. London: Department for Education and Skills.

Department for Education and Skills (DfES) (2004b) *Children Act*. London: HMSO.

Department for Education and Skills (DfES) (2005) *The Youth Matters Green Paper*. London: HMSO.

Department for Education and Skills/Qualifications and Curriculum Authority (DFES/QCA) (1999) *The National Curriculum*. London: HMSO.

Department of Education (DoE) (1970) *The Education (Handicapped Act) 1970*. London: HMSO.

Department of Education (DoE) (1994) *Code of Practice on the Identification and Assessment of Special Educational Needs*. London: HMSO.

Department of Education (DoE) (2005) *Special Educational Needs and Disability Order 2005*. Available at: www.opsi.gov.uk/si/si2005/20051117.htm.

Dickens, C. ([1838] 1985) *Nicholas Nickleby*. Philadelphia, PA: University Library Association.

Disability Discrimination Act (DDA) (1995) *Disability Discrimination Act*. Available at: www.opsi.gov.uk/acts/Acts1995/ukpga_19950050_en_1.

Doyle, B. (1997) 'Trans-disciplinary approaches to working with families', in B. Carpenter (ed.), *Families in Context: Emerging Trends in Family Support and Early Intervention*. London: David Fulton.

Dykeman, B.F. (2006) 'Alternative strategies for assessing special educational needs', *Education*, winter. Available at: http://findarticles.com/p/articles/mi_qa3673/is_200601/ai_n17176206.

Dyson, A. and Millward, A. (2000) *Schools and Special Needs: Issues of Innovation and Inclusion*. London: Paul Chapman.

Dyson, A. and Slee, R. (2001) 'Special needs education from Warnock to Salamanca: the triumph of liberalism?', in R. Phillips and J. Firlong (eds), *Education Reform and the State: Twenty Five Years of Politics, Policy and Practice*. London: RoutledgeFalmer.

Edinburgh Review (1865) 'Idiot asylums', *Edinburgh Review*, 121: 37–72.

Education and Skills Committee (2006) *Special Educational Needs*. Available at: www.publications.parliament.uk. London: House of Commons.

Edwards, A., Daniels, D., Gallagher, T., Leadbetter, J. and Warmington, P. (2009) *Enhancing Inter-professional Collaborations in Children's Services: Multi-Agency Working for Children's Wellbeing* (Improving Learning series). London: Routledge.

Elkins, D.N. (2009) 'The medical model in psychotherapy: its limitations and failures', *Journal of Humanistic Psychology*, 49: 66–84.

Equality and Human Rights Commission (2014) *Equality Act Codes of Practice and Technical Guidance.* Available at: www.equalityhumanrights.com/legal-and-policy/legislation/equality-act-2010/equality-act-codes-practice-and-technical-guidance.

Evans, J. (1995) 'Implementing the 1981 Education Act', in I. Lunt, B. Norwich and V. Varma (eds), *Psychology and Education for Special Needs: Recent Developments and Future Directions.* Aldershot: Arena.

Evans, J. (1996) *Chairperson, European Network on Independent Living, Campaign for Civil Rights Legislation: The Direct Payments Act and the Disability Discrimination Act (DDA).* Available at: www.independentliving.org/docs2/enilevans9610.html.

Evans, J. and Lunt, I. (2005) 'Inclusive education: are there limits?', in K. Topping and S. Maloney (eds), *The Routledge Falmer Reader in Inclusive Education.* London: RoutledgeFalmer.

Farrell, M. (2000) *Special Educational Needs: The Importance of Standards of Pupil Achievement.* London: Continuum.

Farrell, M. (2004) *Special Educational Needs: A Resource for Practitioners.* London: Paul Chapman.

Farrell, M. (2005) *Key Issues in Special Education: Raising Standards of Pupil Attainment and Achievement.* London: Routledge.

Findlay-Williams, R. (2014) 'The representation of disabled people in the news media', in J. Swain, S. French, C. Barnes and C. Thomas (eds), *Disabling Barriers, Enabling Environments* (3rd edition). London: Sage.

Finkelstein, V. (1980) *Attitudes and Disabled People.* New York: World Rehabilitation Fund.

Firkowska-Mankiewicz, A. (2000) *Edukacja wlaczajaca – zadaniem na dzis polskiej szkoly* (Inclusive Education now the task of the Polish school). Available at: www.fio.interklasa.pl/fio7/edukacja.htm.

Fisher, P. and Goodley, D. (2007) 'The linear medical model of disability: mothers of disabled babies resist with counter-narratives', *Sociology of Health and Illness,* 29(1): 66–81.

Florian, L. (2008) 'Special or inclusive education: future trends', *British Journal of Special Education,* 35(4): 201–20.

Foley, P. and Rixon, A. (eds) (2014) *Changing Children's Services: Working and Learning Together* (2nd edition). Bristol: Policy Press.

Forlin, C. (2008) 'Education reform for inclusion in the Asia-Pacific Region: what about teacher education?', in C. Forlin and J.M.G Lian (eds), *Reform, Inclusion and Teacher Education: Towards a New Era of Special Education in the Asia-Pacific Region.* London: Routledge.

Frederickson, N. and Cline, T. (2002) *Special Educational Needs, Inclusion and Diversity.* Buckingham: Oxford University Press.

Frederickson, N. and Cline, T. (2009) *Special Educational Needs, Inclusion and Diversity* (2nd edition). Maidenhead: Oxford University Press.

Fuchs, D. and Fuchs, L. (1994) 'Inclusive schools movement and the radicalisation of special education reform', *Exceptional Children,* 60(4): 294–309.

Gajda, M. (2008) *Dwuglos w Sprawie Edukacji.* Available at: www.niepelnosprawni.pl/ledge/x/27040.

Gargiulo, R.M. and Kilgo, J.L. (2014) *An Introduction to Young Children with Special Needs. Birth Through to Age Eight.* Belmont, CA: Wadsworth.

Gibson, S. and Blandford, S. (2005) *Managing Special Educational Needs: A Practical Guide for Primary and Secondary Schools.* London: Paul Chapman.

Glazzard, J. (2014) 'The standards agenda: reflections of a special educational needs co-ordinator', *Support for Learning,* 29(1): 39–53.

Gleeson, B.J. (1997) 'Disability studies: a historical materialist view', *Disability and Society*, 12(2): 179–202.

Goodey, C.F. and Rose, L.M. (2013) 'Mental states, bodily dispositions and table manners: a guide to reading intellectual disability from Homer to late antiquity', in C. Laes, C. Goodey and L.M. Rose (eds), *Disabilities in Roman Antiquity: Disparate Bodies A Capite ad Calcem*. Leiden, The Netherlands: Koninklijke Brill.

Goering, S. (2010) 'Revisiting the relevance of the social model of disability', *The American Journal of Bioethics*, 10(1): 54–5.

Goodley, D. (2011) *Disability Studies: An Interdisciplinary Introduction*. London: Sage.

Goodley, D. (2014) 'Who is disabled? Exploring the scope of the social model of disability', in J. Swain, S. French, C. Barnes (eds), *Disabling Barriers – Enabling Environments* (3rd edition). London: Sage.

Gove, M., in Sellgren, K. (2011) *Gove: Tougher New Teacher Standards Needed*. Available at: www.bbc.co.uk/news/education-12717061.

Graham, J. and Wright, J.A. (1999) 'What does "inter-professional collaboration" mean to professionals working with pupils with physical disabilities?', *British Journal of Special Education*, 26(1): 37–41.

Grainger, T. and Todd, J. (2000) *Inclusive Educational Practice – Literacy*. London: David Fulton.

Gray, D.E. (2002) 'Everybody just freezes. Everybody is just embarrassed: felt and enacted stigma among parents of children with high functioning autism', *Sociology of Health and Illness*, 24(6): 734–49.

Guralnick, M.J. (2002) 'Involvement with peers: comparisons between young children with and without Down's syndrome', *Journal of Intellectual Disability Research*, 46(5): 379–83.

Haffter, C. (1969) 'The changeling: history and the psychodynamics of attitudes to handicapped children', *European Folklore Journal of the History of Behavioural Sciences*, 4: 55–61.

Hanko, G. (2003) 'Towards an inclusive school culture – but what happened to Elton's affective curriculum?', *British Journal of Special Education*, 30(3): 125–31.

Harpur, P. (2012) 'Embracing the new disability rights paradigm: the importance of the Convention on the Rights of Persons with Disabilities', *Disability and Society*, 27(1): 1–14.

Harasymiw, S.J., Horne, M.D. and Lewis, S.C. (1976) 'A longitudinal study of disability group acceptance', *Rehabilitation Literature*, 37: 98–102.

Hervey, D. (1992) *The Creatures Time Forgot: Photography and Disability Imagery*. London: Routledge.

Hills, G. (2011) *The Equality Act for Educational Professionals: A Simple Guide to Disability Inclusion in School*. London: David Fulton/Nasen.

Hindu Business Line (2007) Available at: www.thehindubusinessline.com/2007/04/16/26hdline.htm.

Hodkinson, A. (2005) 'Conceptions and misconceptions of inclusive education: a critical examination of final year teacher trainees' knowledge and understanding of inclusion', *Research in Education*, 73: 15–29.

Hodkinson, A. (2006) 'Conceptions and misconceptions of inclusive education – one year on: a critical analysis of newly qualified teachers' knowledge and understanding of inclusion', *Research in Education*, 76: 43–55.

Hodkinson, A. (2007a) 'Inclusive education and the cultural representation of disability and disabled people: a recipe for disaster or the catalyst for change? An examination of nondisabled primary school children's attitudes to children with a disability', *Research in Education*, 77: 56–76.

Hodkinson, A. (2007b) 'Inclusive education and the cultural representation of disability and disabled people within the English education system: a critical examination of the mediating influence of primary school textbooks', *IARTEM*, 1(1). Available at: http://alex.edfac.usyd.edu.au/treat/ iartem/index.htm.

Hodkinson, A. (2009) 'Pre-service teacher training and special educational needs in England 1970–2008: is government learning the lessons of the past or is it experiencing a groundhog day?', *European Journal of Special Needs Education*, 24(3): 277–89.

Hodkinson, A. (2010) 'Inclusive and special education within the English education system: historical perspectives, recent developments and future challenges', *British Journal of Special Education*. 37(2): 61–7.

Hodkinson, A. (2011) 'Inclusion: a defining definition?', *Power and Education*, 3(2): 179–85.

Hodkinson, A. (2012a) 'Inclusive education and the cultural representation of disability and disabled people within the English education system: the influence of electronic media in the primary school', *Journal of Research in Special Educational Needs*, 12(4): 252–62.

Hodkinson, A. (2012b) 'All present and correct?' Exclusionary inclusion within the English educational system', *Disability and Society*, 27(5): 675–88.

Hodkinson, A. and Devarakonda, C. (2011) 'Conceptions of inclusion and inclusive education. A critical examination of the perspectives and practices of teachers in India', *Research in Education*, 82: 85–96.

Hornby, G. (2001) 'Promoting responsible inclusion: quality education for all', in T. O'Brien (ed.), *Enabling Inclusion: Blue Skies ... Dark Clouds?*. London: Stationery Office.

Hornby, G. (2002) 'Promoting responsible inclusion: quality education for all', in C.A. Jones (ed.), *Supporting Inclusion in the Early Years*. Maidenhead, New York: Oxford University Press.

Huckstadt, L.K. and Shutts, K. (2014) 'How young children evaluate people with and without disabilities', *Journal of Social Issues*, 70(1): 99–114.

Humphrey, N. and Symes, W. (2013) 'Inclusive education for pupils with autistic spectrum disorders in secondary mainstream schools: teacher attitudes, experience and knowledge', *International Journal of Inclusive Education*, 17(1): 32–46.

Hunt, V. (2013) 'In *loco parentis*?', *TES Connect*. Available at: www.tes.co.uk/article.aspx?storycode=370916.

Hussain, H.D. and Brownhill, S. (2014) 'Integrated working: from the theory to the practice', in S. Brownhill (ed.), *Empowering the Children's and Young People's Workforce: Practice Based Knowledge, Skills and Understanding*. London: Routledge.

Huws, J.C. and Jones, R.S. (2010) 'Missing voices: representations of autism in British newspapers, 1999–2008', *British Journal of Learning Disabilities*, 39(2): 98–104.

infed.org (2007) *The Hadow Reports: An Introduction*. Available at: www.infed.org/schooling/hadow_reports.htm.

Jackson, L. (2002) *Freaks, Geeks and Asperger's Syndrome: A User Guide to Adolescence*. London: Jessica Kingsley Publishers.

Jackson, P. (1983) 'Principles and problems of participant observation', *Geografiscka Anna/er*, 65B: 39–46.

Jacques, N., Wilton, K. and Townsend, M. (1998) 'Cooperative learning and social acceptance of children with mild intellectual disability', *Journal of Intellectual Disability Research*, 42(1): 29–36.

Jahoda, A., Dagnan, D., Jarvie, P. and Kerr, W. (2006) 'Depression, social context and cognitive behavioural therapy for people who have intellectual disabilities', *Journal of Applied Research in Intellectual Disabilities*, 19(1): 81–9.

Jenkinson, J.C. (1997) *Mainstream or Special? Educating Students with Disabilities*. London: Routledge.

Johansson, S.T. (2014) 'A critical and contextual approach to inclusive education: perspectives from an Indian context', *International Journal of Inclusive Education*, 18(12): 1219–36.

Johnstone, D. (2001) *An Introduction to Disability Studies* (2nd edition). London: David Fulton.

Jones, B. (2003) *Childhood Disability in a Multicultural Society.* Abingdon: Radcliffe Medical Press.

Jones, C.A. (2004) *Supporting Inclusion in the Early Years.* Maidenhead: Oxford University Press.

Joseph Rowntree Foundation (1999) *Disabled Children and the Children Act.* Available at: www.jrf.org.uk/sites/files/jrf/scr378.pdf.

Judge, B. (2003) 'Inclusive education: principles and practices', in K. Crawford (ed.), *Contemporary Issues in Education.* Dereham, Norfolk: Peter Francis.

Kaehne, A. (2014) *Multi-Agency Protocols as a Mechanism to Improve Partnerships in Public Services, Local Government Studies, 2014.* Available at: www.tandfonline.com/doi/abs/10.1080/03003930.2013.861819#preview.

Karppi, T. (2013) 'Change name to No One Like people's status. Facebook trolling and managing online personas', *The Fibreculture Journal*, 166: 278–300.

Kavale, K. (2000) 'History, rhetoric and reality', *Remedial and Special Education*, 21(5): 279–97.

Keers, J., Blaauwwiekel, E., Hania, M., Bouma., J., Scholten-Jaegers, S., Sanderman, R. and Links, T. (2004) 'Diabetes rehabilitation: development and first results of a multidisciplinary intensive education programme for patients with prolonged self management difficulties', *Patient Education and Counselling*, 52(2): 151–7.

Keil, S., Miller, O. and Cobb, R. (2006) 'Special education needs and disability', *British Journal of Special Education*, 33(4): 168–72.

Kenworthy, J. and Whittaker, J. (2000) 'Anything to declare? The struggle for inclusive education and children's rights', *Disability and Society*, 15(2): 219–31.

Kirk, S. and Glendinning, C. (1999) *Supporting Parents Caring for a Technology Dependant Child.* Manchester: National Primary Care Research and Development Centre, University of Manchester.

Kristensen, K. (2002) 'Can the Scandinavian perspective on inclusive education be implemented in developing countries?', *African Journal of Special Needs Education*, 7(2): 104–14.

Laat, S., Freiksen, E. and Vervloed, M.P.J. (2013) 'Attitudes of children and adolescents toward persons who are deaf, blind, paralyzed or intellectually disabled', *Research in Developmental Disabilities*, 34(2): 855–863.

Lacey, P. and Ouvry, C. (eds) (2000) *People with Profound and Multiple Learning Disabilities: A Collaborative Approach to Meeting Complex Needs.* London: David Fulton.

Laes, C., Goodey, C.F. and Rose, L.M. (2013) 'Approaching disabilities *a capite ad calcem*: hidden themes in Roman antiquity', in C. Laes, C.F. Goodey and L.M. Rose (eds), *Disabilities in Roman Antiquity: Disparate Bodies* A Capite ad Calcem. Leiden, The Netherlands: Koninklijke Brill.

Lamb Inquiry (2009) *Special Educational Needs and Parental Confidence.* Nottingham: DCSF Publications.

Lees, C. and Ralph, S. (2004) 'Charitable provision for blind and deaf people in the late nineteenth century London', *Journal of Research in Special Educational Needs*, 4(3): 148–60.

Lendrum, A. Barlow, A. and Humphrey, N. (2015) 'Developing positive school–home relationships through structured conversations with parents of learners with special educational needs and disabilities (SEND)', *Journal of Research in Special Educational Needs*, 15(2): 87–96.

Lenney, M. and Sercombe, H. (2002) '"Did you see that guy in the wheelchair down the pub?", Interactions across difference in a public place', *Disability and Society*, 17(1): 5–18.

Lewis, A. (1991) 'Changing views of special educational needs', *Education 3–13*, 27(3): 45–50.

Lloyd, C. (2012) 'Special educational needs', in L. Gearon (ed.), *Education in the United Kingdom – Structures and Organisation*. London: Fulton.

Lockewood, G., Henderson, C. and Thornicroft, G. (2012) 'The Equality Act 2010 and mental health', *The British Journal of Psychiatry*, 200: 182–3.

Longmore, P.K. (1987) 'Screening stereotypes: images of disabled people in television and motion pictures', in A. Gartner and T. Joe (eds), *Images of the Disabled, Disabling Images*. New York: Praeger.

Low, C. (1997) 'Is inclusivism possible?', *European Journal of Special Needs Education*, 12(1): 71–9.

Luke, C. (1996) *Feminisms and Pedagogies of Everyday Life*. Albany, NY: State University of New York Press.

Macleod, F. (2001) 'Towards inclusion – our shared responsibility for disaffected students', *British Journal of Special Education*, 28(4): 191–4.

Madan, A. and Sharma, N. (2013) 'Inclusive education for children with disabilities: preparing schools to meet the challenge', *Electronic Journal for Inclusive Education*, 3(1).

Manion, M.L. and Bersani, H.A. (1987) 'Mental retardation as a Western sociological construct: a cross-cultural analysis', *Disability, Handicap and Society*, 2(3): 231–41.

Mani, M.N.G. (2000) *Inclusive Education in Indian Context*. International Human Resource Development Center (IHRDC) for the Disabled, Hemlata Coimbatore, Belur Math: Ramakrishna Mission Vivekannanda University.

Martlew, M. and Hodson, J. (1991) 'Children with mild learning difficulties in an integrated and in a special school: comparisons of behaviour, teasing and teacher attitudes', *British Journal of Educational Psychology*, 61(3): 355–72.

Mencap (2007) Press release. Available at: mencap.org.uk.

Miles, S. and Singal, N. (2010) 'The Education for All and inclusive education debate: conflict, contradiction or opportunity?', *International Journal of Inclusive Education*, 14(1): 1–15.

Mind (2005) *Mental Capacity Act 2005. A Brief Legal Guide to the Mental Capacity Act, Including Details of Where You Can go for Further Information or Support*. Available at: www.mind.org.uk/information-support/legal-rights/mental-capacity-act-2005.

Mittler, P. and Daunt, P. (eds) (1995) *Teacher Education for Special Needs in Europe*. London: Cassell.

Morgan, H. (2012) 'The social model of disability as a threshold concept: troublesome knowledge and liminal spaces in social work education', *Social Work Education*, 31(2): 215–26.

Morina Diez, A. (2010) 'School memories of young people with disabilities: an analysis of barriers and aids to inclusion', *Disability and Society*, 33(2): 163–75.

Morris, J. (1989) *Able Lives: Women's Experience of Paralysis*. London: The Women's Press.

Morris, J. (1991) *Pride Against Prejudice: Transforming Attitudes to Disability*. London: The Women's Press.

Morris, J. (2005) *Citizenship and Disabled People – the Disability Debate*. London: Disability Rights Commission.

National Association for Special Educational Needs (Nasen) (n.d.) *Draft Special Educational Needs (SEN) Code of Practice. Summary*. Available at: www.nasen.org.uk/uploads/publications/284.pdf.

National Association for Special Educational Needs (Nasen) (2014) *Preparing for Change. New SEN Legislation and What this Means for the Strategic Management of Schools and Front Line Teaching Staff*. Available at: www.rnlcom.com/wp-content/uploads/2014/.../Jane-Friswell-PPoint.pptx.

Nazar, M. and Nikoli, M. (1991) 'Children with development difficulties in regular education', *Primjenjena Psihologija*, 12: 123–7.

National Center for Education Statistics (NCES) (2014) *Fast Facts*. Available at: http://nces. ed.gov/fastfacts/display.asp?id=372.

National Council of Educational Research and Training (NCERT) (2000) *The National Curriculum Framework for School Education*. New Delhi: NCERT.

Nind, M. (2005) 'Introduction – models and practice in inclusive curricula', in M. Nind, J. Rix, K. Sheeh and K. Simmons (eds), *Curriculum and Pedagogy in Inclusive Education: Values into Practice*. Abingdon: RoutledgeFalmer.

Nind, M., Sheehy, K. and Simmons, K. (eds) (2003) *Inclusive Education: Learners and Learning Contexts*. London: David Fulton.

Norden, M. (1994) *The Cinema of Isolation: A History of Disability in the Movies*. New Brunswick, NJ: Rutgers University Press.

Norwich, B. (2000) 'Inclusion in education: from concepts, values and critique to practice', in H. Daniels (ed.), *Special Education Reformed Beyond the Rhetoric*. London: Falmer.

Norwich, B. (2002) 'Education, inclusion and individual differences: recognising and resolving dilemmas', *British Journal of Education Studies*, 50(4): 482–502.

Norwich, B. (2007) 'SEN policy options goup special schools in the new era: how do we go beyond generalities?', Policy Paper 2, 6th series, *Journal of Research in Special Educational Needs*, 7(2): 71–89.

Norwich, B. (2014) 'How does the capability approach address current issues in special educational needs, disability and inclusive education field?', *Journal of Research in Special Educational Needs*, 14(1): 16–21.

Norwich, B. and Kelly, N. (2004) 'Pupils' views on inclusion: moderate learning difficulties and bullying in mainstream and special schools', *British Educational Research Journal*, 30(1): 43–64.

Nowicki, E.A. and Sandieson, R. (2002) 'A meta-analysis of school-age children's attitudes towards person with physical or intellectual disabilities', *International Journal of Disability, Development and Education*, 49: 243–65.

National Parent Partnership Network (NPP) (2013) *Parent Partnership Services in England. Survey on the Extent to which PPS meet the Exemplifications of the Minimum Standards and Additional National Data Collection 2013*. Available at: www.bathnes.gov.uk/sites/default/files/nppn_benchmarking_2013.pdf.

National Union of Teachers (NUT) (2004) *Special Educational Needs Study*. London: National Union of Teachers.

National Union of Teachers (NUT) (2013) *Education, the Law and You*. Available at: www.teachers.org.uk/files/the-law-and-you--8251-.pdf.

Ofsted (2000) *Evaluating Educational Inclusion: Guidance for Inspectors and Schools*. London: Office for Standards in Education.

O'Hanlon, C. (1995) *Inclusive Education in Europe*. London: David Fulton.

Oliver, M. (1988) 'The social and political context of educational policy: the case of special needs', in L. Barton (ed.), *The Politics of Special Educational Needs*. London: Falmer.

Oliver, M. (1990a) *The Politics of Disablement*. Basingstoke: Macmillan.

Oliver, M. (1990b) 'The individual and social models of disability', paper presented at the Joint Workshop of the Luing Options Group, 23rd July.

Oliver, M. (1996) 'Defining impairment and disability: issues at stake', in C. Barnes and G. Mercer (eds), *Exploring the Divide: Illness and Disability*. Leeds: The Disability Press.

Oliver, M. (2013) 'The social model of disability: thirty years on.' *Disability and Society*, 28(7): 1024–6.

Oliver, M. and Barnes, C. (1998) *Disabled People and Social Policy: From Exclusion to Inclusion*. Harlow: Addison Wesley Longman.

Orbe, M.P. (2013) 'The reality of media effects', in A. Kurylo (ed.) *Inter/Cultural Communication. Representations and Constructions of Culture*. London: Sage.

Panda, P. (2005) 'Responsiveness of Pre-service Teacher Education in India: Appraisal of Curricular Dimensions and Practices', paper presented at ISEC conference, August 2005, Glasgow.

Parry, M. (2013) From Monsters to Patients. A History of Disability, unpublished PhD. Arizona State University. Available at: http://repository.asu.edu/attachments/110533/content/Parry_asu_0010E_12951.pdf.

Parton, N. (2011) The Increasing Length and Complexity of Central Government Guidance about Child Abuse in England: 1974–2010. Discussion Paper (unpublished). Huddersfield: University of Huddersfield. Available at: http://eprints.hud.ac.uk/9906.

Payler, J. and Georgeson. J. (2013) 'Multiagency working in the early years: confidence, competence and context', Early Years: An International Research Journal, 33(4): 380–97.

Pearson, S., Mitchell, R. and Rapti, M. (2014) 'I will be "fighting" even more for pupils with SEN: SENCOs' role predictions in the changing English policy context', Jorsen, I: 1–9.

Pearson, C. and Watson, N. (2007) 'Tackling disability discrimination in the United Kingdom: the British Disability Discrimination Act', Journal of Law and Policy, 23(95): 95–120.

Perry, J. (2014a) 'England: SEN measures-implementation', British Journal of Special Education, 41(3): 330–7. Available at: http://onlinelibrary.wiley.com/doi/10.1111/1467-8578.12075/pdf.

Perry, J. (2014b) 'England: Children and Families Act', British Journal of Special Education, 41(2): 215–23. Available at: http://onlinelibrary.wiley.com/doi/10.1111/bjsp.2014.41.issue-2/issuetoc.

Pijl, S., Meijer, C. and Hegarty, S. (eds) (1997) Inclusive Education: A Global Agenda. London: Routledge.

Porter, J., Daniels, H., Feiler, A. and Georgeson, J. (2011) 'Recognising the needs of every disabled child: the development of tools for a disability census', British Journal of Special Education, 38(3): 120–25.

Postlethwaite, K. and Hackney, A. (1989) Organising a School's Response: Special Needs in Mainstream Schools. London: Macmillan.

Pritchard, D.G. (1963) Education of the Handicapped 1760-1960. London: Routledge and Kegan Paul.

Raghavan, N.S. (2014) Inclusion of Students with Disabilities: A Case Study of a Private Primary School in an Urban City in Southern India, unpublished PhD. Austin, TX: University of Texas at Austin.

Reid, K. (2005) 'The implications of Every Child Matters and the Children Act for schools', Pastoral Care in Education, 23(1): 12–18.

Reynolds, M.C. (1989) 'An historical perspective: the delivery of special education to mildly disabled and at-risk students', Remedial and Special Education, 10(6): 11.

Rieser, R. (2014) Disability Equality. Medical Model/Social Model. Available at: www.worldofinclusion.com/medical_social_model.htm.

Roberts, A. (2007) Mental Health History Timeline. Available at: www.mdx.ac.uk.

Roche, J. and Tucker, S. (2007) '"Every Child Matters": "tinkering" or "reforming" – an analysis of the development of the Children Act (2004) from an educational perspective', Education 3-13, 35: 213–23.

Rose, R. (2001) 'Primary school teacher perceptions of the conditions required to include pupils with special educational needs', Educational Review, 53(2): 147–57.

Rose, R. (2003) Strategies to Promote Inclusive Practice. London: RoutledgeFalmer.

Rose, R. and Howley, M. (2007) The Practical Guide to Special Education Needs in the Inclusive Primary Classroom. London: Paul Chapman.

Runswick-Cole, K. (2011) 'Time to end the bias towards inclusive education?', British Journal of Special Education, 38(3): 112–19.

Rustemier, S. and Vaughan, M. (2005) *Segregation Trends – LEAs in England 2002-2004. Placement of Pupils with Statements in Special Schools and other Segregated Settings. Centre for Studies on Inclusive Education (CSIE)*. Available at: http://inclusion.uwe.ac. uk/ csie/segregationstats2005.htm.

Ryan, J. with Thomas, F. (1980) *The Politics of Mental Handicap*. Harmondsworth: Penguin.

Safford, L. and Safford, J. (1996) *A History of Childhood and Disability*. New York: Teachers College Press.

Schonell, F. (1924) *Backwardness in the Basic Subjects*. London: Oliver and Boyd.

Scruggs, T.E. and Mastropieri, M.A. (1996) 'Teacher perceptions of mainstreaming/inclusion 1958–1995: a research synthesis', *Exceptional Children*, 63(1): 59–74.

Sen, R. and Broadhurst, K. (2011) 'Contact between children in out-of-home placements and their family and friends networks: a research review', *Child and Family Social Work*, 16(2): 298–309.

Shakespeare, T. (1994) 'Cultural representation of disabled people: dustbins for disavowal?', *Disability and Society*, 9(3): 283–99.

Shakespeare, T. (2006) *Disability Rights and Wrongs*. London: RoutledgeFalmer.

Shama, K. (2002) 'Attitudinal changes – breaking the psycho-social barriers', *Journal of Indian Education*, 27(4): 85–9.

Sharma, U. and Deppeler, J. (2005) 'Integrated education in India: challenges and prospects', *Disability Studies Quarterly*, 25(1). Available at: www.dsq-sds.org/article/view/524/701.

Sheligevich-Urban, D. (2011) *Integration of Disabled Children in the Social Environment*. Available at: http://archive.kharkiv.org/View/26556.

Singal, N. (2005) 'Mapping the field of inclusive education: a review of the Indian literature', *International Journal of Inclusive Education*, 9(4): 331–50.

Singal, N. (2006a) 'Inclusive education in India: international concept, national interpretation', *International Journal of Disability, Development and Education*, 53(3): 351–69.

Singal, N. (2006b) 'Adopting an ecosystemic approach for understanding inclusive education: an Indian case study', *European Journal of Psychology of Education. Special Issue: Inclusive Education Ten Years After Salamanca*, 21(3): 239–52.

Singal, N. and Rouse, M. (2003) '"We do inclusion": practitioner perspectives in some "inclusive schools" in India', *Perspectives in Education. Special Issue: The Inclusion/ Exclusion Debate in South Africa and Developing Countries*, 21(3): 85–98.

Siperstein, G.N. and Gottlieb, J. (1997) 'Physical stigma and academic performance as factors affecting children's first impressions of handicapped peers', *American Journal of Mental Deficiency*, 81: 455–62.

Skidmore, D. (1996) 'Towards an integrated theoretical framework for research in special educational needs', *European Journal of Special Needs Education*, 11(1): 33–42.

Slee, R. (1998) 'The politics of theorising special education', in C. Clarke, A. Dyson and A. Millward (eds), *Theorising Special Education* (2nd edition). London: Routledge.

Slee, R. and Allan. J. (2005) 'Excluding the included', in J. Rix, K. Simmons, M. Nind and K. Sheehy (eds), *Policy and Power in Inclusive Education. Values into Practice*. London: RoutledgeFalmer.

Slonje, R., Smith, P.K. and Frisén, A. (2013) 'The nature of cyberbullying, and strategies for prevention', *Computers in Human Behavior*, 29: 26–32.

Sloper, P. (2004) 'Facilitators and barriers for coordinated multi-agency services', *Child Care, Health and Development*, 30(6): 571–80.

Smith, M. (2006) 'Teachers urge rethink on inclusion policy', cited in Alexandra Smith, *EducationGuardian.co.uk*, 13th July.

Smith, A. and Thomas, N. (2006) 'Including pupils with special educational needs and disabilities in national curriculum physical education: a brief review', *European Journal of Special Needs in Education*, 21(1): 69–83.

Snyder, L., Garriot, P. and Aylor, M. (2001) 'Inclusion confusion: putting the pieces together', *Teacher Education and Special Education*, 24(3): 198–207.

Soan, S. (2005) *Primary Special Educational Needs*. Exeter: Learning Matters.

Spaling, E. (2002) 'Social acceptance at senior high school', *International Journal of Special Education*, 17(1): 91–100.

Spikins, P. (2014) *The Stone Age Origins of Autism*. Available at: www.intechopen.com/books/recent-advances-in-autism-spectrum-disorders-volume-ii/the-stone-age-origins-of-autism.

Srivastava, M., de Boer, A. and Pijl, S.J. (2013) 'Inclusive education in developing countries: a closer look at its implementation in the last 10 years', *Educational Review*, 67(2): 179–95.

Starczewska, A., Hodkinson, A. and Adams, G. (2012) 'Conceptions of inclusion and inclusive education: a critical examination of the perspectives and practices of teachers in Poland', *Journal of Research in Special Educational Needs*, 12(3): 162–9.

Starczewska, A., Hodkinson, A. and Adams, G. (2014) 'Special education in Poland', in C.R. Reynolds, K.J. Vannest and E. Fletcher-Janzen (eds), *Encyclopaedia of Special Education: A Reference for the Education of Children, Adolescents, and Adults with Disabilities and Other Exceptional Individuals* (4th edition). Hoboken, NJ: John Wiley and Sons.

Stone, B. and Foley, P. (2014) 'Towards integrated working', in P. Foley and A. Rixon (eds), *Changing Children's Services: Working and Learning Together* (2nd edition). Bristol: Policy Press.

Stothers, G. (2008) 'I hate Tiny Tim'. Available at: http://mainstream-mag.com/tinytim.html.

Strogilos, V. and Tragoulia, E. (2013) 'Inclusive and collaborative practices in co-taught classrooms: roles and responsibilities for teachers and parents', *Teaching and Teacher Education*, 35: 81–91.

Sturt, G. (2007) *Special Educational Needs*. Available at: www.garysturt.free-online.eo.uk/Special%20Educational%20Needs.htm.

Subramanian, M. (2014) *Bullying: The Ultimate Teen Guide*. Plymouth: Rowman and Littlefield.

Swain, J. and French, S. (2000) 'Towards an affirmation model of disability', *Disability and Society*, 15(4): 569–82.

Swain, J. and French, S. (2004) 'Whose tragedy?: towards a personal non-tragedy view of disability', in J. Swain, S. French, C. Barnes and C. Thomas (eds), *Disabling Barriers – Enabling Environments*. London: Sage.

Tar, J. (2014) 'Education', in J. Thomas, K. Pollard and D. Sellman (eds) *Interprofessional Working in Health and Social Care: Professional Perspectives*. London: Palgrave Macmillian.

Teacher Training Agency (1998) *Framework for the Assessment of Quality and Standards in Teacher Training*, circular 4/98. London: Teacher Training Agency.

Terzi, L. (2005) 'Beyond the dilemma of difference: the capability approach to disability and special educational needs', *Journal of Philosophy of Education*, 19(3): 443–59.

Terzi, L. (2010) *Justice and Equality in Education: A Capability Perspective on Disability and Special Educational Needs*. London: Continuum.

The Guardian (2009) 'Children Act, 2004', 19th January. Available at: www.theguardian.com/commentisfree/libertycentral/2009/jan/13/children-act.

Thomas, C. (2014) 'Disability and Impairment', in J. Swain, S. French, C. Barnes (eds) *Disabling Barriers – Enabling Environments* (3rd edition). London: Sage.

Thomas, G. (1996) *Teaching Students with Mental Retardation: A Life Goals Planning Curriculum*. New York: Pearson Education.

Thomas, G. and Loxley, A. (2001) *Deconstructing Special Education and Constructing Inclusion*. Buckingham: Oxford University Press.

Thomas, G., Walker, D. and Webb, J. (2005) 'Inclusive education', in K. Topping and S. Maloney (eds), *The Routledge Falmer Reader in Inclusive Education*. London: Routledge Falmer.

Thomazet, S. (2009) 'From integration to inclusive education: does changing the terms improve practice?', *International Journal of Inclusive Education*, 13(6): 553–63.

Timmons, V. (2002) 'International perspectives on inclusion: concluding thoughts', *Exceptionality Education*, 12(2): 187–92.

Tod, J. (2002) 'Enabling inclusion for individuals', in T. O'Brien (ed.), *Enabling Inclusion: Blue Skies … Dark Clouds*. London: Optimus.

Townsend, M.A.R., Wilton, K.M. and Vakilirad, T. (1993) 'Children's attitudes towards peers with intellectual disability', *Disability and Society*, 37: 405–11.

Townsley, R. and Robinson, C. (2000) *Food for Thought: Effective Support for Families Caring for a Child Who is Tube Fed*. Norah Fry Research Centre: Bristol.

Troung, Y. and Ellam, H. (2013) *Educational Workforce Survey 2013*. Available at: http:// dera.ioe.ac.uk/19840.

United Nations (UN) (2006) *Convention on the Rights of Persons with Disabilities*. Available at: www.un.org/disabilities/defau lt.asp?id=259.

United Nations Educational Scientific and Cultural Organisation (UNESCO) (1994) *The Salamanca Statement and Framework for Action on Special Needs Education*. Available at: www.unesco.org/education/pdf/SALAMA_E.PDF.

United Nations Educational Scientific and Cultural Organisation (UNESCO) (2004) Available at: http://portal.unesco.org/education/en/ev.php-URL_ID=28705&URL_ DO=DO_TOPIC&URL_SECTION= 201.html.

United Nations Children's Fund (UNICEF) (2007) *Human Rights-Based Approach to Education for All. A Framework for the Realization of Children's Right to Education and Rights within Education*. New York: UNESCO.

Union of the Physically Impaired Against Segregation (UPIAS) (1976) *Fundamental Principles of Disability*. London: Union of the Physically Impaired Against Segregation.

US Census Bureau (2014) *State and Other Areas Excluding the US Minor Outlying Islands*. Available at: www.census.gov/en.html.

Vanhala, L. (2010) *Making Rights a Reality?: Disability Rights Activists and Legal Mobilisation*. Cambridge: Cambridge University Press.

Vickerman, P. (2007) *Including Children with Special Educational Needs in Physical Education*. London: Routledge.

Wadham, J., Ruebain, D., Robinson, A. and Uppal, S. (eds) (2012) *Blackstone's Guide to the Equality Act 2010*. Oxford: Oxford University Press.

Wapiennik, E. (2005) *Rights of People with Intellectual Disabilities: Access to Education and Employment*. Warszawa, Poland: Open Society Institute.

Warnock, M. (1999) 'If only we had known then', *Times Educational Supplement*, 31st December.

Warnock, M. (2005) *Special Educational Needs: A New Look*. London: Philosophy of Education Society of Great Britain.

Watson, D., Townsley, R., Abbott, D. and Latham, P. (2002) *Working Together? Multiagency Working in Services to Disabled Children with Complex Health Care Needs and their Families: A Literature Review*. Birmingham: Handsel Trust.

Wazna-Pajak, E. (2013) 'Teacher's intercultural competence and teacher education – a case of Poland', *European Scientific Journal*, 2: 318–22. Available at: http://eujournal.org/ index.php/esj/article/view/1343.

Wearmouth, J. (2001) 'Introduction', in J. Wearmouth (ed.), *Special Educational Provision in the Context of Inclusion: Policy and Practice in Schools*. London: David Fulton.

Weinberg, N. (1978) 'Preschool children's perceptions of orthopedic disability', *Rehabilitation Counselling Bulletin*, 21(3): 183–9.

Weiserbs, B. and Gottlieb, J. (2000) 'The effect of perceived duration of physical disability on attitudes of school children towards friendship and helping', *Journal of Psychology*, 134: 343–5.

Welsh Assembly Government (2006) *Children and Young People: Rights to Action Safeguarding Children: Working Together Under the Children Act 2004*. Available at: www.conwy.gov.uk/upload/public/attachments/328/safeguarding_children__english. pdf.

Whittaker, K.A., Cox, P., Thomas, N. and Cocker, K. (2014) 'A qualitative study of parents' experiences using family support services: applying the concept of surface and depth', *Health and Social Care in the Community*, 22(5): 479–87.

Williams, C. (2005) *Old Liverpool*. Available at: www.old liverpool.co.uk/Blind.html.

Wilson, M.C. and Scior, K. (2014) 'Attitudes towards individuals with disabilities as measured by the Implicit Association Test: a literature review', *Research in Developmental Disabilities*, 35(2): 294–321.

Winnick, J. (ed.) (2005) *Adapted Physical Education and Sport* (4th edition). Champaign, IL: Human Kinetics.

Wright-Southwell, W. (2013) 'Past perspectives: what can archaeology offer disability studies?', in M. Wappett and K. Arndt (eds), *Emerging Perspectives on Disability Studies*. London: Palgrave Macmillan.

Wood, K. (2004) *International Perspectives: The USA and the Pacific Rim*. 'Self-assessment of relationships with peers in children with intellectual disability', *Journal of Intellectual Disability Research*, 45(3): 202–11.

World Health Organization (WHO) (1980) *International Classification of Impairments, Disability and Handicaps*. Geneva: World Health Organization.

Zic, S. and Igri, L. (2001) 'Self-assessment of relationships with peers in children with intellectual disability', *Journal of Intellectual Disability Research*, 45(3): 202–11.

INDEX